People's Movements, People's Press

People's Movements, People's Press

THE JOURNALISM
OF SOCIAL JUSTICE
MOVEMENTS

Bob Ostertag

Beacon Press, Boston

BEACON PRESS
25 Beacon Street
Boston, Massachusetts 02108-2892
www.beacon.org

Beacon Press books are published under the auspices of the
UNITARIAN UNIVERSALIST ASSOCIATION of CONGREGATIONS.

09 08 07 06   8 7 6 5 4 3 2 1

This book is printed on acid-free paper that meets the uncoated paper
ANSI/NISO specifications for permanence as revised in 1992.

Composition by Wilsted & Taylor Publishing Services

LIBRARY OF CONGRESS CATALOGING-IN-PUBLICATION DATA
Ostertag, Bob
   People's movements, people's press: the journalism of social justice movements / Bob
Ostertag.
      p.   cm.
   Includes bibliographical references and index.
   ISBN 0-8070-6164-6 (alk. paper)
1. Underground press—United States—History—20th century. 2. Underground press—
United States—History—19th century. 3. Social problems—Press coverage—United
States. 4. Social justice—United States. I. Title.

   PN4888.U5O88 2006
   071'.30904—dc22   2005031735

For a particular aspiring young
social justice activist and journalist

Contents

Introduction

For the last two centuries, Americans whose concerns and interests lay outside the accepted political boundaries of the day have organized social movements as the principal vehicle for advancing their cause. Their journals have been their most important tool and have been applied to almost every task these movements undertook. The history of social movements and the history of their press are often nearly inseparable, and historians frequently peg the birth of a social movement to the founding of the movement's first journal.

It is therefore surprising that the history of the social movement press has been studied so little.[1] I suspect this is largely due to the fact that when judged by the standards typically used to assess the importance of mainstream publications—total circulation, advertising revenue, length of book, longevity, "professionalism," "objectivity," and "lack of bias"—social movement publications appear to have been of negligible importance. Yet even the most cursory review of the social movement press reveals the mistake of judging it by these standards.

It is my contention that the history of social movement journalism can be understood only *in the context of the particular movements of which each journal was a part*: its internal dynamics and strategies, its relation with its immediate adversary, its relation with the state, and its location in the broader culture (for example, the constitution of "abolitionists" as the predominant voice against slavery, the direct conflict between abolitionists and Southern slaveholders, the complex relation between abolitionists and the federal government, and the place of abolitionism in the broader culture, particularly in the North). Each of these four components is highly dynamic; together, they create a context of continuous change.

As a result of this fluidity, there is no schematic framework that can simplify the analysis of social movement dynamics. Therefore, there is no substitute for a nuanced and detailed historical analysis of the social movement press in the context of the movement of which it is a part. Conventional measures of a journal's importance, such as circulation, financial stability, and longevity, may—or may not—be meaningful indicators of the significance of a movement publication. Movement publishers who cling single-mindedly to these objectives may miss crucial opportunities to contribute to overall movement goals, and historians committing the same error may similarly underestimate (or overestimate) the importance of movement journals.

With proper attention to historical detail, however, we find that the social movement press—including journals of seemingly marginal importance at first glance—has played a critical role in the constant process of reinventing American society.

"Objectivity," circulation, longevity, geographic distribution, and advertising revenue are commonly considered universal standards by which the importance of newspapers and magazines can be measured. For the corporate media, however, these measures are tools for maximizing profits, not ends in themselves. As such they are quite useful. Any business plan for running a publication as a profit-making endeavor must incorporate all these tools in a thoughtful and ongoing way. Advertising revenue generates profit. Circulation supports advertising. Longevity keeps the money coming. A large geographic distribution diversifies the profit base and shields against local downturns.

"Objectivity" is the ideological rationale for the whole enterprise. "Objective" and "unbiased" became media buzzwords only as a direct offshoot of the concentration of media ownership. Prior to the giant media oligopolists, these notions were conspicuously absent from American journalism. Newspapers and magazines were published because the people who created them had a point of view they wanted to get across and made no bones about it. The notion that journalists should—or even could—write without a viewpoint or opinion emerged as a necessary ideological underpinning of media oligopoly, the selling point for the idea that media control by the few is not inherently detrimental to democratic institutions or culture.

Social movement journalism seeks to promote ideas, not profits; movement journals seek to challenge corporate control of media, not justify it. They address readers as members of communities, not individual consumers. They cover social movements as participants, not "observers." They exist to make change, not business. If the political context of a given movement at a particular time offers conditions in which a long-lived, large-circulation, profit-making journal can be strategically employed to further movement goals, then these are meaningful accomplishments. If such conditions are not present, these measures may be irrelevant.

This is not to imply that social movement publications always come up short by the standards of corporate journalism. The *Sierra Club Bulletin* (now just *Sierra*) has been in continuous publication for more than a hundred years. The *Earth First! Journal* made a small profit beginning with its very first issue (mainstream publications typically expect a year, or more of red ink on the corporate ledger). Some gay and lesbian publications now produce profits that make the corporate giants envious (and the journals possible takeover targets). The AIDS epidemic, one of the biggest stories of the twentieth century, was first reported by a volunteer writer in the *New York*

Native, a gay community paper less than one year old at the time. Gay papers consistently scooped the mainstream press in coverage of the epidemic for years afterward.

William Lloyd Garrison's *Liberator,* by contrast, had nothing along these lines to recommend it. It was a one-man operation that never had a "scoop." In fact, it rarely had news at all in the conventional meaning of the term. It consistently lost money and at its peak had only three thousand subscribers, yet it remains one of the most influential newspapers in U.S. history. Its demand for immediate, as opposed to gradual, emancipation moved from the outer fringe of the abolitionist movement to its core, and then to national policy with the Emancipation Proclamation. Its uncompromising voice spread well beyond abolitionists to inspire and inform early women's rights activists and many others. It even bequeathed us the term "Garrisonian," an adjective first used to describe the most militant brand of abolitionism and later generalized to indicate an uncompromising willingness to speak one's mind on social-justice issues, regardless of the consequences.

Frederick Douglass, a former slave, had to lecture constantly and mortgage his home simply to keep his papers in print, yet he is considered one of the giants of American political writing. One hundred years later, *Not Man Apart,* published by Friends of the Earth with little money, few volunteer writers, and a circulation of thirty-five thousand, was more influential in its day than any other environmental journal, including the *Sierra Club Bulletin* (which then had a circulation of three hundred thousand) and *Greenpeace* (with a circulation of more than a *million*).

If profitability and circulation are not reliable measures of the contribution of movement publications to the overall goals of the movement of which they are a part, what about other conventional standards, such as longevity? Duration of publication is certainly a measure by which the wheat of American journalism is typically separated from the chaff.

Here again we find influential journals at both ends of the spectrum, with no reliable correlation between longevity and contribution to movement goals. The *Sierra Club Bulletin / Sierra* has been publishing continuously for more than a century. *Walker's Appeal* and the early woman suffrage pamphlets were one-issue affairs. *The Furies* became "legendary" among lesbians in the second half of the twentieth century, despite having published for less than a year.

The Liberator set an early standard with thirty-five years of uninterrupted publication, spanning the period from the earliest articulation of "abolitionism" to the legal abolition of slavery. But what if abolition had been achieved in ten years instead of thirty-five? *The Liberator* would not have entered the historical record with its lofty thirty-five years; but would the reduced life span indicate a *less* successful journal or a *more* successful one?

In both the abolitionist and woman suffrage movements, even the softer-focused, larger-circulation publications went into a tailspin in the period just prior to victory, with many publications closing their doors. In both cases, however, the demise was a consequence of the movements' concerns moving to the front page of the mainstream press. Here again, was the termination of so many publications a sign of the journals' failure or of their success?

Longevity is a particularly interesting conundrum in that it is equally prized by the profit-driven media *and* by most movement publishers. Although nearly all movement publishers acknowledge that making a profit is not what movement publishing is about, many still believe that the longevity of their publication is a certain indicator of their contribution to their cause. This notion is a particular manifestation of the conventional activist wisdom that gives priority to building lasting institutions that can outlive the transitory character of activist upsurges and thus "build for the long haul." The idea is that by outliving the upsurge that created them, institutions such as journals can continue to further their cause and remain at the ready so that when the next upsurge comes, the movement will have seasoned organizations ready to roll and not have to "reinvent the wheel." This notion too does not hold up well under historical scrutiny.

The tiny gay and lesbian papers that emerged in the 1950s and early 1960s assembled a remarkable track record. They fought for and won the right to publish and distribute materials that discussed homosexuality. They developed a dedicated core of increasingly confident and experienced activists and a loyal readership. By conventional reckoning, they should have been perfectly positioned to lead the charge if a real mass movement emerged. But when "gay liberation" exploded in the aftermath of Stonewall, these publications appeared confused and outdated, and they quickly folded. After years of barely eking out an existence in the desert, they starved in the midst of abundance. The movement itself, however, was none the worse for it, as new publications more in tune with the times sprung up.

What of the environmental movement? After decades of "long-haul" journalism as the most prominent voice of "conservationism" and "outdoor enthusiasts," the *Sierra Club Bulletin* should have been perfectly positioned for the 1960s and the birth of "environmentalism." It even had an editor well suited to the job in the form of David Brower, who tried everything within his considerable personal powers to cajole the journal forward into the new era. The result was that Brower was run out of the organization and started a new journal, the aforementioned *Not Man Apart*, with substantially less money, fewer staff—and more clout.

If the record of journals attempting to make the transition from an era of relative quiescence to a time of widespread activism is one of failure, what of those journals which emerged during a movement's heyday and survived the subsequent decline? Here the record is even worse.

The pioneer gay glossy *The Advocate* is a particularly dramatic example. Launched as a community-based journal to track police violence against homosexuals, *The Advocate* reinvented itself as a slick "lifestyle" magazine; it not only managed to survive the decline of gay radicalism but attained a commercial success unparalleled in the history of social movement journalism, with major advertising accounts, Wall Street investors, and substantial profits. Yet in terms of social-justice advocacy, the latter-day *Advocate* has been simply awful. The quality of its content traces a trajectory almost the exact inverse to its profitability.

The underground press of the 1960s fared no better. The few underground papers that survived the waning of the counterculture did so through an increasing reliance on sex ads in the personals, a tradition that began as an expression of "free love" ethics and degenerated into fairly unexceptional pornography. And then there was *Rolling Stone*, which secured an advertising base by explicitly purging the counterculture of radical politics.

Journals that closed when they sensed their time was up appear in a comparatively appealing light. These range from Garrison's *Liberator* to the 1970s' lesbian journal *Amazon Quarterly*. Once abolition was achieved, Garrison abruptly and unceremoniously shut his paper down, despite widespread criticism by his allies. Gina Covina of the *Amazon Quarterly* went straight to the point when she noted, "When we quit to pursue other interests, we didn't feel guilty because we weren't, by any means, leaving a vacuum.... There were lots of other papers. We weren't needed in the same way we had been."[2]

This conundrum is rooted in the very nature of institutions in general and the particularities of movement journals in specific. Social power is always exercised through institutions, be they banks or mafias, armies or churches, states or families, antislavery committees or environmental journals. By creating a stable set of relations among their members and rules for their behavior, institutions make it possible to aggregate social resources and personal energies. These very things, these fixed rules and relations, make institutions by nature resistant to change, to at least some degree. Yet institutions function in a social milieu of constant change. This confrontation between institutional rigidity and social fluidity results in perennial endeavors of institutional reform, and movement publications are no exception. In general, building an institution is a difficult project, and reforming an existing institution is often a more efficient strategy than launching a new one.

As institutions go, however, the start-up costs associated with launching a movement journal are remarkably low; a handful of people (or even one person) and a few dollars have often been sufficient. The cost of reforming an existing journal may be much higher. Movement journals are typically staffed by people who work long hours for little or no pay and who often perceive challenges to their existing way of doing things as invalidating the many sacrifices they have made. This accounts for the conspicuous failure of most movement journals to outlast the particular social and political context in which they emerge, and for the ease with which they are often replaced by new journals more in tune with the times. *Mother Earth News* is one of the very rare exceptions to this pattern; emerging from the widespread "back-to-the-land" movement of the 1970s, the journal managed to transition from an activist-run publication to a professional enterprise without losing focus on its core social and political objectives.

This book is not a chronological history of the varied fortunes of the major social movement publications. Since it is my thesis that social movement publications can be judged only by their integration into a viable movement strategy, the publications are grouped according to movement, not time. Nor do I attempt an exhaustive history of all the journals in all social movements in American history, a mammoth undertaking that would lead us far from the issues on which I wish to focus. Instead, I concentrate on a few movements that, taken together, highlight the complexity of the interplay between the journals, the social movements that produced them, and the social and political conditions the movements sought to address. These include the abolitionist, woman suffrage, gay and lesbian, and environmental movements, as well as the underground GI press during the Vietnam War.

This collection will allow for a broad mix of issues of class, race, gender, and age; of movements whose goals were as specific as abolishing slavery, enfranchising women, ending the American military adventure in Vietnam and as broad and diffuse as countering homophobia throughout the culture or protecting the environment. It will take our gaze to every region in the nation, and then beyond its borders. It will carry us from the sparse, privately owned media environment of the nineteenth century to the corporate media saturation of the present. Last but certainly not least, it will frame the book with the most important innovations in printing technology since the invention of the printing press: the invention of the iron press and machine-made paper at the start of the nineteenth century, which made the abolitionist press possible; the invention of offset printing, which fueled the radical upsurge of the 1960s and 1970s; and the development of desktop publishing in the 1980s and 1990s, which gave rise to the zine explosion. The book will end with the emergence of the Internet, which in some ways signals the end of the era of the social movement *press*. By starting in 1830 and ending in the present, this work will span the entire era.

This approach leaves some venerable publications out of our frame. *The Appeal to Reason,* the standard-bearer of the socialist movement and one of the most successful movement papers ever, will not make an appearance, since the socialist movement of the early twentieth century is not examined. Also absent are journals that contributed to many movements yet were not rooted in any particular one; these include *The Nation* (the granddaddy of them all, which has published since 1865); *The Catholic Worker, Liberation, I. F. Stone's Weekly* (all maintained a progressive voice in the wasteland of the 1950s, but they were lonely voices in the wilderness); and *Mother Jones* (which has consistently published major-impact investigative pieces on environmental issues). More mainstream publications that have made significant contributions to movement objectives are also omitted. *The New Yorker,* for example, played a major role in the formulation of early environmentalism when it published serialized versions of both Rachel Carson's *Silent Spring* in the 1960s and Barry Commoner's *Closing Circle* in the 1970s. Urban weeklies have in many cases published investigative environmental pieces of regional or local significance.

As important as these journals are, their inclusion would have confused this study, not clarified it. The *Washington Post*, for example, was crucial to ending the Vietnam War, since its Watergate reporting was key to bringing down the political coalition that waged it. Yet to conclude that the *Washington Post* was thus somehow a movement journal would be absurd. My interest is not in the professional journalists working for mainstream institutions deeply embedded in the power structures of American society, who were professionally trained for their trade at prestigious institutions of higher learning, and who ultimately are accountable to a corporate board of directors. Rather, I am interested in the "accidental" journalists who, out of a sense of social justice, volunteered to do whatever was needed for a particular cause and ended up as journalists.

People in positions of institutional power, whether generals, politicians, bankers, and even journalists, exercise some degree of social power during the course of their everyday professional lives. For everyone else, if we seek to have a voice in shaping our society beyond our immediate social circle, we have to step outside our daily existence into roles to which we are not accustomed and for which we have little or no institutional support. We have to band together to maximize our very limited time and resources. Before we can do any of that, we have to find each other—identify others with the same interests who are also willing to step outside their daily lives to pursue our long-shot objectives. We have to see who's good at what, who else is doing what, who might rise to the occasion if given half a chance. We have to make plans, formulate strategies, set priorities. We have to agitate, educate, mobilize, confront, and more. In short, we have to constitute ourselves as a political subject, a constituency, a *social movement*. And if we had done this sometime between 1830 and 2000, we would have made a newspaper. In most cases, it would have been the first thing we did.

I stated at the outset that there is no schematic framework that can simplify the analysis of social movement dynamics, no "stages" theory of social movements, and therefore no substitute for nuanced and detailed historical analysis of movement publications in the context of the movement of which they were a part. The movements included in this book demonstrate my point. The trajectory of the abolitionist movement is the most neatly linear. The goal of immediate abolition of slavery with full political rights for slaves emerged as a consensus after years of debate between various alternatives. Once abolitionism took off, it witnessed a relatively steady increase in its number of adherents in its first thirty years—men and women who grew increasingly militant and vocal. The goal of woman suffrage likewise emerged out of a variety of ideas for the advancement of women's rights, accompanied by an upsurge of militant activity. But then the movement fell into decades of "doldrums" during which it adopted an increasingly mainstream, genteel tenor. Final victory came with a whimper, not a bang.

The gay and lesbian movement followed an altogether different trajectory. Accumulating momentum very gradually in the 1950s and early 1960s, it suddenly exploded into a mass movement when its trickle of activists flowed into the mighty river of 1960s radicalism. This momentum lasted well into the 1970s, creating a golden age of "gay liberation" when breathtaking victories were won in a stunningly short period of time. The movement then began to disintegrate, until the AIDS epidemic forced the community back into political mobilization.

The GI movement is even more narrowly bound by the period of U.S. military intervention in Vietnam. The movement grew from nothing at the outset of the 1960s to a power that brought the world's most formidable military to a grinding halt, then quickly dissipated when U.S. combat operations in Southeast Asia ceased.

The environmental movement offers yet another trajectory. The movement's key victories (the creation of the EPA, the Clean Water Act, and the Endangered Species Act, among them) date from the widespread activism of the 1960s and 1970s. Since that time, as the global environmental catastrophe has become increasingly apparent, the issue has gained a more or less permanent place in the corporate media. This has helped create a continuous widespread interest in the issue and broad support in opinion polls, yet most "members" of environmental organizations limit their activities to mailing checks to national organizations. The crisis this movement seeks to address, meanwhile, presents no clear solutions, such as abolishing slavery, enfranchising women, or withdrawing from Vietnam.

The trajectories of the press that these movements created are just as varied as the movements themselves. The abolitionist and woman suffrage press are the most similar. In both cases, extremely radical fringe journals came first (*The Liberator, Revolution*), followed by journals with a progressively softer tone and broader circulation (*National Era, Women's Journal, Women's Column*). Finally, there was an across-the-board decline, and even collapse, of the movements' journals in the period just before victory was won.

Both movements achieved consensus on one very specific policy objective around which everything in the movement then revolved (immediate emancipation without emigration for the abolitionists and suffrage for women). But consensus was not something the movements were born with; it developed over time. Should emancipation happen gradually or all at once? Should the freed slaves be sent abroad or remain in the United States? Should they have the full political rights of citizenship? Should the U.S. Constitution be replaced or amended? All these questions remained unresolved in the early years of abolitionism. Winning the vote for women likewise emerged only gradually as the consensus objective among nineteenth-century American feminists, whose concerns entailed a much broader vision of women's rights.

In both movements, it was in the early period, when ideological and policy consensus was up for grabs, that radical journals could hold sway with tiny circulations and no resources other than the passion of their publishers' convictions and the fire in their words. Once the movement's direction was settled and the task of the day became winning converts to a generally accepted program, uncompromising adherence to principle became a much less valuable asset, and more conventional assets like financial backing, a stable staff, and a more flexible appeal increased in importance. The *National Era*, which dominated the later stages of the abolitionist movement, quickly reached a circulation nearly ten times the peak achieved by either Garrison or Frederick Douglass. In the woman suffrage movement, the later and tamer *Women's Journal* quickly outran the *Revolution* by the same proportion.

The gay and lesbian movement, by contrast, never had one objective that if won would constitute "victory." Even the present-day battles over marriage rights and military service do not represent anything close to a consensus in the gay and lesbian movement, and those activists who do prioritize these issues do not imagine that achieving these objectives would constitute anything more than another step on a long journey. The environmental movement is even farther afield, addressing challenges that will never be "won" but only better managed, and which promise to become only more complex and thorny. The path cut by these movements is thus less linear, and the story of what resources are most valuable to movement journals and when is correspondingly more complex.

The *Sierra Club Bulletin* (now *Sierra*), the flagship of the environmental movement press with a huge circulation and the financial muscle of the Sierra Club behind it, has been enormously effective— *when it has been used as one element of a broader activist strategy*. The publication reached its apogee of influence in the successful fight to prevent the damming of the Grand Canyon, when David Brower used the *Bulletin* in close coordination with grass-roots mobilization, aggressive lobbying, and paid advertising in the *New York Times*. In other periods, when the journal has not been as tightly linked to an audacious political strategy, its clout faded dramatically, despite its having a larger circulation, a more stable staff, and healthier finances.

The *Earth First! Journal* offers another successful example of the strategic use of a journal. The paper was launched with essentially no money and peaked at ten thousand subscribers, yet this was sufficient to achieve the goal its publishers had in mind: not so much to win policy battles per se as to redefine the left fringe of the movement as a magnet that would pull the entire environmental debate to the left.

My main thesis—that the history of social movement journalism can be understood only in the context of the particular movements of which each journal was a part—can be abbreviated as follows: *words do not make history.* No argument, no matter how brilliantly reasoned or beautifully articulated, can create more democracy. Words are central to this book, but this book is not about words. The fact that I regard the history of the social movement press as a crucial and neglected part of the history of social movements does not mean that I think the social movement press—or any other press—is capable of doing *anything* on its own.

Words matter, but only when something is *done* with them, and the specifics of what is done matter too. It is not just a question of whether words are shared but of *how* they are shared. How do words make it to the page (or the screen or the microphone)? How are the pages distributed? By what means do the recipients respond? How are the resources for the whole effort marshaled? What social relationships develop as a consequence? How do these relationships dovetail with other relationships in the constitution of a social movement? How do those relationships fit into the broader culture? How can they be deployed when the movement confronts its adversaries?

The ultimate impact of social movements on society has everything to do with the resources that movements bring to such confrontations. Those resources might include almost anything: money, guns, land, technical expertise, votes, education, social history, cultural coherence, communication channels, access to the means of production, the means of culture, the means to disrupt the social peace. Full-blown theories of social movements and social change must account for all of these. This book examines just one: the press the movements themselves create. Overarching theories of social power and social change are thus beyond the reach of this study.

Although the movement press is just one resource among many, it is a very particular and important one. Because it is simple to establish, a rudimentary press is easily within the reach of even the most resource-poor movements. It is extremely malleable and capable of quick reconfiguration. The fact that it is often the first tool for which a movement reaches should come as no surprise. Words are what we use to think. Without descending into the arcana of academic debates on language and knowledge, we must address the fundamental fact that social actors—whether individual or collective—must constitute themselves through words. For social movements in the period I have studied, the printed word was supreme. The broadcast word, when it appeared, was nearly always beyond their reach, and the digital word did not yet exist.

If context is the key to understanding the social movement press, there is no element of context more important than the increasingly dense web of communications we call media. What it meant for the Sierra Club to have its own magazine was completely different in 1895, 1965, and 2005. Since the appearance of *Freedom's Journal* in New York City in 1827, the media have grown from a handful of newspapers in a few major cities into an environment in which we are so totally immersed that we often don't notice its presence. Media images and sounds are as inescapable to us as the natural environment once was to agricultural societies. For many people, these sounds and images constitute the whole of contemporary culture, defining their nation, their community, and even their families and individual identities. There is, however, nothing natural about this media-drenched world. It has been constructed by people, and overwhelmingly for one central reason: profit.

The limited print media of the nineteenth century was joined by movies, then radio, and then television. Television itself moved from a few homes to all homes, then to multiple rooms in many homes. According to Nielsen Media Research, by the end of the twentieth century 98.1 percent of U.S. households had at least one television, and 50 percent had three or more. These televisions were turned on an *average* of 7 hours and 12 minutes a day. The average American spends the equivalent of 70 days of nonstop TV watching per year, and by the age of sixty-five she or he will have spent nearly 9 years glued to the tube.[3]

Advertising, once largely confined to television, radio, and print, has become a sort of expeditionary force infiltrating every conceivable social space. Banks sell advertising to fill the few seconds at an ATM between a customer's last push of a button and the magical appearance of the requested cash, ensuring that no American spends even a few commercial-free seconds before a screen. Telephone services offer free minutes to customers who are willing to keep the phone to their ear for a few minutes of advertising. Go out for a beer, and chances are your view at the bar will include multiple screens, each with different content. A trip to the bar's restrooms will bring you eyeball to eyeball with small billboards managed by corporate agencies, lest the time you spend there be lost to the world of corporate marketing. Numerous "stealth-marketing" techniques have turned movie plots, concerts, and even private conversations into marketing events.

Who owns all this? In 1983, when Ben Bagdikian published the first edition of *The Media Monopoly*, 50 corporations dominated the U.S. mass media, and the biggest media merger in history was a $340 million deal. By 1987 those 50 corporations had shrunk to 29. By 1997 the 29 had shrunk to 10, one of which was created in the $19 billion merger of Disney and ABC. Just three years later, the end of the century saw the 10 shrink to just 5 amid the $350 *billion* merger of AOL and Time Warner, a deal more than a thousand times larger than "the biggest deal in history" just seventeen years earlier. As Bagdikian noted in his 2004 edition, "In 1983, the men and women who headed the first mass media corporations that dominated American audiences could have fit comfortably in a modest hotel ballroom.... By 2003, [they] could fit in a generous phone booth."[4] After reviewing FCC data, Senator John McCain concurred, "Five companies control 85 percent of our media sources."[5]

These five firms are among the world's largest corporations. All are listed in *Fortune* magazine's Global 500 largest corporations in the world. They have integrated horizontally, acquiring control of many newspapers across the nation, which serve different local markets. And they have integrated vertically, controlling newspapers, magazines, book publishing houses, and movie and TV production studios, as well as print distribution systems, cable and broadcast TV networks, radio stations, telephone lines, satellite systems, Web portals, billboards, and more.

"Censorship" is an entirely insufficient description of the effect of corporate media control on our culture. This is not to say that blatant old-school censorship does not exist. Far more common, however, is the more subtle but much more powerful form of censorship that frames news, entertainment, and advertising so as to limit the range of options for social change to those that are consistent with corporate interests. This kind of censorship tends to be self-reinforcing; for example, it is virtually impossible to find any discussion of corporate control of the media in any media hat are corporately controlled. "Debate" is then confined within this stunted domain. As comedian Jon Stewart noted, to call this *debate* is akin to calling Pro Wrestling an athletic sporting competition.[6] Finally, it is crucial to note that although the forty thousand TV commercials the average child sees per year and the two million commercials the average American has seen by the age of sixty-five advertise a wide range of products, they all sell the same fundamental idea: the route to happiness and a better life is through *buying stuff*, and not through any kind of community or collective action.

Of all the stories that are censored, distorted, or simply ignored by the corporate news media, none suffers more than the story of social movements that challenge corporate power. Most often these are simply ignored. Demonstrations or strikes of thousands of people fail to win a mention. When they are visible at all, they are usually as *spectacle*—violence at a demonstration, arrests at a picket line, the financial problems of an organization, or the flamboyance of celebrity leaders. The *substance* of the movements' concerns is nearly always absent. Even more invisible is anything that accurately represents the experience of being part of a movement: the sense of personal transformation and community, the sense of hope, and the satisfaction of participating in history.

There is a countermovement to the corporate media grab; although not on the same scale as the titans of the mass media, it is real, significant and growing. At the outset of the unprecedented social ferment of the 1960s, only a handful of journals reported on the decade's upheaval from a movement perspective. By the end of the decade, the *Alternative Press Index* listed 72 active periodicals on the "alternative" end of the media spectrum; thirty years later, the *Index* included 270 titles, a nearly fourfold increase; and today the 2004 edition of the *Index* lists 385 titles. Similarly, the membership of the Independent Press Association (IPA) has grown from 20 titles when it was launched in 1996 to more than 575 at this writing.

These publications cover a kaleidoscope of constituencies and ideas. *In These Times,* a biweekly alternative newsmagazine, has a conventionally leftist political perspective, a circulation of 12,000, and a history going back twenty-two years. *Hip Mama,* a quarterly that was started in 1994 by a single mother on welfare, is for parents in nontraditional child-rearing situations and has a circulation of 3,000. *Hues* was launched in 1992 by three nineteen-year-olds for the benefit of "women who don't meet the conventional, airbrushed image found in most magazines."

There is also a vast and growing "ethnic press." In a 2001 study, the IPA identified 250 ethnic and community newspapers in New York City alone. In 2003 the IPA found another 250 in the Chicago metropolitan area. Some of these publications focus on news from immigrants' home countries, and others on local ethnic communities. Although these papers encompass a wide range of political views, many focus on issues of social justice. And none of these numbers include the thousands of newsletters of local activist organizations or the countless Web zines, blogs, and Web sites that defy simple categorization.

In this age of mass media saturation and expansion of corporate power both globally and domestically, the fact that this vast world of independent media remains beyond the grasp of corporate control gains a political and cultural significance that is above and beyond the political platforms of the individual publications. The independent media form a counterculture in the most literal sense: a culture based in community (however that is defined, and there are many ways) and individual creativity that runs counter to the dominant culture of corporate hegemony and mass consumption. This counterculture will be crucial to whatever the future holds for movements for social justice.

Complex human societies are inherently hierarchical and unjust. Movements for social justice challenge the existing hierarchy and pit the weak against the strong. To the dispassionate observer, the odds for success must always seem remote and often so lopsided that participation in social movements, or even belief in the possibility of social change, appears irrational. Choosing to become active in a movement for social justice involves at its core a leap of faith, a stepping out of predefined social roles. Barry Romo, former leader of Vietnam Veterans Against the War, summed up this transformative experience beautifully:

> Someone once said, "How can you change so quickly?" I said, "Well, it wasn't a question of changing quickly; it was a question of being in shock after taking the blinders off. When you take sunglasses off, the sun shines in: it doesn't trickle in, it doesn't take time, it all becomes bright."

The creation of a community and culture that invite and then sustain these transformations is crucial to movements facing irrationally long odds. It is here that the social movement press has played its most important role. Learning to write, publish, and distribute a paper is empowering in all aspects of organizing. Finding the words to express oneself, building enough of an organization to manage the production of a journal, finding the nerve to approach others with the copies—these are experiences that can turn a "nobody" into an agent of social change.

The process snowballs when the finished paper falls into the right hands. Overcoming isolation is often the first step in this transformation, whether the isolation is that of the runaway slave living in fear of the slave hunter, the woman trapped in the social straitjacket of the "housewife," the closeted homosexual, or the soldier under the constant surveillance of his superiors. Isolation is the great inhibitor of political engagement, the problem at which any social movement must begin. Testimonies down through the decades speak of the singular impact that movement journals have had for individuals in this transformation from passive isolation to engaged citizen.

> It sent a thrill of joy [through my soul]. I loved this paper, and its editor. His words were few, full of holy fire, and straight to the point.
>
> FREDERICK DOUGLASS ON THE LIBERATOR

> In the darkness and gloom of a false theology, I was slowly sawing off the chains of my spiritual bondage. . . . A few bold strokes from the hammer of his truth and I was free! Only those who have lived all their lives under the dark clouds of vague, undefined fears can appreciate the joy of a doubting soul suddenly born into the kingdom of reason and free thought.
>
> ELIZABETH CADY STANTON ON THE LIBERATOR

> A woman would read just one article that touched a certain sensibility in her—and suddenly her life was turned upside down. She embraced the lesbian culture as the center of her very existence. When that process is repeated for women in tiny, isolated communities from coast to coast—women who previously trembled in fear but then began asserting their own self-worth—the impact cannot be measured in mere numbers.
>
> LESBIAN HERSTORY ARCHIVES COFOUNDER
> JOAN NESTLE ON THE LESBIAN TIDE

*I was exposed to a lot of dissent in college. I would walk through demon-
strators in my ROTC uniform. [But the GI paper] really impacted on me
personally. I had no other contact at that time with anyone who was
antiwar.*

JIM WILLINGHAM ON YOUR MILITARY LEFT

*I am REALLY psyched to be in on the Homocore deal. I can't tell you
what a fucking great idea the zine is—gay people and hardcores get
such shit and are so pushed down and (the big one) it's SO FUCKING
LONELY!*

LETTER TO HOMOCORE, 1998

The Nineteenth Century

ABOLITIONISTS AND WOMAN SUFFRAGISTS

In December 1830 a twenty-six-year-old printer put pen to paper in a Boston attic to announce the launch of a small journal:

> I determined, at every hazard, to lift up the standard of emancipation in the eyes of the nation, within sight of Bunker Hill, and in the birthplace of liberty. That standard is now unfurled; and long may it float, unhurt by the spoliations of time or the missiles of a desperate foe; yea, till every chain be broken, and every bondman set free! Let Southern oppressors tremble; let their secret abettors tremble; let their Northern apologists tremble; let all the enemies of the persecuted blacks tremble.[1]

Who was this mighty individual who could set such a powerful array of adversaries trembling with desperation at the mere unfurling of his banner? What armies did he command? What vast wealth was at his disposal? What coalition of interests stood behind him?

The writer was William Lloyd Garrison, and he had none of these things. In fact, he was flat broke and virtually alone. He launched his little paper, *The Liberator*, without securing a single subscriber in advance. The very paper it was printed on was obtained on credit. The attic served as his office, print shop, and home, and his meals were largely limited to what he could finagle from a nearby bakery. Yet after a year's publication, *The Liberator*, which still counted its subscribers in the hundreds, had indeed managed to set "Southern oppressors[,]...their secret abettors[,]...and their Northern apologists" trembling with rage. The Georgia state legislature offered $5,000 for Garrison's dead body, and the Vigilance Association of Columbia, South Carolina (composed of "gentlemen of the first respectability"), promised $1,500 for the "apprehension and prosecution to conviction" of any white person caught distributing *The Liberator*.[2]

Thirty-four years later, the corpses of more than six hundred thousand young men lay rotting in shallow graves on battlefields across a country in the flames of war. The Union army that advanced into the abandoned Confederate capital to accept the formal surrender of the Confederacy was more than 10 percent black. Slavery was abolished. Garrison was still publishing *The Liberator*, though its circulation had never surpassed three thousand and it lost money on every issue from the first to the last. Yet when Fort Sumter—the site of the war's first battle—was finally reconquered, the president of the United States invited Garrison to do the honor of hoisting the Stars and Stripes.[3]

To understand Garrison's stature, we must step back into the "media world" of 1831. Strip away the more than 130 million personal computers Americans buy each year.[4] Unplug the 18.7 million Playstation 2s, the 5.7 million Xboxes, the 4.4 million GameBoys, and the millions of other electronic gaming devices.[5] Turn off the projectors at the 36,652 commercial movie screens.[6] Turn off the 428 million television sets in American homes, not forgetting to look around for the 3 or more that we will find in nearly half of American homes.[7] Then turn off the radios that receive broadcasts from the 13,804 broadcast radio stations.[8] Find and destroy all the compact discs, records, cassette tapes, iPods, cameras, PDAs, and other electronic devices. Now remove all the billboards, all the neon signs.

Finally, take away most of the books, magazines, and even newspapers. When Garrison launched *The Liberator*, the combined circulation of *all* U.S. newspapers was somewhere in the neighborhood of 50,000; in 2004, both *USA Today* and the *Wall Street Journal* had nearly 2 million subscribers each, and the Sunday circulation of all newspapers hovered at 60 million. That 60 million comes to 1 newspaper for every 4 people in America; in 1830, the ratio was 1 to 17, and there were no other media.[9]

In the social space that had been occupied by all those media, we would find but one thing: *words*. Garrison's world was one in which words—the printed word in particular—had a power we can scarcely imagine today. When referring to Garrison, abolitionist-turned-woman-suffrage-leader Elizabeth Cady Stanton described words as a "hammer of truth" that could free a person's mind with "a few bold strokes."[10]

Discussions about American democracy, and how it might be reformed for the better, occupied the heart of what we might now consider popular culture. Speeches by traveling lecturers were not only a key element in national politics but a principal form of popular entertainment. The lecturer, however, came and went. The only tangible artifact the speaker could leave behind was the printed word, most often in a newspaper or pamphlet. As Clara Belwick Colby, publisher of the *Women's Tribune*, put it:

> *The spoken word has its power for the day, but for building up a new line of thought in the popular heart there must be the written word. . . . [W]hile the lecture amuses and interests for an hour or two . . . the paper read in quiet moments gradually makes conviction, and the reader instead of being transitorily influenced by the opinion of another, builds up opinions of his own.*[11]

The social weight of these publications bore no resemblance to that of the newspaper that arrives at our doorstep or the pamphlets that clog our mailboxes, both of which are fortunate if even a tenth of their words pass before a human eye on the trip to the recycling bin. As the only mechanically reproducible artifact of human communication, publications of the 1830s enjoyed a near monopoly on the popular imagination and were read from cover to cover. They were pored over, put away for safekeeping, then retrieved and studied anew. They were hoarded, shared, handed off, and discussed. Just as a jury does not vote up or down at the end of a trial but retires to the jury room to deliberate the validity of the claims made at trial, nineteenth-century Americans would retire from attendance at a public lecture to deliberate the truth of the speaker's claims based on the evidence left behind in the newspaper or pamphlet.

One such pamphlet was written by a free black man named David Walker. Commonly referred to as *Walker's Appeal,* the full title of his pamphlet was *Walker's Appeal, in Four Articles: Together with a Preamble, to the Coloured Citizens of the World, but in Particular and Very Expressly, to Those of the United States of America.*

This title was chosen by a man who wanted to get his words *right.* Today such a belief in the power of words would strike us as naive, but in 1829 each of David Walker's words *were* powerful. His *Appeal,* the work of an unknown, first-time, and self-publishing black writer working out of a used clothing store, caused riots, changed laws, resulted in murder and imprisonment, and shifted the frame of the national debate about slavery.

As with the Internet today, the abolitionists rode on the crest of a wave of technological change that profoundly affected how information circulated through American culture. The printing process used to publish American newspapers in the early nineteenth century differed little from that used by the first press established in North America in 1639, which was itself hardly different from that used by Johannes Gutenberg in the fifteenth century. Early American printing used wooden Franklin presses to print on paper made by hand from rags, old clothing, and other newspapers. The entire process was exceedingly laborious and resulted in a product that was expensive by the standards of the day. Newspapers financed their production by selling yearlong subscriptions, payable in advance, at a price that left the publications out of reach for many. Newspapers were thus the province of the wealthy, literate few.

In the 1820s, however, the introduction of machine-made paper and more durable iron presses with a more efficient lever mechanism brought a sea change to printing. Penny Press papers appeared by the 1830s, priced at one cent instead of the typical six and hawked on the street issue by issue instead of via yearlong subscriptions. The Penny Press is considered the beginning of the modern American newspaper, and as such its history has been thoroughly examined. But the advantages of the new technology were hardly the monopoly of the Horace Greeleys of the Industrial Age. The first newspaper published by African Americans (*Freedom's Journal* in 1827), by labor (*The Philadelphia Journeyman Mechanic's Advocate* in 1827), and by Native Americans (the *Cherokee Phoenix* in 1828) date from this transition in printing technology. Broadly speaking, the "sudden availability of cheap, interesting reading material was a significant stimulus to the achievement of the nearly universal literacy now taken for granted in America."[12]

It was at this transition, when the printed word still carried the power of something rare, elevated, and a bit mysterious, yet now suddenly available to a much larger pool of writers and readers, that David Walker, William Lloyd Garrison, and other early abolitionists launched their endeavors in print.

The Abolitionist Press

The birth of the abolitionist press is generally traced to Jonesboro, Tennessee. Although Tennessee would eventually secede from the Union, the economy of its eastern portion did not depend on slave labor, and Quakers in the area spearheaded an active abolitionist movement a full generation before militant abolitionism would emerge in New England. In March 1819 Elihu Embree began publishing the *Manumission Intelligencer,* a weekly that continued for fifty issues. The term "manumission" referred to the legal release into freedom of a single slave by a single slave owner. After one year of publishing, Embree decided this was not what he had in mind and changed the name of his paper to *The Emancipator*—"emancipator" suggesting not the freeing of one slave but the end of slavery as a legal institution.[13]

Embree passed away just months later. By this time, however, another antislavery paper, *The Genius of Universal Emancipation*, was being published out of Mount Pleasant, Ohio, by another Quaker, named Benjamin Lundy.[14] Lundy was slight of stature, weak of constitution, and hard of hearing. He was neither a great orator nor a great writer, but his commitment to ending slavery was absolute. With the admittance of Missouri into the Union as a slave state on the horizon, Lundy decided to dedicate his life to the abolition of slavery in America. He loaded the inventory of his business on a barge and floated it to Saint Louis, where he sold all at a discount. Henceforth his every waking hour would be devoted to his cause. Upon Embree's death, the Quakers in Jonesboro offered Lundy the use of Embree's printing equipment, and Lundy relocated to eastern Tennessee.

To understand Benjamin Lundy, we must imagine not only a world without electronic media, telephones, and nearly all the print media of our time but also a world without cars. For Lundy, spreading the abolitionist creed was fundamentally a face-to-face proposition, and he literally walked around the country talking to whoever would listen. Upon accepting the offer of the use of the press in Tennessee, he walked from Ohio to Greensboro. But he didn't stop there for long. Soon he had walked through nineteen of the twenty-four states. Wherever he could he would organize a local antislavery society, starting 130 in total, all among Southern Quakers. Lundy integrated his work as a publisher and his work as an organizer in a most practical, albeit unusual, fashion. As he traversed the country, he "carried his type with him in his knapsack, set up his paper wherever he happened to find himself and got a printer to run off the edition." This was dangerous work, and his willingness to persevere despite the risks finally caught up with him in Baltimore, where a slave trader assaulted him, leaving him bleeding and unconscious in the street. He recounted the event in his journal without a trace of resentment or self-pity.[15]

While Lundy was walking the countryside, the first African American newspaper appeared in Boston. Samuel E. Cornish and John B. Russwurm, two freeborn African Americans, introduced *Freedom's Journal* on March 16, 1827:

> *We wish to plead our cause. Too long have others spoken for us. Too long has the public been deceived by misrepresentations in the things that concern us dearly. . . . In presenting our first number to our Patrons, we feel all the diffidence of persons entering upon a new and untried line of business. But a moment's reflection upon the noble objects, which we have in view by the publication of this Journal; the expediency of its appearance at this time, when so many schemes are in action concerning our people—encourage us to come boldly before an enlightened publick. For we believe, that a paper devoted to the dissemination of useful knowledge among our brethren, and to their moral and religious improvement, must meet with the cordial approbation of every friend to humanity.[16]*

Among the many notable things about *Freedom's Journal*, none stands out more than its distribution network. The inaugural issue listed fourteen "authorized agents" charged with selling subscriptions and promoting the paper in various parts of the country, including Salem, Massachusetts; Boston; Providence, Rhode Island; Philadelphia; Albany, New York; Washington, DC; and more. An agent in Port-au-Prince, Haiti, was listed beginning in the second issue. The space devoted to the list of agents steadily increased from a small box at the bottom of the page to an entire column. By the final issue, the number of *Freedom's Journal*'s authorized agents had grown to thirty-eight in four countries. Most significantly, the list grew to include a number of agents from Southern states: while in August 1827 there was only one in Virginia, by November there were two agents each in Virginia and Maryland. Three agents in North Carolina were added in January.[17] While Benjamin Lundy was walking the country attempting to personally set up a distribution network for an abolitionist press, *Freedom's Journal* seemed to have arrived on the scene with one already in place.

The "authorized agents" of *Freedom's Journal* were the tip of an iceberg, the publicly visible point at the top of an African American community that had developed considerably over the previous two decades. Free blacks in the North had established stable communities. Community leaders had emerged, usually through the church. These local community leaders were forming regional networks, at first through church denominations, then through the much more explicitly political Massachusetts General Colored Association. These connections gave the community much greater power than it had enjoyed previously.[18]

In keeping with the times, this emerging African American leadership gave importance of the first order to securing access to the printed word for their communities. Just as *Freedom's Journal* was publishing its first issues, reading societies such as the Colored Reading Society of Philadelphia and New York's Phoenix Society emerged in cities throughout the North, on the theory that the "condition" of African Americans could "only be meliorated by their being improved in . . . literature." A white abolitionist describes a visit to "a society of colored ladies, called the Female Literary Association," in Philadelphia:

> The members assemble every Tuesday evening for the purpose of mutual improvement in moral and literary pursuits. Nearly all of them write, almost weekly, original pieces, which are put anonymously into a box, and afterwards criticized by a committee. . . . If the traducers of the colored race could be acquainted with the moral worth, just refinement and large intelligence of this association, their mouths would hereafter be dumb.[19]

Freedom's Journal was conceived as a way of giving this network formal standing through its authorized agents and a permanent presence through its printed word. As Cornish announced in the inaugural issue, "It is our earnest wish to make our journal a medium of intercourse between our brethren in the different states of the great confederacy."[20]

The immediate political target of all these efforts was the American Colonization Society (ACS), which sought to send American blacks to populate its newly established colony of Liberia on the west coast of Africa. Established in 1816, the ACS quickly won the support of several Protestant denominations, fourteen state legislatures, and prominent political figures including Henry Clay, James Madison, James Monroe, and Daniel Webster. It amassed a sizable treasury for the purpose of recruiting black settlers and transporting them to Liberia.[21] Even Lundy, publishing the only white abolitionist paper of the day, envisioned the end of slavery as a gradual process of releasing blacks from servitude a few at a time, loading them onto ships, and sending them to Liberia, Haiti, or some other place acceptably far from the United States. An overwhelming majority of blacks, however, were vehemently opposed. Northern blacks felt little fear that they might eventually be forced into slavery like their Southern brethren, but the prospect of losing family, land, home, and possessions as part of a forced emigration to an unknown land suddenly seemed very real. They fiercely opposed the idea. The first national black convention had been held in Philadelphia in 1817, specifically to condemn colonization, but the convention—and the community at large—had no public voice. *Freedom's Journal* aimed to give them one.

Several years later, an orator addressing an African American convention reviewed the large public meetings blacks had held in Northern cities to denounce colonization and then noted that

> there was not a single public journal...secular or religious, which
> would publish the views of the people of color on the subject.... That
> was a dark and gloomy period. [But then] the united views and inten-

*tions of the people of color were [made] known, and the nation awoke
as from slumber. The* Freedom's Journal, *edited by the Rev. Sam'l E.
Cornish, announced the facts in the case, our entire opposition. Sir, it
came like a clap of thunder.*[22]

Freedom's Journal was not limited, however, to discussions of
slavery and colonization. On the contrary. "Elevating" the race or
"raising our community into respectability" was considered the
top priority, reflected in the motto on the masthead of each issue:
"Righteousness Exalteth a Nation." To this end, the publishers regularly included poetry, sermons, and essays on a wide range of topics. In the eyes of the publishers, none of this was a distraction from
or an addition to the fight against slavery. Rather, forming a literate,
educated leadership of the black community, in regular contact and
discussion, was the most urgent task in that long struggle. As Cornish would later write, "It is for us to convince the world by uniform
propriety of conduct, industry, and economy, that we are worthy
of esteem and patronage.... On our conduct in a great measure,
[Southern slaves'] salvation depends."[23]

Like many black papers to come, *Freedom's Journal* lasted a short
time—two years. By this time Cornish had withdrawn from editing.
Russwurm shocked his readers by announcing his conversion to the
ACS colonization plan, after which he closed the paper and eventually emigrated to Liberia, where he had a long and successful
political career. Outrage among Northern blacks was such that at
one public meeting, Russwurm was burned in effigy. For years after,
Russwurm's critics would allege he had betrayed his people, probably for money offered by the ACS. There is evidence, however,
that he reversed his previous position not for reward but in genuine
despair of ever changing whites' attitudes toward blacks. In his final editorial, Russwurm announced, "We consider it mere waste of
words to talk of ever enjoying citizenship in this country: it is utterly
impossible in the nature of things: all therefore who pant for these,
must cast their eyes elsewhere."[24]

Cornish, however, continued the work he had begun with Russwurm through a series of new papers. In 1828 he founded *Rights for All*, which lasted just six months. *The Advocate* soon followed, followed in its turn by *The Colored American*. Here Cornish finally found some stability. *The Colored American* published continuously for five years and reached a circulation of two thousand, spread across the Northern states.[25] Throughout, he continued to develop the authorized agents' network:

> Let the executive committees employ one general agent, whose duty it
> shall be to continue traveling from one extremity of our country to
> the other, forming associations, communicating with our people and
> the public generally, on all subjects of interest... thereby linking to-
> gether, by one solid chain, the whole free population, so as to
> make them think and feel, and act, as one solid body *[emphasis
> added]*.[26]

* * *

One of *Freedom's Journal*'s authorized agents was David Walker, but
he was much more than that. Walker was instrumental in gathering the resources to get *Freedom's Journal* off the ground. He was
also a major figure in the Massachusetts General Colored Association. Despite exhaustive historical research, we do not know when
or where this key political thinker was born, how or where he was
educated, when he arrived in Boston, or when or how he died.[27] We
have only hints concerning how widely distributed his writing actually was. What we do know is that he was born a free black in the
South, that he traveled extensively, and that by the time he finally
appeared on the pages of history running a used clothing store in
Boston, he wrote and spoke exceptionally well. And in 1829 he put
those skills to use by writing and then publishing his *Appeal*.

Walker's *Appeal* demonstrates an extremely tight integration of
writing, publishing/distribution, and political strategy, an integra-

WALKER'S

APPEAL,

IN FOUR ARTICLES;

TOGETHER WITH

A PREAMBLE,

TO THE

COLOURED CITIZENS OF THE WORLD,

BUT IN PARTICULAR, AND VERY EXPRESSLY, TO THOSE OF

THE UNITED STATES OF AMERICA,

WRITTEN IN BOSTON, STATE OF MASSACHUSETTS,
SEPTEMBER 28, 1829.

―――――

THIRD AND LAST EDITION,
WITH ADDITIONAL NOTES, CORRECTIONS, &c.

―――――

Boston:
REVISED AND PUBLISHED BY DAVID WALKER.
....
1830.

Walker's Appeal: *an integration of writing, distribution,*
and political strategy unparalleled in American journalism.

tion so coherent it has few peers in the history of the social movement press in America. In sharp contrast with *Freedom's Journal*, *Walker's Appeal* was directed to blacks as much in the South as in the North. Instead of arguing against the evil of slavery in general, Walker treated the specifics of slavery as found in the United States at the time. Instead of addressing the racism of the American Colonization Society, he confronted Thomas Jefferson, the icon of democracy for whites of the day.[28]

What earned Walker instant notoriety was his perceived advocacy of armed slave rebellion. For a Northern black to appeal to slaves to rise up and seek retribution against whites was unheard of. To do so in print was still more audacious. To then distribute this text to slaves throughout the South was downright incendiary.

In fact, Walker's text is enigmatic when it comes to violence. Walker was adamant about the *right* of slaves to rebel but uncertain about whether that right should be exercised. His stance toward violence can be seen as a forerunner, for example, of that of Nelson Mandela and the African National Congress (ANC) in South Africa under apartheid. Mandela spent many years in jail for refusing to renounce the right of South African blacks to armed resistance, even though the ANC placed far more importance on the role of strikes, demonstrations, boycotts, and education.

Walker hoped that his essay would bypass "the suburbs, just to enter more fully into the interior of this system of cruelty and oppression,"

> to demonstrate . . . to the satisfaction of the most incredulous mind, that we Coloured People of these United States, are, the most wretched, degraded and abject set of beings that ever lived since the world began. . . . The causes, my brethren, which produce our wretchedness and miseries, are so very numerous and aggravating, . . . so impenetrable, and so notorious, I shall be obliged to omit a large class of, and content myself with giving you an exposition of a few of those, which do indeed rage to such an alarming pitch, that they cannot but be a perpetual source of terror and dismay to every reflecting mind.

Walker took care to address the *particular* character of American slavery, at a time when the conditions of American slaves were deteriorating from an already shockingly inhuman level:

> *Heathen nations of antiquity, had but little more among them than the name and form of slavery; while wretchedness and endless miseries were reserved, apparently in a phial, to be poured out upon our fathers, ourselves and our children, by Christian Americans! . . . I call upon the professing Christians, I call upon the philanthropist, I call upon the very tyrant himself, to show me a page of history, either sacred or profane, on which a verse can be found, which maintains, that the Egyptians heaped the insupportable insult upon the children of Israel, by telling them that they were not of the human family. Can the whites deny this charge? . . . O! my God! I appeal to every man of feeling—is not this insupportable? . . . So far, my brethren, were the Egyptians from heaping these insults upon their slaves, that Pharaoh's daughter took Moses, a son of Israel for her own.*
>
> *Every body who has read history, knows, that as soon as a slave among the Romans obtained his freedom, he could rise to the greatest eminence in the State, and there was no law instituted to hinder a slave from buying his freedom. Have not the Americans instituted laws to hinder us from obtaining our freedom? Do any deny this charge? Read the laws of Virginia, North Carolina, &c. Further: have not the Americans instituted laws to prohibit a man of colour from obtaining and holding any office whatever, under the government of the United States of America?*
>
> *I have been for years troubling the pages of historians, to find out what our fathers have done to the white Christians of America, to merit such condign punishment as they have inflicted on them, and do continue to inflict on us their children. But I must aver, that my researches have hitherto been to no effect. I have therefore, come to the immoveable conclusion, that they (Americans) have, and do continue to punish us for nothing else, but for enriching them and their country.*

Walker's remarks on armed rebellion are indeed incendiary, yet finally enigmatic:

Some [whites] will curse the day they ever saw us. As true as the sun ever shone in its meridian splendor, my colour will root some of them out of the very face of the earth. . . . No doubt some may say that I write with a bad spirit, and that I being a black, wish these things to occur. Whether I write with a bad or a good spirit, I say if these things do not occur in their proper time, it is because the world in which we live does not exist, and we are deceived with regard to its existence. I should like to see the whites repent peradventure God may have mercy on them, some however, have gone so far that their cup must be filled. . . .

Now, I ask you, had you not rather be killed than to be a slave to a tyrant, who takes the life of your mother, wife, and dear little children? Look upon your mother, wife and children, and answer God Almighty; and believe this, that it is no more harm for you to kill a man, who is trying to kill you, than it is for you to take a drink of water when thirsty.

In the end, Walker's priority seems to have been education, not rebellion:

Ignorance, the mother of treachery and deceit, gnaws into our very vitals. Ignorance, as it now exists among us, produces a state of things, Oh my Lord! too horrible to present to the world. Any man who is curious to see the full force of ignorance developed among the coloured people of the United States of America, has only to go into the southern and western states of this confederacy, where, if he is not a tyrant, but has the feelings of a human being, who can feel for a fellow creature, he may see enough to make his very heart bleed![29]

Walker's remarks concerning education were directed to a group of people who had never been addressed in print before: Southern black preachers and literate slaves. Some slaves who worked as artisans learned basic reading skills on the sly through their craft training. More often, slaves were taught to read "by a white person who considered it their religious duty to teach their slaves how to read Scripture." Literate slaves then taught others to read in clandestine reading groups, as Frederick Douglass did before fleeing north.[30] The clandestine reading groups in the South had a counterpart in the aboveground reading societies of the North. It was to this emerging leadership of literate blacks, both north and south, that Walker appealed:

> Men of colour, who are also of sense, for you particularly is my APPEAL designed. Our more ignorant brethren are not able to penetrate its value. I call upon you therefore to cast your eyes upon the wretchedness of your brethren, and to do your utmost to enlighten them—go to work and enlighten your brethren! . . . There is a great work for you to do, as trifling as some of you may think of it.

Through his travels, not only was Walker made uniquely aware of the spread of literacy among Southern blacks, but he also became acquainted with clandestine communication channels between these groups. The hubs of these channels were usually preachers, both black and white, who enjoyed a degree of freedom of movement and could call a public meeting (though not necessarily protect it from harassment or assault). The lines of communication connecting these hubs were generally runaway slaves or mariners, again both black and white, who by the nature of their trade moved from seaport to seaport.[31] Walker's bold plan was to combine the distribution network that *Freedom's Journal* had assembled in the North with clandestine networks in the South to forge a national leadership of literate, politically emboldened blacks.

Walker published his tract on September 28, 1829. It made its first public appearance just three months later, when police in the port town of Savannah, Georgia, seized sixty copies. The steward of a Boston brig that had docked in Savannah had delivered the copies to a prominent black preacher, who became so alarmed upon reading them that he apparently returned them to the steward and notified the police. Within weeks the state of Georgia had new laws quarantining all black sailors entering Georgia ports, punishing the introduction of seditious literature into the state with serious penalties, and tightening laws against educating slaves.[32]

At about the same time, a free black was apprehended while distributing copies of the *Appeal* in Richmond, Virginia. In short order, the police notified the mayor, who notified the governor, who called an emergency closed-door session of the General Assembly to discuss how to handle the situation.[33] Three months later a white mariner from Boston was arrested for distributing copies among black longshoremen in Charleston, and four blacks, all literate, were arrested for distributing the *Appeal* in New Orleans. Within a month the Louisiana state legislature had imposed a penalty of life imprisonment or death on anyone who might "write, print, publish, or distribute any thing *having a tendency* to create discontent among the free coloured population of this state, or insubordination among the slaves therein."[34]

These, of course, were the cases in which Walker's emissaries were caught by Southern authorities. We will never know how many other emissaries managed to slip through and distribute their cargo as planned. We do know that Walker went through three editions of the *Appeal* before his untimely death. Extensive historical research has yielded several accounts by Southern whites concerning blacks seen reading the *Appeal*, including the following, which implies that at least in some cases blacks were shot for reading the pamphlet: "There was a good deal of shooting in Wilmington [NC].... The reason of it was this. A colored Baptist preacher named Spaulding had one of Walker's books. He lent it to another and his master saw him reading it. The white folks got together and read the book, and they had the colored folks up in no time."[35]

The circulation of the *Appeal* was being noticed in the North as well, as in this 1830 account from a Boston newspaper:

> Since the publication of that flagitious pamphlet, Walker's Appeal, for the consequences of which, if we mistake not, some fanatical white man will have to answer, we have noticed a marked difference in the deportment of our colored population. It is evident that they have read this pamphlet, nay, we know that the larger portion of them have read it, or heard it read, and that they glory in its principles, as if it were a star in the east, guiding them to freedom and emancipation.[36]

* * *

William Lloyd Garrison arrived in Boston in the spring of 1830, just as the first copies of *Walker's Appeal* were being discovered by Southern police. Garrison had come from Baltimore, where for some time he had been assisting Benjamin Lundy in editing the *Genius of Universal Emancipation*. Lundy and his paper never took a clear position concerning colonization and the ACS, and though Baltimore had a substantial black population, Lundy and his paper did not have close ties with them.[37] In Boston Garrison found a local black leadership centered around Samuel Cornish and David Walker—mobilized, articulate, and emphatic in its opposition to the ACS and indeed any plan or scheme that did not acknowledge that blacks had the same rights as whites did.

Garrison's encounter with the black movement in Boston had the same epiphanic effect on Garrison that Garrison's own words would subsequently have on so many others. As a white contemporary of Garrison's aptly noted, Garrison "undertook to look at the slave question as the Negro looked at it."[38] This simple shift in perspective was quite without precedent, even among abolitionists. Just a year after arriving in Boston, Garrison was speaking with the clarity of a man who had found God—through finding those whose humanity even abolitionist whites had not fully confronted:

> I never rise to address a colored audience, without feeling ashamed of my own color; ashamed of being identified with a race of men, who have done you so much injustice, and who yet retain so large a portion of your brethren in servile chains. To make atonement, in part, for this conduct, I have solemnly dedicated my health, and strength, and life, to your service. . . . Henceforth I am ready, on all days, on all convenient occasions, in all suitable places, before any sect or party, at whatever peril to my person, character or interest, to plead the cause of my colored countrymen in particular, or of human rights in general. For this purpose, there is no day too holy, no place improper, no body of men too inconsiderable to address. For this purpose, I ask no church to grant me authority to

speak—I require no ordination—I am not careful to consult Martin Luther, or John Calvin, or His Holiness the Pope. It is a duty, which, as a lover of justice, I am bound to discharge.[39]

Such words had never been spoken by a white person, and the effect was electric on blacks and whites equally, though the polarity of the charge was generally felt oppositely depending on the color of one's skin. White mobs became a real peril for Garrison, and at one point his rescue party found him with a noose already around his neck. During its first months of publication, *The Liberator* attracted only fifty white subscribers.[40] Even after two years, it had only two hundred white subscribers, many of whom were the publisher's personal friends.[41] Blacks, by contrast, "underwrote the printing costs, enlisted subscribers, served as agents in most northern cities, purchased the bulk of its advertising, organized the Colored Liberator Aiding Association to coordinate the paper's fundraising efforts, and contributed hundreds of essays and letters to its columns."[42]

Garrison's words were as forceful on the printed page as they were in person, beginning with *The Liberator*'s very first editorial:

I shall strenuously contend for the immediate enfranchisement of our slave population. In Park Street Church, on the Fourth of July, 1829, in an address on slavery, I unreflectingly assented to the popular but pernicious doctrine of gradual abolition. I seize this opportunity to make a full and unequivocal recantation, and thus publicly to ask pardon of my God, of my country, and of my brethren, the poor slaves, for having uttered a sentiment so full of timidity, injustice and absurdity. . . .

I am aware, that many object to the severity of my language; but is there not cause for severity? I will be as harsh as truth, and as uncompromising as justice. On this subject, I do not wish to think, or speak, or write, with moderation. No! no! Tell a man, whose house is on fire, to give a moderate alarm; tell him to moderately rescue his wife from the hands of the ravisher; tell the mother to gradually extricate her babe from the fire into which it has fallen; but urge me not to use modera-

tion in a cause like the present! I am in earnest. I will not equivocate
—I will not excuse—I will not retreat a single inch—AND I WILL BE
HEARD.[43]

Garrison insisted that any critique of slavery must begin with
the acknowledgment that blacks were just as much God's children
as whites, and consequently that slavery was a *sin*. Defeating slavery was thus a matter of turning away from sin, repenting (as Garrison himself had done), and turning back to God. Electoral politics,
in his view, was necessarily about compromise. Renouncing sin
was, in an equally necessary way, an all-or-nothing deal. Thus Garrison abhorred electoral politics as much as he abhorred the Protestant churches for collaborating with the sin of slavery. Finally,
Garrison demanded strict pacifism: just as slavery was a sin, so also
was murder. The proper response to sin was to repent and turn to
God, not to become more deeply mired in evil. He stuck to this view
even in later years when the specter of Southern secession made
war inevitable in the eyes of many. It was this absolute adherence
to a simple set of principles, come what may, that gave his words
such power—that turned his ideas into a "coherent whole" that
came to be known as Garrisonianism.

Just months after the appearance of *The Liberator*, and with
Walker's Appeal still fresh news, Nat Turner led a slave revolt in
Southampton County, Virginia.[44] Southern slaveholders had long
held that the circulation of seditious materials among slaves would
lead to just such an eventuality, and though it has never been determined whether Turner actually came into contact with *The Liber-*
ator, Walker's Appeal, or any other abolitionist literature, the timing
of his uprising convinced many in the South that he had.

As confused rumors and reports connected *Walker's Appeal* and
The Liberator with the events in Southampton County, Garrison became a household name. Garrison had adroitly positioned himself
for such an eventuality by reprinting lengthy selections from pro-
slavery papers in *The Liberator* without comment, implying that the
evil in the slave owners' prose was self-evident. Incensed Southern

editors felt compelled to respond. Garrison would reprint their letters, along with his rebuttal. Southern papers would reprint all that, adding their own commentary, and so on. The debate moved across the South from paper to paper, and the notoriety of *The Liberator* and its publisher went with it. The governor of Georgia gave his approval to an act of the state legislature offering $4,000 to anyone who would bring Garrison to trial. The "vigilance committee" of Columbia, South Carolina, offered $1,500 for the conviction of any white person caught circulating *The Liberator* or *Walker's Appeal*.[45]

Amid the furor, the American Anti-Slavery Society (AASS) was formed in 1833, with Garrison as a key influence. Its initial meeting in Philadelphia drew just 62 people. Five years later, the national organization claimed 1,350 local societies with a membership of some 250,000, concentrated entirely in the free states.[46] (By way of comparison, in 2000 an organization with a membership of the same proportion to the national population as that of the AASS in the North would have had more than 10 million members.)

New periodicals sprang up. *The Colored American* was joined by other black papers: *Mirror of Liberty, Palladium of Liberty, Genius of Freedom, Herald of Freedom, Freedman's Advocate, The Elevator,* and the *Ram's Horn.* The most successful by the conventional standards of journalism was the *Ram's Horn,* which published from 1841 to 1848 and featured articles by Frederick Douglass and John Brown. White abolitionists published the *American Anti-Slavery Reporter, The Emancipator, Slaves' Friend, Anti-Slavery Record,* and *Human Rights.*

This burgeoning press was a cornerstone of abolitionist activity. In its second year the American Anti-Slavery Society announced a six-point program. The third point read, "We shall circularize unsparingly and extensively antislavery tracts and periodicals."[47] These publications were then "circularized" so energetically that a controversy erupted concerning whether Southern postmasters had the right to either censor the mail or demand that Northern postmasters in the cities of the publications' origin do so for them. In 1835, when the controversy was at its height, the combined circulation of abolitionist publications reached a total of more than a million, thousands of which were flooding the Southern mail.[48] In Charleston, when word got out that the mail steamer had brought a cargo of abolitionist periodicals, a mob broke into the post office and burned the bags of mail in the street.[49]

Abolitionists were confronted with mob violence in the North as well. Garrison was attacked in Boston and dragged through the streets, traveling abolitionist lecturers were assaulted on trains and thrown off railroad cars, and Elijah Lovejoy, an abolitionist in Alton, Illinois, was murdered by a mob. Because of their difficulty in finding public spaces for their activities, abolitionists in Philadelphia constructed their own center, Pennsylvania Hall, which was burned down by a mob just days after it opened.

Abolitionists were no longer being ignored; on the contrary, they were now seen as a serious threat to social order, and not just in the South but in the North too. Abolitionists denounced mainstream churches. They were bad for business. They brought women to the platform and allowed them to speak. They brought *blacks* to the platform and gave them center stage.

Attacks on the abolitionists were a two-edged sword, however. As their struggle was increasingly cast in terms of civil liberties, including freedom of the press, they were able to identify their cause with the rights of white Americans as well as black.[50]

The most notable African American to take the abolitionist stage was Frederick Douglass. A former slave who had run away to freedom in the North in 1838, Douglass was one of many for whom their first encounter with *The Liberator* had been a defining moment. Douglass recalled that the paper "sent a thrill of joy" through his soul. "I loved this paper, and its editor. His words were few, full of holy fire, and straight to the point." Each week Douglass made himself "master of its contents."[51]

Douglass and Garrison met in 1841. Garrison immediately hired Douglass as an agent for the American Anti-Slavery Society, and Douglass became an instant hit on the lecture circuit. His eloquence and charisma were so striking that his audiences sometimes questioned his claim that he had escaped from slavery so recently. In response, Douglass penned the autobiographical *Narrative of the Life of Frederick Douglass, an American Slave,* which quickly sold five thousand copies. By the time war broke out, thirty thousand copies had been sold. Douglass's fame was a mixed blessing, however, as the publicity of the details of his escape exposed him to the very real threat of capture and forcible return to slavery in the South. Douglass subsequently fled to England.

Douglass was not the only former slave on the abolitionist lecture circuit; nor was he the only one to write his memoirs. William Wells Brown's autobiography went through four editions in its first year,[52] and Solomon Northup's *Twelve Years a Slave* sold twenty-seven thousand copies in two years.[53]

When two English friends provided him with the money to buy his freedom from his owner, Douglass returned to the United States, determined to start his own newspaper. In 1847 Douglass published the inaugural issue of *The North Star* and continued on a weekly or monthly basis for sixteen years. In 1851 he changed the name of the journal to *Frederick Douglass' Paper,* and later to *Douglass' Monthly.* In eloquence, longevity, circulation, and influence, Douglass's publications marked the pinnacle of the antebellum black press.

By publishing his own paper, Douglass was going out on a limb. Garrison and his inner circle were vehemently opposed to the idea, not least because it was understood that any paper Douglass might launch would necessarily compete with *The Liberator* for the same subscribers. And there was the financial burden such an undertaking would place on a former slave, even one as capable and respected as Douglass. Furthermore, Douglass had numerous opportunities to be read in print without starting his own publication. By 1847, many abolitionist papers would have welcomed the contributions of such a respected voice. But Douglass adamantly insisted that there could be no substitute for a high-quality black abolitionist paper. The inaugural issue presented two editorials, one addressed to whites and the other to blacks.[54] "Facts are facts,"

Douglass wrote. "White is not Black, and Black is not white. . . . The man who has suffered the wrong is the man to demand redress, the man struck is the man to cry out." Blacks themselves were the ones who could render "the most permanent good . . . to our cause."[55]

Douglass returned to the lecture circuit to raise money for his paper. During the first year of publication, he was on the road for six months. In the spring of 1848, he mortgaged his home to keep the paper afloat. During the 1850s, he spent nearly half his time on the road. In the winter of 1855–56 alone, the great orator gave some seventy lectures while traveling nearly five thousand miles.

Douglass's special skill was his ability to voice rage and urgency as eloquently as David Walker, while not losing his patience and connection to his white audience. His keen balancing on this narrow and precarious perch is evident in this famous 1852 address to a Fourth of July gathering in Rochester:

> Why am I called upon to speak here to-day? What have I, or those I represent, to do with your national independence? . . . I fancy I hear some one of my audience say, "It is just in this circumstance that you and your brother abolitionists fail to make a favorable impression on the public mind. Would you argue more, and denounce less; would you persuade more, and rebuke less; your cause would be much more likely to succeed." But, I submit, where all is plain there is nothing to be argued. What point in the anti-slavery creed would you have me argue? . . . How should I look to-day, in the presence of Americans, dividing, and subdividing a discourse, to show that men have a natural right to freedom? speaking of it relatively and positively, negatively and affirmatively. To do so, would be to make myself ridiculous, and to offer an insult to your understanding. . . .
>
> What, am I to argue that it is wrong to make men brutes, to rob them of their liberty, to work them without wages, to keep them ignorant of their relations to their fellow men, to beat them with sticks, to flay their flesh with the lash, to load their limbs with irons, to hunt them with dogs, to sell them at auction, to sunder their families, to knock out

their teeth, to burn their flesh, to starve them into obedience and sub-mission to their masters? ... No! I will not. I have better employment for my time and strength than such arguments would imply. ...

At a time like this, scorching irony, not convincing argument, is needed. O! had I the ability, and could reach the nation's ear, I would, to-day, pour out a fiery stream of biting ridicule, blasting reproach, withering sarcasm, and stern rebuke. For it is not light that is needed, but fire; it is not the gentle shower, but thunder. We need the storm, the whirlwind, and the earthquake. ...

To [the slave], your celebration is a sham; your boasted liberty, an unholy license; your national greatness, swelling vanity; your sounds of rejoicing are empty and heartless; your denunciation of tyrants, brass fronted impudence; your shouts of liberty and equality, hollow mock-ery; your prayers and hymns, your sermons and thanksgivings, with all your religious parade and solemnity, are, to Him, mere bombast, fraud, deception, impiety, and hypocrisy—a thin veil to cover up crimes which would disgrace a nation of savages.[56]

Douglass soon began to give programmatic substance to his assertion that blacks needed their own paper, advocating posi-tions that were increasingly at odds with the Garrisonians. He ar-gued that the Constitution was not necessarily a proslavery docu-ment, that it could even "be wielded in behalf of emancipation." He urged his readers to engage in electoral politics. He abandoned pacifism, as did many white abolitionists when confronted with the Fugitive Slave Act of 1850. A bitter dispute between Douglass and Garrison ensued, lasting into the Civil War.

Garrison's stature notwithstanding, Douglass's positions carried the day. It was toward his ideas that the bulk of the abolitionist movement—and after a fashion, Northern sentiment in general and even the federal government itself—was moving in the final decade before the Civil War. Garrison's insistence on seeing the issue of slavery as bounded by heaven and hell, rather than rooted in actual soil in which real slaves lived and died, seemed increasingly out of date, and his voice more shrill than profound.

* * *

New journals appeared that were in many ways far more success-ful than *The Liberator* or *The North Star*. The most important one was the *National Era*, launched in 1847 by the wealthy abolitionist Lewis Tappan. Tappan hired Gamaliel Bailey to run the paper, chosen for his "meekness and nonsectarian persuasiveness"—in other words, Garrison's opposite. The content of the paper reflected the fact that the goal of ending slavery had moved far beyond the radical fringe. Opposition to slavery was a central theme of the journal, but arti-cles addressing the issue were tossed into a mix of poetry on nature and love, chitchat for "good wives," essays on topics like laughter, letters, and short stories.[57] In just three years the *National Era* ac-quired fifteen thousand subscribers.

The *National Era* then launched one of the great events of Amer-ican journalism, publishing Harriet Beecher Stowe's *Uncle Tom's Cabin* in serial form over forty installments. White abolitionists had already discovered that black speakers—especially former slaves —could move white audiences like no white speaker could. Like-wise, the narratives of former slaves sold in numbers far greater than those of white abolitionists. *Uncle Tom's Cabin* was in essence a fictionalized slave narrative, made even more palatable to the gen-eral white reading public by its author, a white abolitionist.

By the time the entire serialized novel had been published, the number of the *National Era*'s paid subscriptions had hit twenty-five thousand.[58] The novel then moved to book form and created an un-precedented sensation. *Uncle Tom's Cabin* became the great literary event of nineteenth-century America, comparable to the work of Charles Dickens in Britain. The total sales figure for the book is un-known, but it may have approached one million. The *New York In-dependent* described the production of unprecedented quantities of books: "Notwithstanding [that] three paper mills are constantly employed making the paper, and three of Adams' power presses are kept running twenty-four hours per day (Sundays only excepted), and 100 bookbinders are constantly plying their art, the publishers are still some thousands of copies behind their orders."[59]

The racial politics of *Uncle Tom's Cabin* defy easy summary. The story ends with one protagonist deciding to go to Africa, which upset some abolitionists. Beecher Stowe attempted to show the full complexity of human behavior caught up in the tornado of slavery in America. It is this quality that made her work a great novel but also left it vulnerable to continual reenactments, retellings, reinterpretations, and adaptations, exposing it to social forces from which great political speeches and essays are protected. Theater companies put on traveling "Tom shows" around the country, which after the Civil War were often reshaped to convey more a nostalgia for slavery than a condemnation of it. Early silent movies retold small fragments of the story, "partly because the audience already knew the story well enough to fill in all the blanks in the action and the dialogue."[60] By the mid-twentieth century, "Uncle Tom" had become a caricature signifying the exact opposite of what proud black civil rights activists aspired to be.

With the onset of hostilities and the consequent need to mobilize more and more of society for the war effort, abolitionist writers attained a national prominence scarcely imaginable for most social justice crusaders in American history. Harriet Beecher Stowe met Abraham Lincoln at the White House, where the president remarked, "So this is the little lady who wrote the book that made this great war."[61] Lincoln not only conferred with "my friend Frederick Douglass" but enlisted his help to mobilize blacks to join the Union army after this step was finally authorized in 1862. Douglass obliged, but then protested the treatment to which black soldiers were subjected. Following the war, Douglass was appointed to a series of federal posts. In 1870 he began publishing his last paper, the *New Era*, "in the interest of the colored people of America; not as a separate Class, but as a part of the WHOLE PEOPLE."[62]

Garrison remained at the fringe of these events, and historians have generally given him more mixed reviews. His self-righteousness divided the movement. His acrimonious split with Douglass was self-serving. His politics were impractical. Garrison ended his career with as much controversy as he had begun it. In 1865, with the great war over but the political battle over which political rights former slaves would be granted only beginning, Garrison closed The Liberator, announcing "my vocation as an abolitionist is ended.... Most happy am I to no longer be in conflict with the mass of my fellow country-men on the subject of slavery."[63]

But in its day, Garrison's impracticality had a purpose. There was no practical way to envision the demise of slavery. In the end it took a decidedly impractical war that cost more than half a million lives. In 1830 no one seriously contemplated advocating such an apocalypse, except perhaps John Brown, whom many viewed as a lunatic. Garrison's uncompromising adherence to principles of justice had drawn a circle of activists into politics, and they would continue to fight for radical change in the United States for decades to come. Many of these continued to accord Garrison the utmost respect, even as they moved away from Garrisonianism.

Many historians have considered the foregoing events as encompassing not one but two stories, divided by race: the story of the early "black press" and that of the predominantly white "abolitionist press." This approach is not without merit: the life experiences of antebellum whites and blacks, even free blacks in the North, were starkly different. Whites could choose "abolitionism" from several reform movements they might participate in. Northern blacks, however, had no such choice. With friends and family enslaved just a state or two away, white racism constricting every aspect of their lives, and the constant threat of being captured and sent to the South (or to Haiti or Liberia) hanging over their heads, slavery, even if confined to the Southern states, continued to define much of their lives.

Yet when we examine the newspapers produced by these people, who lived in such drastically different circumstances, the separation of a "black press" and a "white abolitionist press" falls down. The two most influential abolitionist newspapers were *The Liberator,* published by a white man with a mostly black readership,[64] and *The North Star,* published by a black man with a mostly white readership. As noted earlier, blacks kept Garrison and *The Liberator* afloat, raising the capital for the launch, representing the paper as its agents, buying most of the advertising, contributing essays and letters, and even organizing "the Colored Liberator Aiding Association to coordinate the paper's fund-raising efforts."[65]

Many black abolitionists were indeed adamant about having their own newspapers. The *Anglo-African,* which appeared in New York City in 1859, just before the Civil War, eloquently expressed this desire: "We need a press—a press of our own. No outside tongue, however gifted in eloquence, can tell [our] story; no outside eye, however penetrating, can see [our] wants."[66]

Yet among the three thousand people who eventually subscribed to *The North Star,* whites outnumbered blacks by five to one.[67] Among subscribers to William Lloyd Garrison's *Liberator,* blacks outnumbered whites by a similar margin. Not only did many blacks honor Garrison for his pioneering work, but "Garrison and Boston's black community developed a political partnership that brought a distinctively anticolonizationist agenda, a patriotic language of civic virtue, and a well-organized network of improvement societies into the New England abolition movement."[68] Garrison's stature among blacks may also be deduced from the fact that David Walker, the most militant black writer of the era, named his only son after the white abolitionist. But while maintaining his base among blacks, Garrison had alienated many white abolitionists.

What we find with *The Liberator* and Frederick Douglass's papers is blacks and whites participating in a sustained, racially integrated political debate—perhaps the most profound such debate in U.S. history. Black publishers sought to have a voice of their own not so they could disengage from the debate but to enter it more fully.

It may have been the early nineteenth-century power of the word, both spoken and especially printed, that sustained this discussion between populations in such utterly different life circumstances.

The Woman Suffrage Press

The roots of the women's rights movement in the United States are deeply intertwined with abolitionism. It was through abolitionism that women first moved into public political roles, with the support of leading abolitionist men like Garrison, Douglass, and others. In fact, many of the best and best-known abolitionist orators and writers were women. If I have omitted them until now, it is not because their skills as writers or their contributions to the cause were in any sense less than those of abolitionist men. Rather, it was so these women could be treated here both as abolitionists and as the early voices of what eventually became the movement for woman suffrage. It was their experience in confronting social barriers, both from outside and within the abolitionist movement, that led them first to consider their own situation in a new light, then to speak out for their own rights, and eventually to form a movement of their own.

The first American woman to speak publicly on a political theme was Maria Stewart, a free black woman from Hartford who in 1826 had married an associate of David Walker's in Boston. Her husband died just three years into their marriage, and Walker's own untimely death in 1830 quickly followed. Stewart had been profoundly influenced by Walker, and after his death she moved into politics on her own, becoming a one-woman explosion of political activity. She wrote. She gave speeches. She helped launch the African-American Female Intelligence Agency in Boston in 1831. She formed a close friendship with William Lloyd Garrison, who published her speeches in *The Liberator* and also in two collections: *Religion and the Pure Principles of Morality, etc.* (1831) and *Meditations from the Pen of Mrs. Maria W. Stewart* (1832).

Like Walker, Stewart (who had no formal education) focused on black education, arguing that if blacks could organize to educate themselves, "Knowledge would begin to flow, and the chains of slavery and ignorance would melt like wax before the flames."[69] *yes!*

> *Tell us no more of southern slavery; for with few exceptions, although I may be very erroneous in my opinion, yet I consider our condition [as free blacks] but little better than that. Yet, after all, methinks there are no chains so galling as the chains of ignorance—no fetters so binding as those that bind the soul, and exclude it from the vast field of useful and scientific knowledge. O, had I received the advantages of early education, my ideas would, ere now, have expanded far and wide; but, alas! I possess nothing but moral capability—no teachings but the teachings of the Holy Spirit.[70]*

Stewart was adamant in her opposition to colonization:

> *Now that we have enriched their soil, and filled their coffers, they say that we are not capable of becoming like white men, and that we never can rise to respectability in this country. They would drive us to a strange land. But before I go, the bayonet shall pierce me through.[71]*

Again like Walker, Stewart addressed herself primarily to other blacks and was thus largely ignored by white abolitionists with the exception of Garrison. She fared no better with her black male contemporaries, who threw tomatoes at her during one of her lectures.[72] After just two years of public advocacy, she withdrew from the public eye to pursue a career as a schoolteacher. In her *Farewell Address*, she bitterly explained her decision before a black audience:

> *On my arrival here, not finding scarce an individual who felt interested in these subjects, and but few of the whites, except Mr. Garrison, and his friend Mr. Knapp; and hearing that those gentlemen had observed that female influence was powerful, my soul became fired with a holy zeal for your cause; every nerve and muscle in me was engaged in your behalf. I felt that I had a great work to perform....*

and I'm sure you did

I am about to leave you, perhaps, never more to return. For I find it is no use for me as an individual to try to make myself useful among my color in this city. It was contempt for my moral and religious opinions in private that drove me thus before a public. Had experience more plainly shown me that it was the nature of man to crush his fellow, I should not have thought it so hard. Wherefore, my respected friends, let us no longer talk of prejudice, till prejudice becomes extinct at home. Let us no longer talk of opposition, till we cease to oppose our own. For while these evils exist, to talk is like giving breath to the air, and labor to the wind.[73]

Stewart maintained her friendship with Garrison over the decades and self-published some of her writings in 1875, but she never sought to connect with the (white) woman suffrage movement that emerged after the war.

The highest-profile women in the abolitionist movement were Sarah and Angelina Grimké, from Charleston, South Carolina. The Grimké family owned a plantation that like many plantations around the South, had dozens of field slaves, numerous house slaves, and a slave nursemaid for the fourteen Grimké children. Each Grimké child was also attended to by a "constant companion," a slave child of roughly the same age. Both sisters, however, came to oppose slavery and moved north, where Angelina became active in the AASS in Philadelphia.

In 1835, with race riots erupting in several Northern cities, Angelina wrote a letter to Garrison, whom she had never met. The letter was extraordinary for the Southern perspective of its author, the passion of its argument, the beauty of its prose, and perhaps above all its clear articulation of the Christian pacifism that Grimké, Garrison, and other abolitionists shared.

Although I expected opposition, yet I was not prepared for it so soon —it took me by surprise, and I greatly feared Abolitionists would be driven back in the first onset, and thrown into confusion. So fearful was

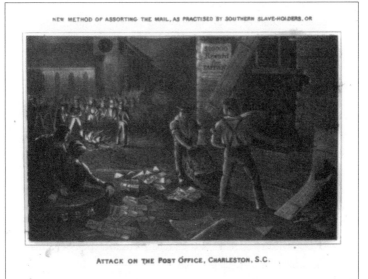

NEW METHOD OF ASSORTING THE MAIL, AS PRACTISED BY SOUTHERN SLAVE-HOLDERS, OR

ATTACK ON THE POST OFFICE, CHARLESTON, S.C.

Abolitionist broadside depicts a mob in Charleston breaking into the post office and burning abolitionist periodicals. The sign reading $20,000 REWARD FOR TAPPAN refers to the bounty placed by the city of New Orleans on the head of Arthur Tappan, president of the American Anti-Slavery Society.

I, that though I clung with unflinching firmness to our principles, yet I was afraid of even opening one of thy papers, lest I see some indications of compromise, some surrender, some palliation.... Judge, then, what were my feelings, on finding that my fears were utterly groundless, and that thou stoodest firm in the midst of the storm, determined to suffer and to die, rather than yield one inch.... The ground you stand on is holy ground: never—never surrender it....

If persecution is the means which God has ordained for the accomplishment of this great end, EMANCIPATION; then...LET IT COME; for it is my deep, solemn deliberate conviction, that this is a cause worth dying for. I say so, from what I have seen, and heard, and known, in a land of slavery....

At one time I thought this system would be overthrown in blood, with the confused noise of the warrior; but a hope gleams across my *mind, that our blood will be spilt, instead of the slaveholders['].... Let us endeavor, then, to put on the whole armor of God, and, having done all, to stand ready for whatever is before us.*[74]

Garrison reprinted the letter in *The Liberator*, from which it was picked up and reprinted by many other papers. Garrison also included it in a widely circulated pamphlet along with some of his own writing. The Grimké sisters suddenly found themselves at the forefront of abolitionism, Southern women in a movement dominated by Northern men. The following year they wrote a series of pamphlets and books, including Angelina's *Appeal to the Christian Women of the South* and Sarah's *Epistle to the Clergy of the Southern States* and *An Address to Free Colored Americans*. The sisters spent much of the following year on the lecture circuit, speaking in sixty-seven cities in twenty-three weeks.

Not long after, Angelina Grimké Weld (now married to fellow abolitionist Theodore Weld) addressed three thousand white and black women gathered at the Anti-Slavery Convention of American Women, part of the festivities celebrating the completion of the abolitionist Pennsylvania Hall in Philadelphia. Angelina struggled to make herself heard over a mob gathered outside, which was raining stones on the building. The mob returned the next day and burned down the building, but Grimké Weld got the last word, as her speech was published in pamphlet form and circulated widely.

What came ye out for to see? A reed shaken with the wind? Is it curiosity merely, or a deep sympathy with the perishing slave, that has brought this large audience together? [A yell from the mob without the building.]...Do you ask, "what has the North to do with slavery?" Hear it—hear it. Those voices without tell us that the spirit of slavery is here,...that slavery has done its deadliest work in the hearts of our citizens.[75]

* * *

By this time, the participation of women in the abolitionist movement was causing such a public commotion that abolitionists felt compelled to address the matter in print, beginning with Sarah Grimké's *Letters on the Equality of the Sexes.* "To me," she wrote, "it is perfectly clear that whatever it is morally right for a man to do, it is morally right for a woman to do."[76] Pamphlets on women's rights were soon included in the baggage abolitionist speakers peddled from town to town. Lucy Stone, another abolitionist speaker, wrote to a friend, "I sell a great many of the tracts, so seed is being scattered that will grow *sometime.*"[77] Soon the occasional tracts evolved into regular columns in abolitionist newspapers, notably supported by William Lloyd Garrison and then Frederick Douglass. In 1847, when Douglass launched *The North Star,* the motto on the masthead read: "Right Is of No Sex—Truth Is of No Color." Women, the former slave argued, as a matter of justice and morality, should be "elevated to an equal position with man in every relation of life."[78]

The women who wrote these pamphlets and columns saw no need for women's newspapers, as they did not perceive their endeavor as constituting an ongoing movement or even a separate subject. Rather than fighting for women's rights per se, they understood themselves to be working to improve their ability to contribute to the cause of abolition. But once debate about the role of women in abolitionism was engaged, it soon overflowed its bounds into a discussion of women's social role in general. If women were as qualified to speak against slavery as men, why were they not equally qualified to address other matters?

The primary locus of pre–Civil War women's rights advocacy, however, was not publications but conventions. Abolitionists Elizabeth Cady Stanton and Lucretia Mott traveled across the Atlantic to London in 1840 to participate in the World Anti-Slavery Convention, but upon arrival they were denied seats because they were women. Locked out of the convention, they occupied their time in London hatching first the general idea and then the actual plans for a women's rights convention.[79]

women's rights

It took a full eight years for their dream of a national convention of abolitionist women to be realized, in Seneca Falls, New York. Between 1850 and 1860, national conventions became a nearly annual event.[80] The conventions were a crucial laboratory in which ideas were developed, contacts were made, and experience in lecturing and debate was obtained.[81]

The first periodical to emerge from these efforts was *Una*, published in 1853 by Paulina Kellogg Wright Davis, a wealthy socialite who also funded and organized one of the early conventions. Wright Davis argued:

> *The idea is false that political papers do not . . . represent this movement, no other class of reformers have been so unwise. The Temperance people with a work far less delicate and subtle in its character, far less likely to be misunderstood, have their papers in every part of the country. The anti-slavery people . . . have their organs and feel that without them they can do but little, while this work . . . is left with no other medium of communication than the chance notices of political or other papers.*[82]

Wright Davis conceived of the *Una* as an alternative to the "ladies journals" of the day and adopted their standard mix of poetry, fiction, proverbs, and useful tidbits. Sprinkled among them were items such as the texts of speeches given at women's rights conventions. Wright Davis was ahead of her time, however, and the pages of her paper expressed growing frustration that women were not embracing the *Una* with subscriptions at a rate that could sustain it. In fact, very few women had their own spending money, and those who did were reluctant to spend it on a newspaper—especially one that could cause serious problems if found around the house. The *Una* folded after just two years.

With a newspaper and annual conventions, a movement for women's rights was acquiring an identity of its own, but it was a gradual, difficult process. The abolitionist cause benefited from having a clearly defined target (slavery), opponent (slave owners), and goal (abolition). The early women's rights advocates had none of these. They did not even have an adequate *language*. They did not, for example, have the word *feminist*, which made its debut in the United States only in the twentieth century.[83] Just as they had no word for themselves, they had none for their opponents. Even the slang with which they labeled their enemies was ambiguous. Abolitionist foes were slave owners, or, in movement jargon, "slavers." The opponents of expanding women's rights were simply called "antis," leaving exactly *what* their opponents were against undefined.

Not only could they not easily describe themselves or their opponents, it was not immediately clear exactly what they wanted. Suffrage only gradually emerged as the lead banner in their march, in part precisely because it was a concrete end that could be succinctly declared, and everyone would know if and when it was won.

Their opponents were neither geographically nor culturally distant, as the white citizens of the South were to their counterparts in the North. More often, they were members of their own families. Frequently their most pronounced opposition came from their husbands, who controlled not only the women's property and finances but also what church they went to, what meetings they could attend, what visitors they could entertain even within their home, and much more.

Like the early abolitionists, early women's rights campaigners were shut out of the mainstream press. When not ignored entirely, women's rights events were reported briefly, with disgust and condescension. Some newspapers even refused to publish paid advertisements concerning lectures or meetings.[84] (This treatment would be repeated, almost exactly, with early gay and lesbian activists a century later, as we will see in a later chapter.)

The lack of words, the family control, the lack of independent social networks, and the banishment from the press formed a web of constraints that denied women not only a *public voice* but even a *private community*. In an era in which anyone with a modem and a computer can send uncensored messages to millions in seconds, it is difficult to comprehend the degree to which these early activists were hemmed in and marginalized. When the first Seneca Falls convention finally came off, not one of the women's rights pioneers, despite having the audacity to organize this groundbreaking event, felt competent to chair the meeting, and the job was handed off to Lucretia Mott's husband. When faced with the task of writing a manifesto for the convention, firebrand Elizabeth Cady Stanton, who would soon become the most prominent of early suffragist writers, reported feeling "as helpless and hopeless as if [I] had suddenly been asked to construct a steam engine."[85]

The arrival of the Civil War effectively put the women's rights movement on hold, as abolitionist women threw their energies into supporting the Union war effort. After the war, the question of voting rights for freed slaves moved to the top of the national agenda. The war had shattered slavery as a legal institution, but whether the freed slaves would be granted the full rights of citizens, particularly the right to vote, was anything but certain. To women such as Elizabeth Cady Stanton and Susan B. Anthony, the debate on voting rights was an open door for a push to extend the vote to *all* adult citizens regardless of race or gender. They took it as a given that the political coalition that had pushed through abolition and was now poised to campaign for the Fourteenth Amendment would see things the same way. It was inconceivable to them that the nation might grant the vote to black men yet leave black women—and white women—disenfranchised.

Most abolitionist leaders, including prominent women such as Lucy Stone, took the opposite tack, arguing that it was the "Negro's hour" and women would have to wait. In their view, although black suffrage and woman suffrage might be linked logically, the political reality was that the fight for black male suffrage was shaping up to be a very difficult struggle, and complicating the matter further by raising woman suffrage put the fruits of the tremendous sacrifices of the war in jeopardy. Victory for black suffrage, they believed, would open the door for women, whereas a defeat for black suffrage would close all possibility of enlarging the franchised population for years to come. Advocates of linking the enfranchisement of women and blacks were shocked to find prominent allies like Garrison and Douglass, who had consistently been far ahead of the pack in their support of female abolitionists, arguing that women's suffrage had to wait.

The question of whether Kansas would join the Union as a free state or a slave state had been a trigger issue in the buildup to civil war. In 1867 Kansas was a flashpoint once again when its citizens were asked to vote simultaneously on two separate constitutional amendments, one enfranchising blacks, the other women. The outcome would finally decide the debate over whether the political rights of slaves would be defined as the "[male] Negro's hour" or a "more complete democracy." With so much on the line, the split between those campaigning for just one or both amendments became predictably bitter. On Election Day black suffrage won, whereas woman suffrage lost overwhelmingly: 21,000 to 9,000. For the woman suffragists who had campaigned extensively in the state, even more devastating than the loss itself was their impression of being betrayed by their former allies, the Republican Party in particular. For the party of "free soil, free labor, and free men" had actively sought to isolate the woman suffragists in its campaign to enfranchise the former slaves.

Elizabeth Cady Stanton and Susan B. Anthony had been the most prominent woman suffrage advocates in the Kansas campaign, and they were righteous with rage. They emerged from the debacle with some radical conclusions. Strategically, they resolved that advancing the cause of women's rights required an independent women's movement that could push forward even when allies vacillated. Practically, the first thing they felt such a movement would need was its own newspaper. "Our three most radical papers...were closed against us," they later wrote of the campaign. "We could not get an article in either...demanding the recognition of women in the new government. Thus ostracized, we tried to establish a paper of our own."[86]

During the Kansas campaign, when Anthony and Stanton realized the Republicans were undermining their efforts, they reached out to Democrats. The move yielded few votes for woman suffrage but did result in a close relationship between the suffragist leaders and one very particular Democrat, George Francis Train, who stumped for them around the state. Train was a low-class politician and first-class character: a financial schemer, railroad promoter, one-man campaigner for the presidency, and flamboyant racist. Attacks on the intelligence of blacks were fundamental to his standard appeal, and he employed them as an argument for voting rights for women. The collaboration between two top woman suffragists and such a blatant racist horrified many other suffragists. Stanton and Anthony shocked their friends by refusing to budge in the face of withering criticism. "So long as opposition to slavery is the only test for your platform," Stanton angrily wrote to the abolitionists, "why should we not accept all in favor of woman suffrage to our platform and association, even though they be rabid pro-slavery Democrats?"[87]

The break with the abolitionist movement left Stanton and Anthony in near complete isolation and thus more dependent on Train than ever. Anthony began 1868 by writing in her diary, "All the old friends, with scarcely an exception, are sure we are wrong."[88] Working essentially alone, the following year Stanton, Anthony, and Train launched the *Revolution,* the "paper of our own" they had dreamed of. Train promised to provide financing, then disappeared to Ireland.

Not only were the two women now isolated from their previous allies, they were cut off from their previous ideological framework as well. They set out to use the *Revolution* to forge a new one. Freed from concern for the views of others, they created "the least trammeled and most daring feminist paper that had yet—and perhaps has ever—appeared."

The Revolution *reported on female farmers, inventors, sailors, and thieves, on any woman who disproved that "nature contended them all*

Elizabeth Cady Stanton and Susan B. Anthony: The editors
of the Revolution left an ambiguous legacy of women's
rights and racism, democratic reform and elitism.

for the mission of housekeepers." The editors wrote and reprinted articles on prostitution, infanticide, the need for sex education, cooperative
housekeeping, and the nonmonogamous practices of Oneida commu-
nitarians and Utah Mormons. They . . . discovered a feminist heritage
that was many centuries old. Friends advised them to change the paper's name to something more in keeping with the genteel tradition of

women's journalism, but only the Revolution *would suit them. It in-dicated their goal of building woman suffrage into a movement that promised women total revolution in every aspect of their lives.*[89]

The *Revolution* opened its editorial doors so wide that even overtly racist arguments were allowed in. "American women of wealth, education, virtue, and refinement," Stanton warned, "if you do not wish the lower orders of Chinese, Africans, Germans and Irish, with the low ideas of womanhood to make laws for you and your daughters, . . . to dictate not only the civil, but moral codes by which you shall be governed, awake to the danger of your present position."[90]

The *Revolution* never had more than three thousand subscribers. For many of these, however, reading the paper was a defining moment in their lives, which gave the paper an influence far greater than its number of subscribers would imply. The *Revolution* inspired its readers to action, even to the establishment of new suffrage publications, including the *Women's Tribune* and the *Agitator*.[91] The *Revolution's* pages were quickly filled with letters like this one:

> *I send you by this mail a petition for Equal Suffrage [copied from the pages of the* Revolution*], signed by one hundred and eighty-five names, with the exception of forty, I have obtained them myself by going house to house. It is a slow process, so few have heard anything of the movement, and the whole thing has to be explained to each person.*[92]

The influence of the *Revolution* as a paper, and of its editors as public figures, fed off each other in a virtuous circle. Stanton, Anthony, and the small group around them lectured, traveled, organized, and agitated without rest. At this time there was no strong national women's rights organization. In the void, the *Revolution* seemed to function as one. At the 1868 National Labor Congress, four women "connected with the *Revolution*" were awarded delegate status.[93] The following year, when the National Women Suffrage Association (NWSA) was finally constituted, it was organized at a reception for the editors of the *Revolution*.[94]

* * *

The wild and erratic course charted by the *Revolution* left a huge space open for a steadier player to take the field. In 1870 the American Women Suffrage Association (AWSA) was formed. AWSA leaders immediately established their own competing paper, the *Women's Journal*, featuring Lucy Stone, her husband, Henry Blackwell, abolitionist publisher Julia Ward Howe, and William Lloyd Garrison on its editorial board. The *Women's Journal* not only was fiercely critical of the racist aspects of the *Revolution* but explicitly supported the Republican Party's position that woman suffrage had to wait until suffrage for freed slaves had been secured. The *Women's Journal* also stuck more closely to the single theme of woman suffrage instead of the sweeping "revolution" envisioned by Anthony and Stanton.

The *Women's Journal* was everything the *Revolution* was not. It had stable financial backing, a respected editorial board, and a sharply defined focus on woman suffrage. It quickly became the most widely distributed and longest-running woman suffrage paper. By 1915, the *Journal* reached twenty-seven thousand subscribers in forty-eight states and thirty-nine countries. It did not miss an issue in nearly five decades of continuous publication.[95]

Radicals from the circle around the *Revolution* found the more cautious, narrowly focused approach of the *Women's Journal* "dull, timid, and uninspiring,"[96] but Lucy Stone and her colleagues were attempting to reach women not yet ready to embrace a broad radical agenda. Where the *Revolution* spoke in strident tones calling women to action, the *Journal* aimed for a gentler voice and a more intimate tone.

One original approach the *Journal* used was to give each of its four editors a regular column. The editors were free to express themselves as they wished and to respectfully disagree—which they often did. Readers were invited to consider the contradictory opinions and to address their correspondence to a particular editor as appropriate. The style the *Journal* developed in many ways foreshadowed the techniques the feminist movement would much later come to term "consciousness-raising."[97]

Shortly after the appearance of the *Women's Journal*, the *Revolution* folded. Beginning in 1883, the *Women's Tribune* functioned in its place as an unofficial organ of the NWSA. The paper continued until 1909, as the more or less personal platform of its ambitious editor and publisher, Clara Belwick Colby. The *Women's Tribune* maintained a fairly high profile, primarily because Elizabeth Cady Stanton chose to publish much of her writing there. But it remained a distant second to the AWSA's *Women's Journal* in importance.[98]

The first two decades in which the *Women's Journal* published were the most difficult of the woman suffrage movement, referred to by contemporaries as the "black hole" or the "doldrums." Woman suffrage, it was becoming clear, would not follow quickly on the heels of black suffrage. The *Journal* resolutely stuck to the strategy of pushing a constitutional amendment for woman suffrage on a state-by-state basis, a strategy the *Revolution* lambasted as hopelessly piecemeal. From 1870 to 1890 the movement did not win a single state referendum and lost many. To make matters worse, woman suffrage publishing was becoming an increasingly crowded field, with thirty-three suffrage papers addressing an increasingly consolidated but frustrated prosuffrage minority.[99] These included the *Pioneer* (San Francisco), *New Northwest* (Portland), *Woman's Herald of Industry* (San Francisco), *Queen Bee* (Denver), *Woman's Exponent* (Salt Lake City), and *Woodhull and Claflin's Weekly* (New York City).[100]

Woodhull and Claflin's Weekly was a sensational journal that advocated not only woman suffrage but "free love," spiritualism, and socialism. The *Weekly* was published by Victoria Woodhull, one of the most colorful characters in American political history. Known widely for her physical beauty, Woodhull grew up as a traveling child faith healer, then became the first female to own a Wall Street brokerage house (which she obtained after a session of the healing art of "animal magnetism" with millionaire financier Cornelius Vanderbilt). She went on to become the first woman to testify before Congress, where she made a constitutional case for woman suffrage (this time with arrangements by Civil War general and Massachusetts congressman Benjamin Butler, who had also written her speech). In 1872 she became the first woman to form her own political party and the first woman to run for president.

Her *Weekly* published the first English translation of Karl Marx's *Communist Manifesto*. She herself advocated communism, and she joined the International Workingmen's Association. She was eloquent in her commitment to the ideal of "free love," and she spoke openly of her many lovers. Her *Weekly* also included her thoughts on what most people would consider quack philosophy and medicine, and she was president of the American Spiritualist Association. If the *Revolution* was on the cutting edge for its time, *Woodhull and Claflin's Weekly* was over the edge and left most of the woman suffrage movement—and even the editors of the *Revolution*—running for cover. They didn't run far enough.

Angry both that the suffragists had not supported her presidential run and that they would not join her advocacy of "free love," Woodhull decided to expose what she saw as the hypocrisy of her critics in a way that would "burst upon the ranks of the moralistic camp like a bombshell."[101] She succeeded admirably in this pursuit when she published an account of an affair between the wife of a prominent prosuffrage journalist and Henry Beecher Stowe. Beecher Stowe was a hugely influential abolitionist, woman suffragist, advocate of the theory of evolution, and extremely successful American Congregational preacher with a high-profile congregation in New York City. The scandal of the century ensued.

Woodhull insisted she was not muckraking; instead, she announced, Beecher shared her beliefs in the "most advanced doctrines of free-love and the abolition of Christian marriage." Moreover, Woodhull insisted, Beecher *practiced* free love, though he was afraid to say so publicly. Her motive, she explained, was to force him and "moralistic" leaders to lead on this question as well.

Even before Woodhull's bombshell, "free love" had become something of a national panic issue, akin to communism in the 1950s. "Free Lovers" were alleged to have an "avowed program—first to de-

stroy the institution of marriage; second to abolish the Christian religion; and third, to inaugurate a reign of lust... [thus] destroying all
morality."[102]

Woodhull succeeded spectacularly in her goal of linking "free
love" and woman suffrage in the national political imagination, but
the backlash for the woman suffrage movement was catastrophic.

By 1890 the bleak political outlook the movement faced had created
a consensus on the need for change, and old passions had subsided
to the point that the NWSA, AWSA, and their respective leaders
could merge into the National American Woman Suffrage Association (NAWSA). The *Women's Journal* served as its official organ, along
with the newer *Women's Column*. The *Column* was conceived not as
a newspaper at all but as a way of providing mainstream newspaper editors with regular news and opinion pieces relating to woman
suffrage—a kind of woman suffrage news service. The *Column* soon
evolved into a subscription newspaper, but one that was distributed
widely for "missionary work."[103] Free copies were provided to min-
isters, politicians, teachers, and editors. In 1888 hundreds were sent
to the Ohio Centennial Exposition, and in 1892 and 1893, fifteen
hundred were sent to prominent citizens of Alabama.[104] The pre-
cise circulation of the *Column* is thus hard to reconstruct, but it was
certainly distributed in greater numbers than any other suffrage
periodical.

As a tool for reaching out to the unconvinced rather than mo-
tivating the militant, the *Women's Column* was even more conservative than the *Women's Journal* and antithetical to the *Revolution*.
Where the *Revolution* held that woman suffrage was just one element in a revolution of gender roles, the *Women's Column* held that
a woman could be prosuffrage yet conventional in every other way.
Where the *Revolution* argued that the female perspective was inherently radical, the *Women's Column* argued that women would
be a good influence on public life due to their intrinsically virtuous and conservative nature. Political activity was presented to

conservative women as an extension of domestic concerns and chores. The paper profiled politically active women who were married, raised children, and adhered to accepted norms of feminine beauty.[105]

The last two decades of the nineteenth century saw a rapid growth in the class of professional women. More than three thousand "women's clubs" emerged, with associated journals such as the *Journal of the American Association of University Women,* the *Business Woman's Journal,* and more.[106] The tenor of the *Women's Column* was well tuned to these developments and succeeded in bringing the discussion of women's rights in general, and suffrage in particular, into mainstream political discourse. After decades of experimentation, the woman suffrage movement was finally hitching its wagon to an ascending constituency.

This strategy was a winner. The turning point came when New York passed a woman suffrage amendment in 1917, which quickly led to victories elsewhere, and to final victory on August 26, 1920, seventy-two years after the first Seneca Falls convention.

Ironically, as the movement toward ratification accelerated, the suffrage press collapsed. Of the fourteen major suffrage papers published after 1900, only two survived past 1917.[107] With woman suffrage now a centerpiece of mainstream news, the era of the woman suffrage press had come to a close.

The trajectories of some woman suffrage papers mirrored those of some abolitionist papers. When the *Una* set the cart in motion by publishing speeches from women's rights conventions, it was following the precedent of the early abolitionist press by aiming to provide a more lasting presence for the spoken words of lecturers. After the *Una* came the *Revolution,* a journal with a small circulation but shrill tone and uncompromisingly radical stance, which played a crucial role in constructing an independent ideological center around which core movement activists could identify themselves to each other. In this regard, Elizabeth Cady Stanton, Susan

B. Anthony, and the *Revolution* inherited the mantle of William Lloyd Garrison and *The Liberator*. The two journals even peaked at the same small circulation of three thousand.

In both movements, once a radical benchmark had been set, new journals with greater tactical savvy took the fore (Frederick Douglass's papers and the *Women's Journal*). Once the issue moved into the national spotlight, the movement press faded in importance, while journals geared almost exclusively to "missionary work" (though of little interest to core activists) became central (the *National Era* and the *Women's Column*).

These parallels break down, however, if taken too far. Garrison's commitment to principles was absolute, even when these conflicted with his political goals. He clung resolutely to pacifism, for example, although it became increasingly clear that slavery would be abolished only through war. Stanton and Anthony were willing to jettison any beliefs that seemed to hinder the immediate advancement of (white) women's rights, even their own previous beliefs in racial equality. As it turned out, they were spectacularly wrong in this assessment. The *Revolution*'s flirtation with overt racism and appeals to class privilege did nothing to advance their cause and much to hinder it. In retrospect, one can see the *Revolution* as an early—and thus very raw—expression of the tension between race, class, and gender that has been a constant theme of American social movements ever since. But the *Revolution* leaves another legacy as well, which has to do not so much with the content or consistency of its positions but rather with the editors' insistence of their right to voice them at all: that militant, strong-minded women had the right and ability to address *all* the subjects of their day, and not just woman suffrage; that *feminism,* in the broadest and most radical sense of the word (a word that again would appear much later), could constitute an entry point into a radical politics.[108]

The results of the abolition and woman suffrage movements could hardly be more different. The abolition of slavery did, in fact, liberate the slaves. To be sure, racism in America did not disappear, but chattel slavery did, and the lives of nearly four million men and women were transformed. Woman suffrage had no such impact. On the contrary, U.S. electoral politics hardly registered a change; nor did relations between the sexes alter. Stanton and Anthony's belief that woman suffrage would bring about an earth-shattering social "revolution" turned out to be profoundly wrong.

Over the long term, however, the development of a feminist ideology, and women's engagement with that ideology and with each other through movement activities, did indeed lead to a sea change in gender relations. It would take decades more, however, before these things would come to fruition.

There is one final remark to be made about the particular contribution of the woman suffrage press. Though nineteenth-century women's lives were broadly similar, at least within a given class and race, this similarity was not *shared*. Many women lived very isolated lives; the fact that the isolation one woman suffered was similar to that of others did nothing to relieve the isolation. Indeed, in part the increasing isolation of women in the ever more elaborately demarcated "home" sparked the movement for women's rights. To become a social movement, these common experiences had to become shared experiences, and to this end the early feminist leaders traveled tirelessly. Usually, they traveled alone. The hostility they faced for daring to step outside their assigned role was constant and inescapable.

As Antoinette Brown complained, "I am forever wanting to lean over onto somebody but nobody will support me."[109] For Brown and many others, the woman suffrage press was the support they turned to. As the movement developed beyond its original core, its press replaced the traveling agitator as the principal vehicle through which a constituency was brought together.[110]

The Gay and Lesbian Press

We are a revolutionary group of men and women formed with the realization that complete sexual liberation for all people cannot come about unless existing social institutions are abolished.

GAY LIBERATION FRONT STATEMENT
OF PURPOSE, JULY 31, 1969

Gays are the epitome of capitalism.

STEVEN SHIFFLETT, FORMER PRESIDENT
OF HOUSTON'S GAY POLITICAL CAUCUS

I'm going to Disneyland!

ELLEN DEGENERES,
"COMING OUT" ON ELLEN

One cannot tell by looking whether a person is queer. Before queers can build community, fight for civil rights, or even form friendships or more intimate relationships, they have to find each other. Before they can find each other, they have to find themselves in a culture that tells them in myriad ways to hide. "Coming out," the personal act of identifying oneself as queer, also forms the basis of the queer community, political constituency, and market niche. The gay and lesbian press has been the primary vehicle of this multidimensional coming-out process. This gives the movement press a centrality to the gay and lesbian movement unique among modern social movements. The history of the struggle for the *right* to discuss homosexuality at all, the history of *how* it was then discussed, and the history of the formation of the gay and lesbian *person, community,* and *movement* are largely one and the same.

The gay and lesbian press has recently undergone a breathtaking transition. In the first half of the twentieth century, people went to jail for publishing material in any way relating to homosexuality. By the end of the century, the gay press exploded into a lucrative niche market where Fortune 500 corporations spent lavishly on ads aimed at a "dream market" allegedly worth hundreds of billions of dollars. No other social movement has been so successfully commercialized. In between came a radical, even zany, "gay liberation" movement that hoped to use the gay experience of oppression as a springboard for transforming American society. As the saying goes, *Be careful what you wish for.*

As the identity-based social movement par excellence, the naming of the identity itself has been the subject of constant struggle and change. The term *lesbian* originally referred to an inhabitant of the island of Lesbos, where the ancient Greek lyric poet Sappho wrote poems of love between women. It has been embraced by homoerotically inclined women throughout the twentieth century. The word *homosexual* was first used in the mid-nineteenth century by advocates for the right to same-gender love, then migrated to psychiatry, and then was carried back to the movement by activists who wanted to give an air of medical authority to their claim for equal rights. At the start of the twentieth century, urban street slang included *queers, fairies,* and *trade,* each denoting a particular subgroup of homoerotically active men.[1] African Americans who were homoerotically active simply said they were "in the life." *Homophile,* literally "friend of homosexuals," was how the activists of the 1950s described their organizations. After the Stonewall riot of 1969, *homo* anything was dismissed as a relic of the oppressive pseudoscientific psychiatric tradition then being challenged, and it was replaced by *gay*. In the late 1960s, there was a brief moment when it was up for grabs whether the term *gay* included women. Many women found that the male-dominated gay world was an inadequate answer to their quest for community, and *gay* became *gay and lesbian*. The following generation, reacting against the increasingly superficial mainstream gay and lesbian culture, rejected *gay and lesbian* for the all-inclusive *queer*. By the start of the twenty-first century, there were many who considered themselves part of a "GLBTQ community" (for Gay, Lesbian, Bisexual, Transgender, and Questioning) as the list of included identities grew to where the mere enunciation of all of them seemed to require abbreviation.

For now, I will use whichever term or terms were in use during each particular period I discuss. There is more reason for such an approach than mere convenience: *fairies, homosexuals, lesbians, gays, queers,* and *GLBTQs* thought and think of themselves in different terms and actually *were* and *are* different people.[2] To make the discussion more manageable, when referring to the movement's course over time periods sufficiently long to have spanned different terminology, I will simply use *gay and lesbian*.

The peculiar history of the gay and lesbian movement begins with the startling fact that until the twentieth century gays and lesbians did not exist. It is a matter of historical record that people of the same gender have been sexual partners in nearly every culture at every time in history that we know of. Every culture has had its own way of regulating this (and all other) sexual behavior. In ancient Greece, love between men and boys was revered as the highest form of romantic love.[3] In some indigenous cultures in New Guinea, multipartner, multigeneration male-male sex is a rite of passage critical to the formation of fierce warriors—in other words, male-male sex is how one attains "manhood," not how one loses it.[4] "Gays" and "lesbians" entered the stage of world history in twentieth-century European cultures (Europe, Great Britain, the United States, Canada, Australia, New Zealand) when people who engaged in same-sex love and sex felt compelled to *declare* this to the society at large. And not just to declare it as a behavior, but as an *identity*: to proclaim that this desire, this passion, defined a fundamental truth about who they were.

What exactly is this truth? What does it mean to be gay or lesbian? It doesn't mean men who have sex with men, or women who have sex with women. Thousands of Americans who engage in same-gender love and sex do not identify themselves as gay or lesbian. Conversely, some gays and lesbians have no sex or romance at all. And what of the gays who have sex with women? And the lesbians who have sex with men? The only definition of *gay* or *lesbian* that does not fall apart in contradiction is this: people are gay or lesbian if they say they are. This may sound flippant, but it has profound implications. "Coming out" is the defining act of "becoming gay." What is "coming out"? It is not having sex. It is not falling in love. It is the act of declaring one's "gayness." "Gay" and "lesbian" are *confessional identities,* and as such are profoundly Western, in the same sense that Christianity is a confessional religion and psychotherapy is a confessional medical practice.

Coming out was taboo in the United States until the latter half of the twentieth century. Those who made their same-gender desire known, even to a few friends, risked losing their jobs, their families, their freedom, and even their lives. Coming out in print was actually illegal. In fact, *any* mention in print of same-gender sex or love was punishable by five years of hard labor.

In 1873, as urban life was taking shape in the great population centers of the country, Congress passed the Comstock Law. Best known as the law that banned contraception in the United States, the law covered a much broader range of activity, making it illegal to "sell...or offer to sell, or to lend, or to give away, or in any manner to exhibit, or...otherwise publish or offer to publish in any manner, or...have in his possession, for any such purpose or purposes, an obscene book, pamphlet, paper, writing, advertisement, circular, print, picture, drawing or other representation, figure, or image on or of paper or other material." The penalty for such an offense was "hard labor in the penitentiary for not less than six months nor more than five years for each offense, or fined not less than one hundred dollars nor more than two thousand dollars." Many states followed the lead of the federal government and passed Comstock laws of their own.

It is therefore not surprising that very little is known about the pre–World War II antecedents of what later became the gay and lesbian press. Due to recent scholarship (which is itself the fruit of the movement press we are examining), we now know that in major urban areas, the period from 1890 to 1940 saw the emergence of a very rich and diverse culture of same-sex desire that was quite different from its contemporary counterpart. That such a developed subculture was until recently largely lost to history is testimony to the effectiveness and severity of the repression of that culture in the 1940s and 1950s.[5]

The only publication we have a historical record of is *Friendship and Freedom*, distributed in Chicago in 1924 and 1925 by Henry Gerber. Gerber was a German immigrant to the United States who served in the American army in occupied Germany following World War I, where he became active in the German homosexual emancipation movement of the time.[6] Gerber returned to the United States and organized the Society for Human Rights, the first known homosexual rights organization in the United States. Describing the organization as an advocacy group for people with "mental abnormalities," Gerber secured a charter for the society from the state of Illinois on Christmas Eve, 1924. The society managed to publish two issues of *Friendship and Freedom* before the police raided the Gerber home. Gerber and other society members were arrested. At trial the prosecution produced a powder puff and a diary entry that read "I love Karl" as proof of Gerber's homosexuality. Gerber lost his job, many of his possessions, all the materials of the society, and his life savings over the course of three costly trials before the charges were finally dropped.

After his ordeal, Gerber moved to New York City, where he reenlisted in the U.S. Army and served for seventeen years. During the 1930s he managed a personal correspondence club, which became a national communications network for homosexual men. But Gerber never returned to print under his own name. Using a pseudonym, he wrote prohomosexual articles for an underground magazine named *Chanticleer* and often wrote letters to editors in response to antihomosexual articles that appeared in various journals in the 1930s and 1940s. When new "homophile" publications appeared in the 1950s, Gerber contributed articles, still using a pseudonym. Gerber died in 1972.[7]

Police destroyed all the copies of *Friendship and Freedom* that they found. At least some copies must have been distributed before the police got their hands on them, for a photograph of *Friendship and Freedom* appeared in a German gay magazine, and the publication was reviewed in the 1924 French gay magazine *L'Amitié*.[8]

The experience of repression continued to define the environment and provide the impetus for much of the gay press for years to come. As writer Rodger Streitmatter has noted, "Dale Jennings created *ONE* in 1952, and [Robert T. Mitch] launched *The Advocate* in 1967, both after being arrested on morals charges. Frank Kameny founded the *Gazette* in 1966 and David Goodstein put $3 million into *The Advocate* after being fired from their previous jobs. Even as late as 1992, Michael Goff became founding editor of *Out* after passing the foreign service exam but then being rejected by the State Department for being gay."[9]

* * *

This is one kind of publication which would, I am sure, have a great deal of appeal to a definite group. Such a publication has never appeared on the stands. Newsstands carrying the crudest kind of magazines or pictorial pamphlets would find themselves severely censured

were they to display this other type of publication. Why? Because So-
ciety decrees it thus. Hence the appearance of VICE VERSA, *a maga-*
zine dedicated, in all seriousness, to those of us who will never quite be
able to adapt ourselves to the iron-bound rules of Convention.[10]

With these simple and understated words, VICE VERSA announced itself to the public in 1947, the first known postwar "homophile" publication. VICE VERSA was the creation of a young
secretary who was discovering her own sexuality and whose principal goal was to use her paper as a means to meet others like
her. While she thought of herself as looking for friends and dates,
in contemporary vernacular she was building community. "I put in
an original plus five sheets of carbon paper. That made a total of six
copies from each typing. So when I typed the pages twice through,
I had my twelve copies. If anyone came around I had to zip it into
my briefcase real quick."[11]

She never put her name or address in the paper, nor those of any
contributors or business establishments. Even fifty years later, this
pioneer of the movement press, whose real name was Edithe Eyde,
declined to identify herself by name to an explicitly supportive gay
historian, instead using Lisa Ben, a pseudonym she had taken in
1962 (an anagram of lesbian).[12]

Eyde took her mission of creating a social space for homosexuals quite literally. Her policy was to publish everything submitted.
Yet her mix of editorials, letters, poems, fiction, and book reviews
set a pattern that still holds in much of the gay press. After only nine
issues, VICE VERSA ceased publication: Eyde had found the friends
and love she was looking for.[13]

During the McCarthy era, more Americans were hunted down,
blacklisted, and fired from their jobs for being homosexuals than
for being Communists.[14] Communists and homosexuals were imagined to be linked in a vast conspiracy to undermine the moral fiber
of America. It is one of the great ironies of the era that this mass
delusion came to contain an element of truth: the earliest homo-

phile activists of the postwar period *were* Communists. In November 1950, Harry Hay gathered a group of five men in Los Angeles to launch what became the Mattachine Society. Three of the group were members of the Communist Party. They were hardly working to undermine the American character on orders from Stalin, however, for the Communist Party was just as homophobic as the U.S. government, and as the Mattachine Society grew, the founders withdrew from the party.

The climate of fear among homosexuals in the 1950s was so great that the new organization was structured in quasi-underground cells. Members knew only those who shared their cell, as well as one contact person in another cell one step up the clandestine pyramid. The need for secrecy was felt to be so acute that when one of the leaders was arrested the following year on an entrapment charge, the activists formed an ad hoc Citizens Committee to Outlaw Entrapment rather than make the existence of the Mattachine Society public.[15] The organization grew quickly, however, and when its leaders launched the journal *ONE* in 1953, its circulation immediately shot up to two thousand.[16]

The growth of the society produced immediate political tensions along a fault line that would define the movement for the next fifty years. Were they a minority building their own unique culture based in the particular nature of same-gender love? Or were they simply citizens fighting for the recognition that they were no different from anyone else, aside from the small detail of the gender of their sexual partners? Was the first step to "disenthrall ourselves of the idea that we differ only in our sexual directions and that all we want or need in life is to be free to seek the expression of our sexual desires," as founder and former Communist Chuck Rowland put it in his keynote address to the first Mattachine Society convention in 1953? Or was it to assert that "we are the same, no different from anyone else," as Marilyn Rieger argued? "Our only difference is an unimportant one to the heterosexual society, *unless we make it important*."[17]

The radicals withdrew from the organization after the convention, taking ONE with them as an independent publication. Without the vision and organizing skills of the radicals, the society went into decline. The new leadership persevered, however, and in 1955 it began publishing the *Mattachine Review* out of San Francisco.

The following year *The Ladder* also appeared in San Francisco. The only periodical of the 1950s directed to lesbians, it was published by the Daughters of Bilitis, a group of just eight women headed by two lovers, Phyllis Lyon and Del Martin.[18] The Daughters' Statement of Purpose stressed deferring to the opinions of experts and teaching lesbians to accommodate to society rather than vice versa, indicating that *The Ladder* would land toward the conservative end of the spectrum being defined in the struggles within the Mattachine Society: "(1) Education of the variant... to enable her to understand herself and make her adjustment to society... (3) Participation in research projects by duly authorized and responsible psychologists, sociologists, and other experts directed toward further knowledge of the homosexual."[19]

Despite its lack of organizational affiliation, ONE had by far the largest reach of the three journals. Headlines like the first issue's "Proud and Unashamed" were typical of ONE's tone, offering a simple, forthright antidote to the homophobia of the day.[20] The issue carried a first-person account of editor Dale Jennings's arrest and trial, concluding: "Were all homosexuals and bisexuals to unite militantly, unjust laws and corruption would crumble in short order."[21] The practical information that the journal included was invaluable for homosexuals living during McCarthyism: an explanation of the legal limits of police entrapment, what information one is legally required to tell a cop, and more.

Throughout the decade, ONE cut a path that was unique in many ways. While its editors continued to espouse the gays-as-minority position, they relished keeping their pages open for genuine, freewheeling debate. The core staff remained a mixed-gender group of three men and three women. ONE grew more confident as the decade progressed. In 1956 the ONE Institute began publishing a more scholarly journal, *Homophile Studies*. By 1958 its editor declared, "The time has come when ONE must LEAD. Solutions must be found for the present intolerable minority status of millions of American men and women who refuse any longer to tolerate suppression, subjection, and abuse from every side.... The Weather Forecast for the Magazine's future might read: thunder, lightning, frequent high winds, occasional sunshine."[22]

Mattachine Review took a more conservative, even apologetic tone, working from the assumption that homosexuals needed heterosexual "experts" to speak on their behalf. The least negative social research on the subject of homosexuality was summarized and presented with a positive spin. The *Review* ran pieces about various "cures" for homosexuality and included articles that routinely labeled homosexuals "sexual psychopaths."[23] The fact that such articles referenced the *least* homophobic psychology of the day, and that homosexual-rights advocates would republish and circulate such opinions as a worthy alternative to even cruder characterizations of same-sex desire, speaks loudly to the situation in which homosexuals in the 1950s found themselves.

The women publishing *The Ladder* saw their publication as less political than social. *The Ladder* "wished to enlighten the public about the Lesbians and to teach them that we aren't the monsters that they depict us to be."[24] Poetry, fiction, and biography figured prominently in its pages. The "Lesbiana" column provided useful summaries of current lesbian literature. Politics, the publishers felt, were for activists. *The Ladder* was intended more for isolated women in smaller cities and rural areas.

The Ladder's cautious stance concerning lesbian visibility in America, however, did not translate into a similar caution when discussing the role of women within the movement. In remarks at the 1959 Mattachine Society convention that were published in *The Ladder,* Del Martin announced,

> *I find I must defend the Daughters of Bilitis as a separate and distinct women's organization. First of all, what do you men know of Lesbians? In...* [Mattachine] *Review, you speak of the male homosexual and fol-*

low this with—oh yes, and incidentally there are some female homo-
sexuals too, and because they are homosexuals this should apply to
them as well. . . . Lesbians are not satisfied to be auxiliary members or
second-class homosexuals. . . . You are going to have to learn something
about the Lesbian, and today I'd like to give you your first lesson.[25]

As the decade progressed, both *The Ladder* and the *Mattachine Review* took an increasingly admonishing tone toward their own readers. *The Ladder* advised lesbians not to go to bars or wear pants. Mattachine Society president Ken Burns went a step further, telling the *Review*'s readers, "We must blame ourselves for much of our plight. When will homosexuals ever realize that social reform, in order to be effective, must be preceded by personal reform?"[26]

These journals never reached large circulations. ONE peaked at 5,000, the *Mattachine Review* at 2,000, and *The Ladder* closer to 500. Their impact, however, went far beyond what these numbers might imply. Their first victory was that they existed at all. They published at a time when the mainstream media would not use the word *homosexual*—even in a negative context. When the *Miami Herald* reported a raid on a homosexual bar, for example, it referred to those taken into custody simply as "men with a feminine bent."[27]

Three months after ONE appeared, the FBI opened an investigation of the journal and soon expanded the investigation to the *Mattachine Review* and *The Ladder*. FBI agents visited the employers of everyone working on all three papers. In 1954 the Los Angeles postmaster seized copies of ONE and refused to mail them on the grounds that they were "obscene, lewd, lascivious and filthy." ONE filed an appeal, the first time such censorship was challenged in American history. The action was upheld in both the federal district court and the appeals court, which characterized the magazine as "cheap pornography" simply because it discussed homosexuality. Finally, in January 1958, the United States Supreme Court unanimously reversed the findings of the lower courts, ruling that homosexuality is not, per se, obscene. ONE editor Don Slater proclaimed,

"ONE *Magazine* no longer asks for the right to be heard; it now exercises that right."[28]

For the first time, Americans could legally identify themselves in print as homosexual. It is hard to overstate the importance of this victory. A sea change was on the horizon. Previously, "coming out" meant discreetly identifying oneself as homosexual to other, equally discreet, homosexuals. Within a few years, "coming out" came to mean defiantly telling one's family, church, employer, and society in general that one was claiming the right to be a gay or lesbian. The legal right to make this claim was won in 1958 in the U.S. Supreme Court by ONE.

Who would make these radical new claims that would soon appear? Homosexual society, even in the major urban areas, was a very local affair. But streams of letters to the three homophile journals revealed that despite their small circulations, the journals were reaching a nationwide audience. Two letters sent anonymously to *The Ladder* in San Francisco were from noted black writer Lorraine Hansberry in New York.[29] The beginnings of a national constituency were being formed. The "sexual minority" that the radical founders of the Mattachine Society dreamed of was taking shape. The next generation of activists was finding its way to the movement through these journals.

Most prominent among the newcomers was Frank Kameny, an astronomer who in 1957 had been sacked from the U.S. Army Map Service for being homosexual. Kameny decided to fight back. He took his case first through departmental appeals, then to the House and Senate Civil Service Committees, then to the U.S. District Court and the U.S. Court of Appeals, and filed his own petition to the Supreme Court. In March 1961 his case was denied. Then he really got down to business.

Soon Kameny was spearheading the new Washington, DC, chapter of the Mattachine Society and leading it into uncharted terrain. In contrast to previous homophile groups, who had carefully hidden from public officials, Kameny's chapter hounded them relentlessly, demanding face-to-face meetings to discuss homosexual grievances. The group did not wait for the FBI to come knocking; when they launched their newsletter, *The Gazette*, they sent copies to leading judicial officials including FBI director J. Edgar Hoover himself. An FBI agent paid Kameny a call and requested that Hoover's name be taken off the mailing list. Kameny refused, and *The Gazette* continued to be mailed to Hoover until his death in 1972.

At Kameny's urging, first the Washington, DC, Mattachine chapter and then the chapter in New York passed resolutions asserting that same-sex attraction was a matter of sexual "preference" and "orientation"—ideas that form the core of the gay and lesbian identity today. The members resolved that "homosexuality is not a sickness, disturbance, or other pathology in any sense, but merely a preference, orientation, or propensity, on a par with, and not different in kind from, heterosexuality."[30]

Meanwhile, *The Ladder* found a new home in New York and a new editor in Barbara Gittings. Soon *The Ladder* became *The Ladder: A Lesbian Review*.[31] Photographs of real women replaced line drawings on the front cover, at first in poses that obscured their faces. By 1966 Gittings "had a list of women willing to be cover subjects with full face."[32] Her "Living Propaganda" series filled the journal's pages with their "coming out" stories, changing the definition of "coming out" from a private act to a public one. She went further and opened *The Ladder* to the debate Kameny had been pushing.

> When Kameny said that in the absence of scientific evidence to the contrary, we are not sick—homosexuality is not a sickness—many people disputed him, saying[,] "We have to leave that up to the experts." DOB's own research director . . . engaged in a written debate with him which I published in The Ladder. . . . She strongly felt we did not have the credentials or the right to stand up and say this for ourselves.[33]

Under Gittings's direction, "experts" were tossed aside. "I set out to show that we could speak perfectly well for ourselves, thank you very much," Gittings remembered. "We came to the conclusion that the 'problem' of homosexuality isn't a problem at all. The problem is society. Society had to accommodate us."[34] Before the end of the decade, Gittings was forced out of *The Ladder* by the old-guard Daughters, which sent the journal into a tailspin from which it never recovered.

The activity in New York and Washington was noticed by the *New York Times,* in an article entitled "Growth of Overt Homosexuality Provokes Wide Concern." "The homosexual has a range of gay periodicals that is a kind of distorted mirror image of the straight publishing world...publications offering intellectual discussion of his problem."[35]

While Kameny and Gittings were organizing the movement's first picket lines on the East Coast, in San Francisco the newly formed Society for Individual Rights (SIR) was throwing the movement's first party. SIR's newsletter, *Vector,* spelled out just what sort of party the San Franciscans had in mind: "There is not now, and has never been, a 'Homophile Movement.' Our work is to create a Community feeling that will bring a 'Homophile Movement' into being."[36]

SIR went about this work with gusto, organizing dances, parties, brunches, drag shows, bridge clubs, bowling leagues, country outings, meditation groups, art classes, a thrift store, a VD-testing program, and, in 1966, the country's first homophile community center. All of these activities were reported, along with more directly "political" news, in *Vector,* which now featured a glossy cover and a second color and was available in newsstands around the city. Instead of receiving journals mailed in plain brown envelopes which reviewed oppressive psychiatric research, homosexuals in San Francisco were running to the corner to pick up *Vector* so they could find out what was *happening.* The plan worked. By 1966 SIR was the largest homosexual group in U.S. history, with more than a thousand members.[37] The public presence of such a large—and fun—group was already beginning to transform San Francisco politics.

At the same time, a new publication appeared across the country in Philadelphia. *Drum* became the first periodical to include homoerotica, or what was taken as homoerotica at the time: photos of men in swim trunks. Similar images, but pitched to a heterosexual sensibility, were available on virtually every billboard or magazine cover, but the effect on homosexual men was immediate. In just two years, Drum's circulation shot up to ten thousand, more than all movement papers combined.[38]

Ironically, Drum also became the movement's first periodical to feature news regularly, as editor Clark Polak hired a clipping service to monitor homosexual-related news from around the country. Drum also joined Vector in supporting bar culture, arguing that "the gay bar is the only consistently and readily available homosexual gathering place."[39]

By the late 1960s, it was obvious that change was afoot. In the nearly two decades from the appearance of VICE VERSA to the picket lines of 1965, the press had grown in circulation from a dozen carbon copies to 20,000. In the four years from 1965 to 1969, that 20,000 almost tripled to 55,000.[40] The readers of Vector were building community; in a few urban pockets there was a political movement, and the 55,000 readers across the country were starting to look like a national constituency.

Those readers were beginning to look like a market as well. And there was a newspaper to serve the market. The Los Angeles Advocate had begun publishing in 1967. The paper was run by Robert T. Mitch, a venture he began after being arrested in a bar raid in 1966. By 1968 the Los Angeles Advocate was a full-fledged monthly newspaper: offset printed on tabloid newsprint, full of actual news, and available at newsstands. Its initial press run of 500 had jumped to 5,000 on its first birthday, then to 23,000 a year later, with distribution in New York, Chicago, Boston, and Miami. And it had an ad salesman who brought in real advertising.[41]

The famed Stonewall riots in New York City in the summer of 1969 marked a watershed for the homosexual movement. A police raid on the Stonewall Inn, a Greenwich Village gay bar, triggered several days of street fighting and riots as homosexuals, led by transvestites, fought back. What followed were the brief but golden years of "gay liberation."

Gay papers suddenly seemed to be coming from everywhere. "Homosexual," the term inherited from an oppressive psychiatric tradition, was tossed into the dustbin of history: "homosexual" became "gay." New York City alone saw the appearance of GAY, Come Out!, Gay Times, and Gay Flames. San Francisco had Gay Sunshine and the San Francisco Gay Free Press. The Gay Liberator appeared in Detroit.

By 1972, 150 gay periodicals were being published in cities across the nation.[42] Most came from political groups, like the Gay Liberation Front, which formed one month after the Stonewall riots and spread across the country. Like other gay liberation papers, the Front's Come Out! had no paid staff, and contributors worked for free, yet its circulation reached 6,000.[43]

As with the rest of the radical press of the late 1960s, the extremity of the views expressed in the gay liberation papers can seem scarcely credible to the contemporary reader. In the same way that it is difficult for present-day readers to imagine the power of the printed word to the abolitionists who lived in a world without mass media, it is difficult to imagine what seemed possible to people in the midst of the upheaval at the end of the 1960s. Martha Shelly, who shifted from The Ladder to the new Come Out! explains, "It was that marvelous moment at the very beginning of a new adventure when everything—absolutely everything—seems possible. Every topic was on the table."[44]

Gay journals rode the tide with everyone else, earnestly debating issues such as the role of violence in gay liberation, the role of gay liberation in social revolution, whether to build a separatist "gay nation," whether to support the Black Panther Party, and more.[45] In the long run, the particulars of the debates were less important than the act of engaging in them, of making and distributing the papers, and of fully participating as gays and lesbians in one of the great historical moments of liberation in human history.

Although the most visible activists were on the radical fringe, the loudest voices in the gay press were comparatively conservative. GAY was launched in New York City in December 1969. The bi-weekly had twenty-five thousand subscribers after one month and went weekly after six months. Yet this flagship of the new gay press wrote of those who had instigated the Stonewall rebellion: "The drag queen is doing for homosexuality what the Boston Strangler did for door-to-door salesmen."[46]

The sexual revolution of the era did not arrive with a place already set at the table for gays. They had to claim one. In 1969, two years after the "summer of love," and with the "sexual revolution" in full swing, the Village Voice, the bastion of all that is left and liberal in New York City, was still referring to the Stonewall protesters as the "forces of faggotry." When Come Out! tried to place an ad soliciting articles in the Voice, the Voice refused the ad on the grounds that its heading, "Gay Power to Gay People," was obscene.[47]

The explosion of radicalism that had burst forth from Stonewall could not sustain itself. By 1972 the Gay Liberation Front had folded, and the papers its chapters published went along with it. Many other publications died as well, including The Ladder, which ended its sixteen-year run.[48] But it would be wrong to conclude that gay liberation was a failure, as many writers do. Like a match that bursts into flame when struck and then quickly fades before settling into a steady burn, gay liberation, like the broader social upsurge of which it was a part, brought stunning advances in an incredibly short time. It then briefly faltered, but the explosion drew thousands of gays and lesbians into a life of activism. These people would go on to lead the feminist movement of the 1970s and the AIDS movement of the 1980s.

In the heyday of gay liberation, gays and lesbians had worked side by side in the movement, particularly within the Gay Liberation Front. But lesbians found themselves increasingly uncomfortable working alongside gay men, mirroring a similar development in the straight left. When the post-Stonewall papers folded, most of the lesbians who had worked on them were not interested in any new project dominated by men, gay or straight.

Motive, a long-standing liberal Methodist journal that was ship-wrecking on the rocky reef of the new radicalism, decided to give its final issue a gay and lesbian theme. Reflecting the schism of the times, the issue turned into *two* final issues, one gay, the other lesbian. The lesbian issue featured "Is That All There Is?"—a fiery denunciation of the sexism of the gay movement and a call for lesbians to strike out on their own, to say "goodbye to the wasteful meaningless verbiage of empty resolutions made by hollow men of privilege" who "neither speak for us nor to us."[49] The author was Del Martin, the founder of the recently defunct *Ladder,* who had closed out the 1950s telling the men of the Mattachine Society, "You are going to have to learn something about the Lesbian, and today I'd like to give you your first lesson." By the end of the 1960s, by Martin's estimation the lesson remained unlearned, and she was out of patience. The 1970s would be different.

The women who assembled and edited the lesbian issue of *Motive* formed the Furies, a commune in Washington, DC, whose members ranged in age from just 18 to an "elderly" 28 and who went on to publish a journal of the same name.[50] The Furies published just ten issues over one year, with all expenses paid out of the group's communal pocket. Members started dropping out after just a few issues, and by the final issue only two 18-year-olds remained. Yet the journal's influence was such that contemporary lesbian writers usually remember it as *The "Legendary" Furies.*

Just a few years earlier, Frank Kameny had caused a stir in *The Ladder* for suggesting that homosexuality was a sexual "preference" instead of a disease or abnormality. *The Furies* now argued that "lesbianism is not a matter of sexual preference but rather one of political choice, which every woman must make if she is to become woman-identified and thereby end male supremacy," launching a decade of what came to be known as lesbian feminism.[51]

In Los Angeles these ideas were embraced and developed by *Lesbian Tide. Lavender Vision* began publishing in Boston and *Killer Dyke* in Chicago. By 1975 there were fifty lesbian papers with a total circulation of fifty thousand, the most influential of which were the

Lesbian Connection, out of Chicago; the more intellectual *Amazon Quarterly,* in Massachusetts; *Off Our Backs,* in Washington, DC; and the flagship *Lesbian Tide.* Lesbian feminist publishing, however, encompassed more than these journals. Members of the Furies collective went on to launch Diana Press and Olivia Records. Former Fury Rita Mae Brown published a highly successful lesbian feminist novel, *Rubyfruit Jungle.* The Boston Women's Health Collective published *Our Bodies, Ourselves.* Naiad Press published lesbian fiction, poetry, and essays. The records and books were sold in collectively run women's bookstores and to a public that gathered at annual women's music festivals, which appeared in several parts of the country.

The transition from old school to new was personified by Jeanne Córdova, a twenty-three-year old former Catholic nun whose life changed the day she walked into her first Daughters of Bilitis (DOB) meeting in Los Angeles. She quickly became president of the chapter. "I realized I was too radical and wouldn't be reelected president, so I became newsletter editor," Córdova remembers. She then discovered she was too radical to be the newsletter editor and broke with DOB, taking with her the newsletter, an eighteen-page mimeographed publication with a circulation of one hundred. Thus was born the *Lesbian Tide.* By 1977 *Lesbian Tide* was printing three thousand copies, which were sold nationwide. "We were in between feminism and gay liberation," Córdova remembers. "We did show that lesbians are not the same as gay men; the only thing that is similar is our oppression. We raised the whole issue of monogamy as a form of social control of women."[52]

These papers had a profound effect on their readers. "A woman would read just one article that touched a certain sensibility in her —and suddenly her life was turned upside down," says Lesbian Herstory Archives cofounder Joan Nestle. "She embraced the lesbian culture as the center of her very existence. When that process is repeated for women in tiny, isolated communities from coast to coast —women who previously trembled in fear but then began asserting their own self-worth—the impact cannot be measured in mere numbers."[53]

The late 1970s were a time when many of the most committed activists took their politics to an extreme that would later cause them chagrin, and the lesbian feminists were no exception. *Village Voice* journalist Jill Johnston's highly influential book *Lesbian Nation: The Feminist Solution* equated romance with "dope" and monogamy with slavery: "It begins when you sink into his arms, and ends with your arms in his sink."[54] Sex involving vaginal penetration was politically suspect. In 1977 *Tribad* proposed that lesbian mothers give male children up for adoption. *Dyke* devoted an entire issue to lesbians and their pets, including six sex-with-pets stories. "The animals issue seemed to just dumbfound readers," says editor Penny House. The journal folded.[55]

By 1980 most of the other lesbian feminist journals had folded as well. Exhausted by years of poverty and struggling to keep the *Lesbian Tide* afloat, Córdova launched the *Gay Yellow Pages* and went from making $7,000 to $70,000 a year.[56] Many "political lesbians" went back to relationships with men. Lesbian feminism became something of a lightning rod for easy criticism, known for boring sex and boring music. By 1984 a new generation of lesbians who felt that the narrow world of lesbian feminism had nothing to offer them had launched *On Our Backs,* a lesbian porn magazine that celebrated vaginal penetration, dildos, sadomasochism, butch-femme roles, and just about everything else that *Off Our Backs* had denounced.

A closer look, however, reveals lesbian feminism to be less fleeting than is often imagined. As of this writing, both *Lesbian Connection* and *Off Our Backs* were celebrating more than thirty years of continuous publication. Naiad Press had a thirty-one-year run, from 1973 to 2004. (*On Our Backs* was still publishing as well.) The Michigan Womyn's Music Festival celebrated its thirtieth anniversary in 2005, offering five days of music on several stages, ranging from the original Olivia Records star Holly Near to Tribe 8, a screaming dyke punk rock band whose supremely hedonistic singer, Lynn

Breedlove, often careens around the stage topless, breasts flapping wildly, with a strap-on dildo protruding through her unzipped fly, trying to entice gay boys onstage to fellate her silicon appendage.

Lesbian feminism spawned "herstory," a reconstruction of history from a feminist perspective which began in the lesbian feminist press and has now secured its place in academia.[57] The most lasting and profound contribution of all, however, was the idea that women's bodies belong to women themselves, that women can become their own health experts, and that the process of women asserting control over their own health can be a catalyst for social change. *Our Bodies, Ourselves* is now in its eighth edition. It has been translated or adapted into eighteen languages, including Chinese, Thai, Serbo-Croatian, Spanish, Romanian, and Polish. Books inspired by *Our Bodies, Ourselves* but tailored to local circumstances and published with advice and assistance from the Boston Women's Health Book Collective include *Our Body, Our Health: Sub-Saharan Women's Health and Sexuality* (a French-language book published in Senegal), *A Hundred Thousand Questions about Women's Health* (a Telugu-language book published in India), and *Women's Lives and Health* (an Arabic-language book published in Egypt). Closer to home, the lesbian-feminist approach to health, politics, and community laid the groundwork for much of the AIDS activism that would emerge in the following decade.

Jeanne Córdova says that in retrospect lesbian feminism and its press "really helped women to learn to be independent of men. A lot of my friends went back to straight men, but their life was forever changed.... In the lesbian feminist culture, you were supposed to look into yourself and examine all of your habits, personality, relationship, practically the very ground you walked on.... What I notice much later now is that...there is a real quality of depth of intimacy, and of seeing our world as political."[58]

The gay male press, meanwhile, was developing in a parallel but separate universe of some three hundred publications with a circulation of two hundred thousand.[59] Publications such as *Gay Sun-*

shine in San Francisco, which featured lengthy profiles of writers and artists, and *Christopher Street,* a literary review in New York, gave voice to the more erudite, cultured segment of the community. *Gay Community News* in Boston continued its thoughtful mix of community news and politics, making it one of the very few publications of the gay liberation period to make the transition to the 1970s with its editorial stance intact. It also remained one of the few publications of the era in which lesbians and gay men continued to collaborate.

Like the "herstory" being reconstructed in the lesbian press, the gay press brought to light a history that gay men could claim as their own, including the theretofore-ignored place of homosexual men in the Holocaust. The pink triangle emerged as a symbol of gay militancy.

The radical fringe of the era's lesbian press found a male counterpart in Boston's *Fag Rag,* with headlines progressing from "Cocksucking as an Act of Revolution"[60] to "Rimming as an Act of Revolution"[61] to "Indiscriminate Promiscuity as an Act of Revolution,"[62] the latter arguing that *any* discretion in the selection of one's sexual partners constituted bigotry. Just as lesbian feminists sought common cause with the broader feminist movement, *Fag Rag* situated itself in the male-dominated counterculture, counseling readers on how to use homosexuality to stay out of the army, then later how to participate in antinuclear protests.[63] Whereas headlines like "Molestation of the Young Is the Start of All Politics" were clearly designed to provoke, others, such as "To Be 27, Gay, and Corrupted," showed a sincere and even profound effort to find personal and spiritual meaning amid the whirlwind of the sexual revolution.[64]

The highest-profile developments in the world of the mainstream (white) gay male press, however, were pushing in quite the opposite direction. In the wake of gay liberation, the public presence of gay culture was exploding. Gay bars, formerly small, unobtrusive, and even unmarked establishments, began their transformation into vast discos for hundreds or even thousands of patrons. Men's bathhouses had long been a sexual place where men looking for sex with men could find it, though it was most often a furtive, even dangerous affair. Now the baths became specialized, high-profile playgrounds for hedonistic celebration and experimentation.

In 1974 Wall Street investment banker David B. Goodstein bought the Los Angeles Advocate for the unthinkable sum of $1 million, then pumped millions more of his own money into a total remake of the publication as a slick lifestyle magazine, renamed simply The Advocate. Goodstein knew what he was doing. Twenty-five hundred gay bars and 150 bathhouses with receipts of $120 million were now open for business in the United States.[65] By making The Advocate into a national magazine and stripping it of meaningful political content, Goodstein put himself in a position to do business with them.

The new Advocate focused on fashion, cuisine, and travel. Needing feature writers instead of reporters, Goodstein fired the entire editorial staff.[66] The revamped magazine introduced gay men to what would eventually become the sprawling gym culture of the 1990s. "Do some chair dips. All you need is any chair in your pad, and you can build your chest fairly well. Place your hands on the outer edges of the seat."[67]

The watershed year was 1976. The Advocate jumped from thirty-six pages to more than eighty. The bathhouse and bar ads were joined by Jimmy Carter's presidential campaign, which bought a full page. After Carter was elected, Goodstein was invited to dinner at the White House, where Carter accepted a gift subscription.[68] In the same year, the soft-core porn magazine Blueboy went from a press run of 26,000 to 160,000. Its publisher took out a full-page ad in Advertising Age.[69]

By the end of the decade, The Advocate was not only turning a profit but was declaring that those profits themselves were the next step in the advance of the gay movement: "As the gay press taps into mainstream advertising dollars...these periodicals will serve as examples of successful gay businesses, advancing, in their own way, the business of liberation."[70]

*　*　*

An entirely new space in the movement press was opened with the appearance of *Blacklight* in Washington, DC, at the end of the seventies. *Blacklight*'s writing was exceptional. It sought to redirect radical gay and lesbian thinking in a way that pointed beyond both the increasingly rigid beliefs that had come to characterize the radical stance of the fringe and the commercialization of the center. It was also the country's first black gay and lesbian publication.

Editor Sydney Brinkley announced his intentions in the first issue: "Our struggle to be free as Gay people could never be divorced from the struggle to be free as a race. Unfortunately there exist a number of Blacks who refuse to realize that the reverse is also true, we could not be free as a race as long as one segment of that race continues to be oppressed."[71]

Brinkley built his publication around these ideas. The lead issue featured three front-page stories. One concerned a meeting of gay leaders with the DC police chief to complain of police discrimination against gays. Another dealt with discrimination against blacks at gay bars in the DC area. But the lead story was a lengthy educational piece about the struggle for majority rule in the former British colony of Rhodesia, which would soon become Zimbabwe.[72]

Another issue featured an essay by S. Diane Bogus titled "The Black Lesbian." Bogus's vision of who black lesbians were, and what they wanted, flew directly in the face of almost everything that had been done and said in the (predominantly male) (predominantly white) movement since the 1950s and is worth quoting at length:

> I [am] an overt Black Lesbian.... I [want] the public to know that one sister did not want or need the association with group Gays.... Once one is a part of an identified group, Black, Gay or whatever, all of one's perception, self-definitions, and energies have to flow through the filter of the group ideal. I could never be wholly enmeshed in a single group ideology. I have come to prefer not to spend all my time defining or explaining my right to be Black, Gay or whatever. I am of varied interests, both Black and beautiful and Gay and proud.... Once visible, a Black Lesbian, like all open Gays, will be a sinner in the eyes of the church,

sick in the eyes of the psychiatrists, and perverted in the eyes of society. If she presently is able to function without being attached to a Gay organization, or involved in an ongoing consultation with a psychiatrist, she no doubt considers herself well off. And to the open Black Lesbian, being well off might be living with another woman, going to work, maintaining a household, and partying within one's Gay clique. It does not involve making one's self obvious to one's straight coworkers and neighbors. Yet it is not living in the closet, for any of the above are free to inquire as to your sexuality, and receive an unfettered, "Yes, I'm Gay."[73]

Across the country, in Los Angeles, another black writer/publisher was also pushing in a new direction. *Dowager* (1972–1975) and *Crude* (1976–1980) were the work of "black ghetto drag queen" Vaginal Davis, the initial entries in what has become a vast, wildly offbeat, stunningly original body of work. Eventually these publications would be superseded by *Fertile La Toyah Jackson* (1982–1991), *Shrimp* (1993), *Yes, Ms. Davis* (1994), and *Sucker* (1995–1997). But publishing was just the beginning of Davis's extraordinary output, which also includes films, installations, performance art, books, and music. Davis's flair for the outrageous is extraordinary by any standard. Her rock band Pedro, Muriel and Esther (or PME) features Davis (who is approximately the size and build of an NFL linebacker) onstage in a white first-Communion dress with a phony ZZ Top–style beard. The shtick of the act is that Davis is taking testosterone, as she is allegedly a pre-op transsexual preparing to become a man. *And* she is bleaching her skin, as she wants to become a white man, for she intends to become a white supremacist. The title of PME's CD, the cover of which features a white supremacist in a Budweiser-littered living room cleaning a shotgun under a Confederate flag, is titled *The White to Be Angry*. With her publications and music, Davis anticipated the queer punk movement and the zine explosion by fifteen years.[74]

Dowager was created before the word "zine" was even coined. It was a mimeographed literary periodical. I wrote all the articles but used dif-

ferent names like the magazine had a staff of writers. I sold it at one store in Los Angeles called George Sand Book Shop, and I sent copies to my pen pals from all around the world. No issue of the magazine survives because of my family having moved so much during that time from one housing project to another.

I never called my publications 'zines—that was applied to them later. To me they were literary periodicals and each one had a different focus though Crude shared some similarities with Fertile La Toyah Jackson, but mainly Crude was a poetry journal. When the focus of a publication changed it had to become an entire new entity. Dowager was prose with drawings, Crude was poetry with punk rock infused interviews. Fertile was punky black urban art and social criticism channeled through gossip.[75]

Blacklight and the publications of Vaginal Davis sketch the outlines of a profoundly different politics, sensibility, and identity. They also represent roads not taken: a possible world, not a realized one. They simply had too few resources, and the preponderance of the mainstream movement was too overwhelming, for their voices to be heard in a substantial way.

And of course the publishers were the wrong color. Despite her prodigious output, Davis is rarely mentioned in discussions of gay or queer writers, even discussions focusing on black writers, which is just fine with Davis.

Thank God I'm not mentioned in such things. I don't believe in being ghetto-ized as a black or queer writer. Major groan groan groan and roll of the eyes way back into the forehead. . . . The majority of "The Gays" are clueless and middle class oriented, and don't get me at all, I never came out of the gay world. I came from the punk world.[76]

The exclusion of Blacklight and its progeny such as Blackheart: A Journal of Writing and Graphics by Black Gay Men (New York City), Onyx: Black Lesbian Newsletter (Berkeley), and BLK (the most ambitious black gay publication to date) from histories of the gay and lesbian press is more problematic. These were highly articulate, thoughtful journals from writers who saw themselves as a distinct but integral part of the gay and lesbian community. It is unfortunate that their (white) contemporaries ignored them so thoroughly. It is even more unfortunate that even now, (white) historians ignore them as well.[77]

By 1980 the country had six hundred gay and lesbian publications with half a million subscribers,[78] but the movement was confronting an ugly backlash. Harvey Milk, the first openly gay elected official in the country, had been murdered in his office in San Francisco.[79] Former Miss America Anita Bryant was on a national crusade to save the nation from homosexuals. Jerry Falwell was building his televangelist empire on crude attacks on gays and lesbians. In 1980 the U.S. Department of Commerce rejected *Gaysweek*'s trademark application, stating that the newspaper was "immoral and scandalous." In Boston the offices of *Gay Community News* were reduced to ashes in a seven-alarm fire attributed to arson.[80] All of this was covered in the mainstream media; gays and lesbians had finally made it into the corporate press, but as targets and victims, not citizens.

One result was that gay journalism and lesbian journalism came back together. "We were outnumbered and outflanked by a very wealthy, very powerful, and very mean-spirited group of bigots," explains Jeanne Córdova. "We weren't real sure we would survive at all, but we were damned sure we wouldn't survive if our ranks were divided."[81]

Another result was a turn to actual news reporting, as the movement press tried to keep up with events. San Francisco's *Bay Area Reporter* (BAR) was the first to have a paid correspondent, sending a reporter to Miami, where Bryant was leading a campaign to repeal local anti-discrimination legislation. The correspondent was promptly beaten up.[82] Even *The Advocate,* which now featured the subhead *Touching Your Lifestyle,* got into investigative reporting. Its correspondent, Sasha Gregory-Lewis, received telephone death threats at both her home and her office, and her apartment was broken into and ransacked.[83] Adversity of far greater, even unimaginable, proportions was in store.

In 1976 a number of men who had met at an American Legion convention in Philadelphia were struck by a mysterious respiratory illness, later dubbed Legionnaire's Disease. The New York Times published sixty-two stories on the outbreak, which killed 29 people and sickened another 182. Eleven of these stories were on the front page. Six years later, in 1982, cyanide was discovered in Tylenol capsules in the Chicago area. The New York Times covered the story every day in October, and then ran twenty-three more stories in November and December. In the end, seven people died from the tainted capsules.

By that time, 260 Americans had died of AIDS, and 374 more cases of the illness had been diagnosed. The Times published only three stories on AIDS in 1981, and only three more in 1982, none of which were on the front page.[84]

Covering the onset of one of the great epidemics of human history was left to the gay and lesbian press. The first was the New York Native, a biweekly that had launched in 1980 with the standard mix of news, entertainment, and erotica, including a regular column on the sexually transmitted diseases raging through the gay scene in New York. In May 1981 Dr. Lawrence Mass, writing as a volunteer contributor, published the world's first story about what would eventually be called AIDS in the Native, but the paper was highly uncertain about how to handle the story. "Disease Rumors Largely Unfounded," declared the headline. "Last week there were rumors that an exotic new disease had hit the gay community in New York."[85]

Two months later the Native editors had lost their timidity. The follow-up made banner headlines on page one: "Cancer in the Gay Community." Dr. Mass's extensively researched story reported a troubling outbreak of Kaposi's sarcoma (KS) among gay men whose immune systems were found to be severely defective, and it included lengthy interviews with several medical researchers, as well as graphic photographs showing readers how to identify KS lesions. The willingness of the editors to jettison their usual cultural coverage for dry medical details, grisly photographs, and somber tales of illness and death signaled a new era in the gay press.[86] *The Advocate* also ran a story reporting that health authorities had said the troubling issue was not the disease but the victims' depressed immunity. Eerily, *The Advocate* dedicated the issue to associate editor Brent Harris—one of the first eight reported fatalities of the still-unnamed disease—without mentioning anything about the cause of his death.[87]

Dr. Mass tried to move the story into the mainstream press. He called the *Village Voice*, where he was told, "It's not a *Voice* piece." He tried the *New York Times* but was rebuffed with the explanation that the *Times* was not an "advocacy journal."[88] It would take the *Times* two more years to put AIDS on the front page.

In San Francisco, the weekly *Sentinel* ran early AIDS coverage that closely mirrored the *Native* in its reporting of the few verified facts that were available. But where the *Native* ran Dr. Mass's medical column, the *Sentinel* gave the emerging epidemic a human face with a weekly column by the eloquent Bobbie Campbell, one of the first Americans to speak publicly as someone living with AIDS. Editor Randy Alfred moved Campbell's column to the front page, from where it was picked up by television's *Phil Donahue Show*, and then *Newsweek*. Alfred was breaking national news as well, running the first stories on the deliberations that resulted in federal guidelines asking gay men to stop donating to blood banks. When he ran his scoop on page one, he was told to "keep cancer news off the front page." When he nevertheless ran a follow-up on the front page, Alfred was fired.[89]

The bathhouses quickly became the flashpoint issue. There was enormous pressure to do *something*, and closing these hubs of the formerly vibrant gay sex scene seemed to many an obvious first step. Others defended the baths as pillars of gay culture and a vehicle for public health officials and community activists to reach the most sexually active gay men whom the baths attracted. As the scale of the disaster became clearer, emotions boiled over. It did nothing to help matters when the bathhouse owners revealed themselves to be an extremely crude bunch of businessmen pouring more fuel on the fire at every turn. Even twenty years later it remains difficult to have a reasoned discussion about the role of an institution so unimaginable in straight culture yet so central to the gay culture of the time.[90] Some have pointed to pressures from the bathhouse owners in the *Sentinel's* sacking of Alfred.[91] But Alfred himself claims the commercial pressures were much wider. "It was not just the bathhouses. The bars and restaurants were suffering too. And tourism. If you went to the Castro to eat, it wasn't for fine dining. It was the aura of sexual possibility that brought in the street traffic."[92] With AIDS, that aura of possibility became an aura of sickness and death.[93]

In 1983 the *Native* published "1,112 and Counting" by playwright Larry Kramer, a seminal article that signaled the beginning of AIDS activism.[94]

> *If this article doesn't scare the shit out of you we're in real trouble. If this article doesn't rouse you to anger, fury, rage, and action, gay men have no future on this earth. Our continued existence depends on just how angry you can get.... Unless we fight for our lives we shall die. In all the history of homosexuality we have never been so close to death and extinction before.*[95]

Kramer ended by listing the names of his friends who had died. There were twenty-two, "and one more who will be dead by the time these words appear in print."

Kramer's words exploded into the silence, hesitancy, fear, and denial that hung over the early days of the epidemic. An entire generation of activists, and organizations such as ACTUP and Gay Men's Health Crisis, trace their genealogy to "1,112 and Counting," making it one of the single most influential articles in the history of American journalism.

Two weeks later, across the country in San Francisco, Paul Lorch, editor of the gay weekly BAR, published an answer to Kramer that was downright bizarre:

> The unscrupulous will line up for the giveaway as readily—if not more readily—than the scrupulous. Braying at the government can get quickly tiresome. Already one crowd has demanded that the mayor come up with tens of thousands for an AIDS victims' house—or warehouse—as would be assumed under the aegis of a crew I wouldn't trust my sick goldfish to. What a wonderful way to secure a prolonged free lunch.[96]

A group of men with AIDS wrote to the BAR criticizing its "sensational approach to reporting that only fuels the fire of fear, guilt, homophobia and adds to the everyday stress patients must face in dealing with this illness." Lorch wrote in reply, "I sense your experiences have failed in making you bigger men. The letter reveals a reverse trend, a trend towards peevishness. What a time in your lives to be without honor. Taken to tattling. Exiting with a whimper.... For most of the names on your list, the only thing you have given to this gay life is your calamity."[97]

The epidemic quickly grew to proportions that overwhelmed the limited resources of the gay and lesbian papers that chose to address it, leading to a spontaneous division of labor: the Native focused on medical developments; in Boston, Gay Community News highlighted legal issues; and the Washington Blade covered policy. The Blade repeatedly scooped the Washington Post and the rest of the mainstream press on major stories relating to federal policy and the epidemic.

They all raised money, beginning with the Native's first front-page story.[98] With Alfred gone from the Sentinel, the San Francisco papers did essentially nothing.

By 1985 the amount of medical news people with AIDS had to digest in order to keep up with the latest developments in their sadly limited treatment options had grown beyond the capabilities of the general-purpose movement press. Specialty publications emerged, run by volunteers who worked at all hours training themselves on the job in medical minutiae, federal regulations, and alternative therapies.

The biweekly newsletter *AIDS Treatment News* grew out of volunteer research and writing for an AIDS archiving organization in San Francisco. In little over a year, its circulation grew to more than 3,500, almost entirely by word of mouth.[99] Project Inform opened its doors in 1985 as a national, nonprofit, community-based HIV/AIDS treatment information and advocacy organization. Its *PI Perspective* continues publication to this day and is distributed free of charge to 65,000 individuals and organizations. A second, women-specific HIV/AIDS publication, *Wise Words*, reaches 3,500 individuals and organizations.[100] The value of these publications to people with AIDS, particularly those located in parts of the country without specialized doctors and services, is enormous.

In a league all its own was the darkly humorous *Diseased Pariah News*, described by editor Wulf Thorne as "somewhere between *Spy* magazine and *Good Housekeeping* for the HIV set."[101] As a launch promotion, the first ten subscribers were offered an eventual bonus of paperweights containing the ashes of *DPN* cofounder Tom Shearer (after his death Shearer stayed on the masthead as "the deaditor").

Among *DPN*'s many flashes of brilliance was an ad for an "AIDS Barbie—*and she thought math class was tough!*" Pictured were three versions of the doll, "one with CMV Retinitis and Wasting Syndrome, one with Malignant Lymphoma and Gynecological Complications, and one with Kaposi's Sarcoma and Shingles." The ad duly noted that "Barbie is a registered trademark of Mattel, Inc.," and added that "AIDS is a trademark of Burroughs Wellcome, Inc." (Burroughs Wellcome is the pharmaceutical giant that sold AZT, the first HIV drug.) With no office, staff, or budget, *DPN* eventually reached twenty-five hundred subscribers, nearly all of them gay men with AIDS, before folding after the last of its founders died.

* * *

Diseased Pariah News (DPN): *the blackest of humor for the darkest of times. DPN published eleven issues before all of its founders had died of AIDS.*

Even in the midst of the AIDS catastrophe, the gay and lesbian press continued to grow at breakneck speed. At the end of the 1980s, total circulation broke the one-million milestone, divided among more than eight hundred periodicals. And there was much more to come: by the year 2000 total circulation would double again to more than two million, the lion's share going to a new generation of glossies that dominated the 1990s.

The first tentative foray came from San Francisco, where *Out/Look* was published from 1988 to 1992. *Out/Look* attempted to stake out a high ground on the gay cultural map by combining a quasi-academic writing with popular-culture content and by combining lesbian and gay male perspectives. "We didn't think of ourselves as a glossy; we thought of ourselves as well designed," explained co-founder Kim Klausner.[102] Despite reaching a circulation of seventeen thousand, *Out/Look* was both above and ahead of the curve. "We were on the crest of the change of mainstream advertising," Klausner remembered. "But it was not really available for us. We were too highbrow."[103] *Out/Look* folded after four years.

Just as *Out/Look* was shutting down, *Out* appeared in New York City, announcing itself in June 1992 as the *Vanity Fair* of gay publishing, replete with launch parties, a nonstop marketing campaign, and a designer hired from *McCall's*. *Out* became the first gay product advertised on national TV and the first to participate in Publishers Clearing House, alongside *Reader's Digest* and *TV Guide*. An additional office was opened in Los Angeles—to increase entertainment advertising. The publishing schedule changed from quarterly to bimonthly to ten issues a year—to get more ads. As publisher George Slowik explained, "With greater frequency, we will be able to catch timely ads for movies and home videos."[104]

Out was quickly followed by *Square Peg, 10 Percent, Deneuve, Genre,* and *Victory!* Corporate advertisers began to take notice. Just between 1991 and 1993, the *Wall Street Journal*, the *New York Times*, *Advertising Age*, and others featured news of the gay market. *Advertising Age* also produced "Special Report: Advertising to the Gay Market." An entire book on the subject, *Untold Millions: Positioning Your Business for the Gay and Lesbian Consumer Revolution,* appeared in 1995.[105]

Beginning in 1994 with a total of $53 million, ad revenue in the gay and lesbian press jumped by 16.2 percent in 1995, 19 percent in 1996, 36.7 percent in 1997, 20.2 percent in 1998, 29 percent in 1999, and 36.3 percent in 2000.[106] These accounts were coming from corporations like American, Continental, and United Airlines; British Airways; Citibank; Merrill Lynch; Dean Witter Reynolds; Prudential Securities; Subaru; Saab; Saturn; dealerships for Acura, Audi, BMW, Buick, Mercedes-Benz, Porsche, Toyota, Volkswagen, Volvo; Bass Ale; Budweiser; Coors; All State; Farmers; MetLife; State Farm; American Express; Shell; Starbucks; Swatch; and many more.[107] When people living with HIV got their own lifestyle glossy, POZ, Calistoga, Perrier, and Benneton bought a page or more each in the first issue.[108]

As corporate dollars flooded in, the gay and lesbian media underwent a consolidation of their own, mirroring on a much smaller scale the megamergers and acquisitions of the giant corporate media. *The Advocate* formed Liberation Publications, Inc. (LPI), which bought *Out* in 2000, giving LPI control of the two largest and slickest gay publications. LPI also owns two other magazines, *Out Traveler* and *HIV Plus,* as well as Alyson Publications, the oldest gay and lesbian book publisher in the United States, and Advocate Books, an imprint of Alyson Publications. All in all it was a stunning result for an endeavor that began in the 1960s among activists who published the *PRIDE Newsletter* as part of their campaign against homophobic police brutality.

Meanwhile, William Waybourn, cofounder of the Gay and Lesbian Victory Fund (the nation's largest gay and lesbian political action committee) and former managing director of the Gay and Lesbian Alliance against Defamation (GLAAD), left what he calls "the PR side" of things to form Window Media, which promptly began gobbling up gay and lesbian publications.[109] Window's holdings include the *Washington Blade* (the nation's longest continuously published gay newspaper with more than 100,000 readers), the *New York Blade* (100,000 readers), *Eclipse* (a glossy entertainment guide distributed throughout the South with more than 100,000 readers), the *Houston Voice* (Houston's gay and lesbian paper, 30,000 readers), the *Southern Voice* (55,000 readers in Atlanta and throughout the Southeast), the *South Florida Express Gay News*, the glossy "lifestyle" magazine *Genre*, and various Web sites.[110]

A similar process was unfolding on the Internet. In 1999 OnlinePartners.com (the parent company of Gay.net) merged with Gay.com and then purchased OnQ (AOL's original gay service). Just a year and a half later, the newly bloated OnlinePartners.com bought the PlanetOut Corporation, resulting in PlanetOut Inc., which trades on the NASDAQ under the ticker symbol LGBT. PlanetOut claims more than 3.3 million active members on its Web sites, who have posted more than two million personal ads. PlanetOut's ventures include the Families Channel ("offering parenting and wedding content tailored to the LGBT community"), a Britney Spears CD, and the *Corporate Pride Directory*.

In the world of advertising, the "gay market segment" became one of the biggest stories of the nineties. As television's VH1 exclaimed, "Corporate America has been checking out the bulge in Gays' pants. And guess what? Gays are loaded."[111] How loaded? By 2005 Witeck Combs Communications, a firm that "provides expert counsel to Fortune 500 companies in designing marketing communications strategies for the gay consumer market," estimated the "gay market segment" at $610 billion spent by 16 million people.[112]

These figures have been hotly contested by activists, who say they reflect only a narrow slice of the "GLBTQ community," as marketing surveys are skewed toward people living in a few trendy urban gay ghettos who are overwhelmingly male, white, and wealthy. To advertisers, however, it is of no importance whether these wealthy white males are the tip of the iceberg of a much bigger "community" or an island in a sea of heterosexuals. What matters to advertisers is that the target market buys their products. And the gay market does. The "dream market" composed of white gay men is a fact. They have disposable incomes (the ultimate "DINKs," or dual income no kids); they read a very narrow range of publications, so they can be easily reached; they are highly responsive to companies that appear to be gay-friendly; they are brand loyal; and they are "early adopters" of new consumer trends. It is difficult to find a better match between community demographics and advertiser wish lists in American culture.

What's more, advertisers have discovered that selling stuff to gay men is an effective way to market their goods to *straight* men. Sexualized male bodies entered mainstream advertising through what became known as "gay vague," the use of ambiguous homoerotic images in mainstream advertising. Being bombarded by images of gay men who look sexier than they do has made straight men uncomfortable and has led many straights to look for fashion cues in the gay world.

The exploding advertising revenue has resulted in a generation of slick, glossy magazines that turn a profit but give superficiality new depth. The March 2005 issue of *Out* sports a banner headline reading "Unhung Men: How They Cope." Readers are also promised "175 Must-Have Items" (what *kind* of "items," from the known universe of items, is not specified) and actor Keanu Reeves revealing, "I'm Not Gay, but You Never Know."[113] In the same month, the cover headline of *The Advocate* read, "Gay at the Top: Corporate Success Stories." The cover also announced "An Advocate Investigation." What important issue had the magazine assigned to its investigative staff? "How the world media turned Internet chatter into news and forced *Desperate Housewives* star Marcia Cross to come out—as straight."[114]

Out editor Brendan Lemon speaks for many of his peers in the glossies when he writes that editorial content has not been supplanted by corporate advertising; rather, he claims, the corporate advertising *is* the editorial content.

Another reason to cheer: Corporate America increasingly supports us. . . . Corporations know that they must market their products and services in our direction. This magazine just had its best year ever, as more and more Middle America–based companies like General Motors advertise in our pages. We're thrilled to have them join the industries that have recognized the power of the gay dollar. . . .

The cynically minded might not see corporations' advertising as fundamentally pro-gay at all but only an attempt to increase their profits by adding us to their customer base. To which I would reply: And what's wrong with making money? Love of the dollar is pushing positive change for gay people just as much, if not more, than our advocacy of any specific social legislation.[115]

Sam Shahid of Abercrombie and Fitch, credited as the pioneer of "gay vague," succinctly summarized this view: "I like the idea that you can really change people's minds through advertising, you can make them see a better world."[116]

These developments are harshly criticized by many queer activists and writers as a "sell out"[117] and have even resulted in the formation of an anticorporate activist group called Gay Shame.[118] It is worth noting, however, that gay and lesbian political activists have been just as adamant as gay and lesbian entrepreneurs in their insistence that one crucial measure of the progress of the movement is the "visibility" of gays and lesbians in the mass media.[119] One of the most prominent movement organizations, the Gay and Lesbian Alliance Against Defamation (GLAAD), "is dedicated to promoting and ensuring fair, accurate and inclusive representation of people and events in the media as a means of eliminating homophobia and discrimination based on gender identity and sexual orientation."[120]

In a culture in which the line between advertising and content in the mass media is fast disappearing, if "gay role models" are going to be visible in the mass media, they have to be sponsored by someone, and they will have to be selling something.

" 'Visibility' was the first *sell*," says Jeanne Córdova, "the beginning of the long slide toward commercialism. . . . There is something vacuous about that. . . . Visibility of *what?*"[121]

"Betrayal" and "selling out" are inadequate descriptions of what is happening at the complex interface of gay identity and corporate marketing. The issue goes much deeper. The problem is not unique to gay identity. Modern political identities have always been tightly linked to marketing, both conceptually and historically. As writer and activist Alexandra Chasin has noted, "When women were granted the constitutional right to vote, in 1920, advertisers began to address women as consumers in an unprecedented way. Likewise, the civil rights movement won the passage of the Civil Rights Act and the Voting Rights Act within two years of the first time an African American was pictured in an ad in a general circulation publication in 1963."[122]

Although the relationship between market and identity is shared by all identity politics, this connection is nevertheless uniquely tight in the case of the gay identity. It is no accident that gay identity emerged from capitalist society just as mass marketing was developing, when family ties were loosening, and urban populations were exploding. Regarding the body as private property is the basis for both a capitalist economy (the "right" to sell the body's labor in a labor market) and the present-day gay identity (the bodily pleasures are each private person's "private business"). Furthermore, although nearly all identities function as markets as well, no other identity offers such a jackpot combination of attributes to advertisers.

Finally, as I discussed at the outset, the gay identity (or the GLBTQ identities) is unique in the centrality of public declaration, or "coming out," to the identity. As a result, issues of identity and market, which are confronted by everyone in our ever-more-commercial society, are thrown into particularly sharp relief. If "coming out" is the basis of the movement and visibility the goal, why come out to just family, friends, or coworkers? Would it not be politically preferable to come out on television, in front of millions, and sponsored by Disney?

On April 30, 1997, before 43 million viewers, Ellen DeGeneres did just that. On the famous "coming-out episode" of *The Ellen DeGeneres*

Show, the character Ellen came out. "What are you going to do now?" her therapist asks. Ellen replies, "I'm going to Disneyland!" The program was aired on ABC, which is owned by Disney. The broadcast was sponsored largely by ads for Disney movies.[123]

The alternative queer press did not disappear. On the contrary, its new role as an antidote to the superficiality of the glossies seemed to reenergize it. If the early homosexual press was made by and for homosexuals who felt marginalized from straight culture, the alternative queer press was made by and for queers who felt marginalized from *gay* culture. The movement press had come full circle.

RFD, "a country journal for gay men everywhere," is so far from the mainstream of gay culture that generally it is not even mentioned in histories of the gay and lesbian press despite the fact that its thirty-one years of continuous publication (as of 2005) make it one of the longest-running gay publications in U.S. history. RFD began in 1974 as a journal for gay men starting rural communes as part of the "back-to-the-land" turn of the broader youth counterculture. By the 1980s, the communes had coalesced into the Radical Faeries, an amorphous yet somehow coherent network brought together by none other than Harry Hay, former Communist Party organizer and founder of the original Mattachine Society.[124] Based on an eclectic mix of a back-to-the-land environmentalism, hippie paganism, voracious sexual appetite, and belief that gay men are a unique people with their own spirituality, the Radical Faeries grew to encompass a nationwide network of communes, or "sanctuaries," that host "gatherings," which are the lifeblood of the movement. The sanctuaries also host the publication of RFD, the only gay journal that suffers publication delays when there is not enough sunshine to provide the computer with solar power.

Regular RFD columns include topics such as homesteading (later dropped), gardening, cooking, art, poetry, fiction, astrology, pen pals (both for isolated rural gay men and for "brothers behind bars"), and spirituality. Jumbled in throughout are homoerotic photographs of the very particular Faerie sort: men with bushy beards in Victorian dresses rolling in the mud, naked men in the forest doing campy re-creations of scenes from the Bible, and more. Although many outside the Faerie movement may smirk at RFD's pseudohistorical discussions of paganism and articles on topics such as a "vibrational approach" to curing AIDS,[125] the fact remains that RFD has outlasted almost all other gay publications, and the Faerie sanctuaries have outlasted almost all straight communes launched at the same time. For decades, RFD and the Faeries have been a reliable refuge for gay men seeking a more spiritual approach to their sexuality, cross-generational mentoring relationships, and relief from the trendy commercialism of urban gay culture.

Other gay men's journals focus on spirituality as well. The *James White Review*, a gay men's literary quarterly, has looked at spirituality through poetry, art, and fiction for fifteen years, with a much more refined scholarship than can be found in RFD. *The White Crane Journal*, "a quarterly forum for exploring and enhancing gay men's spirituality," is more rooted in the Christian tradition.

The 1990s also saw new journals for Latino gays and lesbians, including *Perra!* (a Latino gay male magazine published in Miami), *Jota!* (a Chicana lesbian poetry review in Los Angeles), and *esto no tiene nombre* and *Conmoción* (both Miami-based lesbian publications). *Esto* began as the newsletter of Las Salamandras, a Latina lesbian social club in Miami. Most Salamandras were women for whom "to be able to live in a fashion that allowed lesbianism to coexist with being a functioning member of family, society, and the workforce was the ultimate goal," but the committee that worked on *esto* had "lived elsewhere [than Miami and] had participated in or at least been exposed to a wider gamut of lesbian culture." Content that seemed appropriate to the latter group offended many in the former. Even within the little group working on *esto*, the diversity of life experience far exceeded what was typically found at predominantly white gay and lesbian publications. Tatiana de la Tierra was a self-described "free-thinking leftist earth mama" from Colombia. Her colleague and lover Margarita Castilla

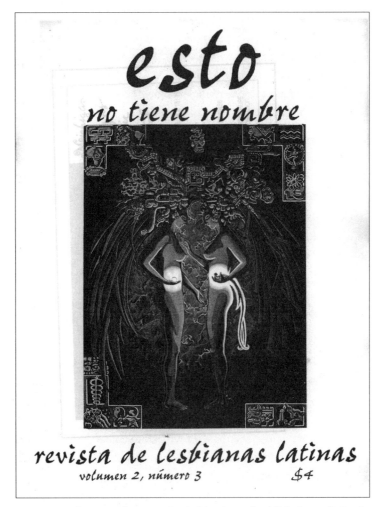

esto

no tiene nombre

revista de lesbianas latinas
volumen 2, número 3 $4

Esto no tiene nombre: *a Latina lesbian journal published out of Miami until Hurricane Andrew literally blew it away.*

had come to Miami during the Mariel exodus in 1980, had walked the streets of La Habana arm-in-arm with her female lovers in a country where being homosexual was a crime. She lived by laws of her own making. She was, according to the biographical note that we published in every issue of esto, "an anti-communist, a Christian, and a lover of women, sexuality, and communication." She was also eurocentric and thought President Bush and Pinochet were the greatest, and she was one of the strongest characters anyone could ever imagine knowing.[126]

Esto split with Las Salamandras and published nine issues before Hurricane Andrew literally blew the journal, and the house that served as its office, away. The project was resurrected as *Conmoción:* "commotion" (conmoción) and "with motion" (con moción), "a powerful combination that alludes to social disturbances, earthly tremors, and all kinds of tumult. *Conmoción* is a fury, a fervor, an endless fuck, a tempest you don't wanna tango with unless you're *conmocionada,* too!" *Conmoción* made an inspired attempt to be "a lesbian megaphone" for Latinas. Partly in English and partly in Spanish, it covered activism, culture, and eroticism and did exceptionally well at each category. It launched Teleraña, a national network of lesbian Latina writers. It was funny and sexy. It took eighty-four contributors from thirty-eight cities to fill the first three issues.

And then it died in a morass of distribution nightmares, in the same way that countless other alternative publications die. De la Tierra began selling *esto* "on consignment at a few bookstores and through a few individuals across the country. But in almost every single case, we were never paid, or we had to chase the bookstores down for a few bucks, and it wasn't even worth the phone calls." She then went through a slew of distribution companies, several of which never paid for their copies.

I didn't even have the energy, in the end, to continue chasing after them all. . . . There was something worse than not getting paid, though. Our print run of esto was very small to begin with (200–500), so the issues were precious and I was guarded about sending them out. We had an agreement with Fine Print that unsold issues would be returned. At that point, Fine Print was the main distributor of esto, *and they had what amounted to* esto's *archives. They destroyed our archives. Today, there are very few original copies of* esto no tiene nombre left; *I do not even have an original set right now.*[127]

Most of the activity in the alternative queer press in the 1990s, however, involved even smaller publications that were much farther out on the fringe: queer zines. Homemade, no budget, deliberately amateur, and brimming with anger and attitude, the zine movement exploded when personal computers developed to the point where "desktop publishing" was feasible and economical. The first queer zines were the work of queer-identified youth who felt more in common with straight punk rockers than with established gay and lesbian culture. Zines were typically simple affairs of a few pages and a tiny circulation, produced by a group of friends for a few months or so. Yet in some ways they wielded more influence than their glossy counterparts in the mainstream gay and lesbian press. Among the dozens of titles were *Clit Rocket* ("an anarcha feminist punk zine into a more specific homo art, gender fuck, lesbian poetry & literature feminist zine"), *Parterre Box* (the queer opera zine), *Homoeroticon* ("queer horror comix zine"), *Fat Girl* (for "fat dykes and the women who want them"), and eventually a queer zine distributor, Xerox Revolutionaries ("trans-run, anti-authority, sex-obsessed, pro-thought, un-funded and dedicated to do-it-yourself ethics").[128]

The early stages of the abolitionist, woman suffrage, and homosexual movements all featured small but passionate periodicals whose effect on readers was life-changing. At the end of the twentieth century, in a culture awash in more information than any individual could possibly absorb, and with the gay and lesbian press now a multimillion-dollar industry, one might imagine it would be impossible for printed words to be so liberating. But the words of San Francisco's *Homocore* zine were.

You don't have to be a homo to read or have stuff published in HO-MOCORE. One thing everyone in here has in common is that we're all social mutants.... *You don't have to be gay; being different at all, like straight guys who aren't macho shitheads, women who don't want to be a punk rock fashion accessory, or any other personal decision that makes you an outcast is enough.*[129]

Homocore was a tiny zine with no budget or advertising, but already the second issue included letters like this one:

I am REALLY psyched to be in on the Homocore deal. I can't tell you what a fucking great idea the zine is—gay people and hardcores get such shit and are so pushed down and (the big one) it's SO FUCKING LONELY![130]

By the third issue letters had arrived from San Antonio and Yugoslavia; by the fifth issue from Brazil and Guam. Among them was this:

Dear HomoCore Dudes, etc, Hey, I'm not gay but I'm only 15 so how would I know? ... awesome zine.[131]

Issue six included this missive:

Your 'zine is fantastic! I love it! It couldn't have come at a better time either 'cause I'm sitting in solitary right now for some real bullshit and I'm starved for stimulation.[132]

After seven issues, the *Homocore* crew had had enough and moved on to other things. By that time, passionate letters had taken over most of the zine.

Although I am not a "punk rocker" type of guy, I am a 26 year old homosexual and I can relate to many instances described by many of the letters. I see the parole board next week and hope to be out soon, so I am glad, even overjoyed, in finding out about Homocore when I did.[133]

The Underground GI Press
and the Vietnam War

In 1971, as a boy of thirteen, I sat with my parents in the family room and watched an extraordinary event unfold on television. Some two thousand Vietnam War veterans were marching to the nation's Capitol. Dressed in faded uniforms and combat fatigues, the veterans had come to return their war-won honors. Finding a fence erected to block their passage, the marchers gathered around the Capitol steps and cleared a space for the ceremony.

One by one, the citizen-soldiers approached the microphone. Pronouncing declarations of anger and peace, the veterans hurled their honorable discharges, medals, and ribbons over the barricade that had been hastily erected to block their access to the politicians who had sent them to war. "My name is Peter Branagan. I got a Purple Heart, and I hope to get another one fighting these motherfuckers." An African American soldier approached the microphone. "I pray that time will forgive me and my brothers for what we did."[1]

Another young man spat out his words in the staccato rhythms of an automatic weapon: "[name indistinct] *died* for these medals. Lieutenant [name indistinct] *died,* so I got a medal. Sergeant [name indistinct] *died,* so I got a medal. I got a Silver Star, a Purple Heart, an Army Commendation Medal, eight Air Medals, National Defense, and the rest of this *garbage*. It doesn't mean a *thing*." He heaved a heavy handful of medals over the barricade and walked away, his body convulsed with sobs.[2]

For three hours, vets paraded by, tossing decorations won with blood, bravery, and pain back at the government that had sent them to Vietnam. The pile of medals grew bigger. No one came out to speak with them. They never got past the fence.

My father served as a medic in World War II. I don't think I have ever seen him as moved by anything else in his life. He and my mother tried to explain to me what these medals meant to these men and how profound this act was. The image is etched in my mind forever. It fundamentally shaped my understanding of war, of government, and of what constitutes meaningful protest.

What I did not know at the time is that the return of the medals had been organized through a vast underground GI press.[3] What's more, this underground press was the backbone of an antiwar movement within the military itself, which had brought the U.S. war effort in Vietnam to the point of collapse. This movement was more militant than its civilian counterpart, and more widespread as well. By the early 1970s, GIs opposed the war in proportionally greater numbers than students ever did, and at far greater risk to themselves.[4] Although the military brass was acutely aware of the threat this movement posed, it went largely unnoticed by the public. It was almost entirely clandestine and had no identifiable organizations. To the degree that active-duty GIs had an organizational vehicle at all, the underground GI press was it.

The 1960s brought a wave of social upheaval such as the world had never seen. Capitalist/socialist, developed/underdeveloped, first/second/third worlds, north/south, old/new—no matter how one sliced up global human society, every piece of the puzzle experienced radical upheaval. Independence movements throughout Africa. Cultural revolution in China. Armed rebellion throughout Latin America. Nearly simultaneous student uprisings in Paris and New

York City, then Mexico City and Tokyo. The Prague Spring. The Italian Hot Autumn. And, of course, the Vietnam War.

As time has passed, the sharp edges of the violence and brutality of the Vietnam War have been polished into the smooth surfaces of national myth. To understand the sixties at all—the depth of the rage, the extremity of the radicalism—we must try to see the Vietnam War as it appeared to its contemporaries, without the gloss of time. More than fifty thousand Americans died in Vietnam, which pales in comparison with the more than five million Vietnamese who perished.[5] The United States dropped more than three times the total tonnage of bombs dropped by both sides in World War II. Chemical agents dropped by U.S. planes defoliated 10 percent of the land, much of it permanently. And, for the first time, viewers back home saw the action unfold on television thanks to recently developed broadcast technology.

Ray Mungo, who went on to become one of the founders of the Liberation News Service, spoke for many of his generation when he wrote, "From Vietnam, I learned to despise my countrymen, my government, and the entire English-speaking world, with its history of genocide and international conquest. I was a normal kid."[6]

In the space of a few short years, and in some cases just months, campuses moved from informational "teach-ins" to protests to strikes and revolts. This was *mass movement*: everywhere and all at once, people—mostly young people—were *doing things*. One of these things they were doing was publishing underground newspapers.

Like so much else in the sixties, the underground-newspaper boom was located at the intersection of technological progress and social unrest. Newspaper copy had previously been set in hot type on a Linotype machine, a process that was laborious, skilled, and expensive. In the early 1960s, the introduction of offset printing put newspaper production within the reach of anyone with a few dollars, a pot of glue, a typewriter, and a circle of friends.[7]

In 1964 Art Kunkin launched the first (and ultimately most successful) of the decade's underground papers, the LA Free Press, with a budget of $15. The Berkeley Barb was launched the following year, as was the East Village Other in New York. The next year saw the emergence of The Oracle in San Francisco's Haight-Ashbury district and The Paper in Lansing, Michigan. The five newspapers, with a combined circulation of fifty thousand, joined together to form the Underground Press Syndicate (UPS). UPS announced its intention "to warn the civilized world of its impending collapse, [and] to offer as many alternatives as the mind can bear."[8]

Within a year UPS was servicing nineteen papers, but this was just the tip of the iceberg.[9] The emerging black power movement was supporting the Black Liberator and the Black Panther, the United Farmworkers had La raza, and militant Chicanos in New Mexico were publishing El grito del norte. Later, Akwesasne Notes would act as the voice of the American Indian Movement. The High School Independent Press Service formed, as the movement drew in younger and younger kids.[10]

By 1968 the LA Free Press alone had a circulation of 50,000, and the Black Panther's passed 85,000. At the start of the year, the recently formed Liberation News Service (LNS) was sending packets of articles to 125 "underground" papers, 80 "peace" papers, and 75 college papers. Before the year was out the packets were going out to 400 papers in total.[11]

By the end of the decade, the flagship LA Free Press was a $2-million-a-year, 150-employee operation with a circulation of 100,000. LNS had 600 regular subscribers.[12] But the movement had grown so fast and large that it was hard to keep track of it all. The Wall Street Journal estimated the underground press' total readership at 330,000, Newsweek estimated it at 2 million, and both LNS and UPS claimed 4.5 million. In 1971 an even larger and more chaotic state was reached. One estimate held that the underground press included 800 papers with 10 million readers; another found 400 papers with 20 million readers. UPS claimed 30 million readers.[13]

The uneasy coexistence of the "counterculture" and the "new

left" that pervaded the youth culture of the time was mirrored in the underground press, sometimes through competing papers such as the countercultural *Oracle* in the Haight-Ashbury district and the more political *Barb* in Berkeley, or the *East Village Other* and the *Rat* in New York City. In other places both tendencies coexisted in the same paper, like the *Seed* in Chicago and the *Great Speckled Bird* in Atlanta.

For most of those involved, organizing "the movement" and publishing the paper were indistinguishable activities. In San Francisco the same energy that spawned the *Oracle* organized the first "Human Be-In" in Golden Gate Park a few months later, with twenty thousand people in attendance. LNS emerged out of the march on the Pentagon in 1967. In Chicago the *Seed* became the key source of information and debate in the lead-up to the apocalyptic demonstrations at the Democratic Convention in 1968.

These papers were produced in a spirit of daring, naïveté, and sheer chaos that is almost unfathomable to those looking back from a distance of several decades. UPS was dreamed up by a few people in their early twenties while acid tripping on a beach north of San Francisco. LNS was funded largely by theft and published between acid trips on a production schedule organized by "magic."[14]

Magic apparently was sufficient for getting stories out but not for fact-checking them. "We were not sticklers for accuracy," wrote LNS's Ray Mungo. "Neither is the underground press in general, so *be advised*. But our factual errors were not the product of any conspiracy to mislead the young, but of our own lack of organization, shorthandedness, and impatience with grueling research efforts.... All we say: tell the truth, brothers, and let the facts fall where they may."[15]

Tom Forcade of UPS neatly summarized the spirit of the movement in his testimony before the Commission on Obscenity and Pornography, where he denounced the "walking antiques...trying to stomp out *our*...working model of tomorrow's paleocybernetic culture, soul, life, manifesting love, force, anarchy, euphoria... flowing new-consciousness media on paper, from our lives to the streets.... So fuck off and fuck censorship," he concluded before tossing a pie at the panel.[16]

The government's response to the underground-press explosion was not nearly as humorous. Especially after Richard Nixon took office in 1969, the FBI targeted these publications. FBI agents pressed record companies to cancel the ads that financed many underground papers.[17] The *Nola Express* in New Orleans and the *Rat* in New York City were under extensive FBI surveillance. During 1969–1970 the editor of Miami's *Daily Planet* was arrested twenty-nine times and acquitted twenty-eight times, posting a total of $93,000 in bond (a staggering sum for an underground activist in 1969). The FBI sent phony letters designed to exacerbate internal tensions within LNS[18] and even launched three phony underground papers of its own, as well as three phony news services. Army intelligence got into the act and burglarized the *Free Press* in Washington.[19]

This was not the abolitionist movement or the woman suffrage movement or even the civil rights movement. Activists saw themselves simply as members of "the movement." So what, exactly, did "the movement" want? It wanted an end to the Vietnam War and to all war; an end to racism and black power; civil rights and students' rights, and then women's rights and gay rights; to Bring the Troops Home and to Be Here Now; free universities, free love, free music, and free drugs. Each one of these demands and desires was addressed at length in the underground press, sometimes all at once.

As the war in Vietnam escalated, stopping it increasingly came to dominate (though never eclipse) other concerns. But it was not clear how students could accomplish this, what leverage they could bring to bear. Workers can bring factories to a halt with strikes. Blacks concentrated in urban areas can threaten urban peace. What could students do? Even strikes that closed down major universities didn't seem to bring results. A feeling of powerlessness in the face of war began to drive some sectors of the movement "crazy."[20] It created a glorification of violence in some, a retreat from the "new left" into the worst kind of sectarianism and old-school "vanguardism" in others, and for still others, a retreat from politics altogether.

Yet the youth had more power than they knew. There *was* one thing for which the state was absolutely dependent on them: fighting the war.

Dissent within the military against U.S. policies in Vietnam began almost the moment American military personnel set foot on Vietnamese soil and before the war was even on the radar of the sixties generation back home.

Jan Barry was an army radio technician in Vietnam from 1962 to 1963, before the introduction of combat troops. Barry recounts, "Some of the special forces people would come back from their missions and say we should be supporting the other side, because these people have legitimate grievances and the other side is the only one ... trying to do something for these people."[21] In 1967 Barry would go on to found the Vietnam Veterans Against the War.

Among the Special Forces people Barry had noticed was Master Sergeant Donald Duncan, who left the Green Berets in September 1965 and wrote "The Whole Thing Was a Lie" for the radical *Ramparts* magazine in February 1966.[22]

On March 8, 1965, the first U.S. combat troops arrived in South Vietnam. Just three months later, Special Forces lieutenant Richard R. Steinke refused a direct order into a combat zone because of his opposition to the war. Before the year was out, Lt. Henry Howe, at Fort Bliss, Texas, became the first known GI to demonstrate in the United States when he marched in a small peace rally carrying a placard reading "End Johnson's Fascist Aggression." Howe was court-martialed and sentenced to two years' hard labor. Neither Steinke's refusal nor Howe's protest and incarceration were publicized.[23]

Four months later, three privates from Fort Hood, Texas, refused to ship out to Vietnam. Puerto Rican David Samas, African American James Johnson, and Italian American Dennis Mora announced a press conference, but federal agents arrested them en route to the church where the event was planned. Civilian supporters managed to publicize their manifesto nevertheless, and the "Fort Hood Three" became the first public face of GI resistance to the war: "We have made our decision. We will not be a part of this unjust, immoral, and illegal war. We want no part of a war of extermination. We oppose the criminal waste of American lives and resources. We refuse to go to Vietnam!!"[24] The men were placed in solitary confinement and threatened with the death penalty. Eventually, they received three years' hard labor.

Soon after, Ronald Lockman, a black GI and the son of a steelworker, refused orders to go to Vietnam with the slogan "I Follow the Fort Hood Three. Who Will Follow Me?" Captain Dale Noyd refused to train bomber pilots for Vietnam duty. Captain Howard Levy refused to train Green Beret medics and got three years' hard labor.[25]

In June 1967 Levy received a telegram of support from five GIs at Fort Sill, Oklahoma. One of the signatories was Andy Stapp. When Stapp was found to have antiwar literature in his foot locker, the army charged him with a minor offense, but Stapp insisted on a full court-martial in order to publicize his views at trial. The military judge was stunned to find himself confronted with both soldiers and civilians chanting antiwar slogans together in what was probably the first antiwar demonstration on a military base.[26]

Stapp announced his intention to organize GIs into a union, the American Servicemen's Union (ASU). The army was uncertain how to respond to the unprecedented situation and finally booted him out with a dishonorable discharge. Stapp began publishing *The Bond*, and the GI underground press was born.[27]

The civilian activists who came to Stapp's support were members of the Workers World Party, one of many Marxist miniparties trying to fit the round peg of sixties activism into the square hole of Trotskyism. Their support helped Stapp generate publicity for his union and funded his paper. But *The Bond* came to look much like the other papers of the dogmatic party left: lots of small type pontificating on jargonistic positions at great length. Attempts to organize local union chapters frequently degenerated into sectarian turf fights. To many dissident GIs, the very idea that their organizing should take the form of a union was a dogmatic misstep. Nevertheless, the ASU signed up a paper membership of twenty-thousand over the life of the organization, an indicator of how fertile the ground for antiwar organizing was inside the U.S. military.[28]

The Bond was not the only paper to appear in 1967. A group of deserters who had fled to Paris formed Resistance Inside the Military (RITA). The RITA newsletter, ACT, encouraged soldiers not to desert but to stay in the military and actively resist. ACT's circulation eventually reached ten thousand.[29]

The year of these events, 1967, is significant. Draftees were required to serve two years in the military, and enlistees three to four. Combat troops were introduced into Vietnam only in 1965 and typically did one-year "tours." Veterans speaking out in 1967 were thus among the very first veterans to return from Vietnam and muster out of the service. Among them was a group that met at an antiwar rally in New York City in the spring and decided to form Vietnam Veterans Against the War, which would become the most important organization of the GI movement.[30]

It is notable that these developments all occurred *before* the Tet offensive of early 1968, which is often seen as the beginning of the demoralization of the U.S. military in Vietnam.

While Stapp was fighting his court-martials in Oklahoma, Jeff Sharlet was struggling at college in Bloomington. At twenty-five, Sharlet was older than most students, having already completed two tours of duty in Vietnam. He had seen a lot. The army had noticed that Sharlet was a smart kid and taught him Vietnamese before assigning him to intelligence. In 1963 he was in Saigon during the CIA-backed coup that overthrew South Vietnamese president Ngo Diem. Later he did top-secret work monitoring, decoding, and translating North Vietnamese radio transmissions. And everywhere he went, he spoke about the war to everyone he could, in Vietnamese. In 1964 he returned to the United States firmly opposed to the war. Soon he was the chair of the Students for a Democratic Society (SDS) chapter at Indiana University but was also increasingly critical of the "shallowness and snotty attitude" of the student movement, which he felt made it ineffective.[31]

"The chemistry was not working too well," remembers Thomas Barton, a conscientious objector who was also a student in Bloomington. "He just didn't feel like he fit in. . . . Jeff wanted to do a newsletter for people back in Vietnam."[32] He spent a summer in New York City working with the newly formed Vietnam Veterans Against the War, then enrolled for graduate school at the University of Chicago. He stayed at school one day—just long enough to pick up his Woodrow Wilson Scholarship check, which he used to launch *Vietnam GI* in January 1968.

Vietnam GI set a standard of excellence unmatched in the underground GI press. It was also unique in that its target audience was soldiers in Vietnam, not on bases back home.[33] "Jeff still had friends getting shot at; these were for them," says Barton. By August the paper had grown into two editions, the main Vietnam edition and a second, "Stateside" edition addressing GI issues on domestic bases.

Sharlet traveled constantly, visiting military bases and recruiting GIs willing to write for the paper or distribute it. Production of the paper was handled by a group of about a dozen volunteers in Chicago. Distribution to Vietnam, however, was done by mail, according to procedures carefully designed to avoid the attention of military authorities.

Bundles were sent to civilian committees and individual GIs around the country. The local group would then mail the papers to soldiers in Vietnam, in a plain brown wrapper with an inconspicuous return address, such as the Presbyterian Pen Pal Club. The return addresses had to be changed constantly to avoid detection by authorities. Using fake return addresses would have simplified things, but the addresses had to be valid. Soldiers' addresses in Vietnam were good for only short periods of time, and postage to Vietnam was costly, so it was crucial that the organizers receive notice when a soldier's address went out of date. Arranging a constantly changing series of valid return addresses from which the organizers could collect mail was their only option. The complete address list was a secret that only the core people in Chicago had access to.

Vietnam GI's content was even more extraordinary than its production and distribution. The tabloid was written entirely by vets and soldiers, "from the point of view of the grunt," remembers GI activist Dave Cline.[34] It never strayed from the voice of the GI on the ground who was concerned about his buddies first and who always spoke from immediate experience.

Each issue led with a long, thoughtful interview with a GI who was either just back from Vietnam or had recently been involved in an act of resistance. The second issue featured such an interview with Pete Martinsen, frankly discussing torturing Vietnamese prisoners with beatings and electric shocks. "I never dug beating up women. I saw it done a lot of times and even did it myself a couple of times." Martinsen reflected on how ineffective interrogations were: "It was a real victory if we got any information at all."

> When we first moved into our area, the Vietnamese were about 50–50 for and against us. Not really extremely against us and not really extremely for us. Just a "wait-and-see" attitude. Then people started getting killed indiscriminately by Americans, all the girls turned into whores, the men into pimps, the kids into thieves and beggars. Long Khanh Province was more against us when I left than it was when I came in. We did this, not the VC.[35]

The same issue featured an insightful letter from a medic with the First Infantry Division:

> I thought of all the oddities I'd seen since coming here. The things I couldn't understand, and couldn't believe. . . . The new Americanized, uplifted people! Living in fallen shacks made of flattened beer cans and scrap wood, riding Honda motorcycles. The begging children who fought viciously over a Hershey bar we won't even eat. . . . Beautiful

*young girls turned into prostitutes for the American GI "Joe." The dis-
gusting treatment of the people by the average GI, taking his animosi-
ties for being here out on them.... It's a strange, beautiful, untouched
land. I'm sickened by it, because I'm forced to it. I'm learning from it.
Finding I want no others here. I only want my fellow Americans in one
war. The war at home. The war for peace.*[36]

The paper had a letters section, but apart from the lead interview and an editorial, the entire paper was made up of letters. "Articles" were often simply letters that the editors had decided to top
with a headline.

*We know that war is ugly all the way around. But too much really bru-
tal shit goes on in Nam, and the responsibility for this goes right to the
Brass.*

  *Troops who are serving in the III Corps probably heard that the
2/27th Inf. ("Wolfhounds") is a pretty tough outfit. Well and good. But
they also have a rep as an outfit that takes damn few prisoners back.
If you don't know why, you should hear it.*

  *Going into the field, 2nd Bn. CCs pass the order down that if any
man takes a Vietnamese alive, he is personally responsible for that
prisoner's security and well-being. In other words, that troop must feed
the prisoner out of his own rations, guard him, and personally transport him back to base camp. Since the 2nd Bn. is often in the field as
long as 30 or 40 days, this order is telling the men to kill all prisoners....*

  *If the Brass want troops to kill prisoners and stray civilians, then
they should tell the American people that this is their policy. Of course,
that is asking the Brass to openly take responsibility for the dirty side
of war, like men.*

  As we well know most officers don't have the guts to do that.[37]

What is most extraordinary is how the paper managed to remain
unflinching in its opposition to the war while positioning itself as
the key forum for uncensored discussion among GIs with an exceedingly diverse range of views. *Vietnam GI* never limited its pages

to views that its editors agreed with. The May 1968 issue led with an interview with George H. Travis, who was wounded twice and despite being active duty asked that his name be used.

> If they want to win this war, they should go on and win it instead of babying around. I really feel that if the Vietnamese that we are fighting had the equipment we have we would just lose automatically because they're messing us up pretty good already.[38]

The following month's paper interviewed a door gunner on a chopper:

> Q: How do you feel toward the anti-war movement?
>
> A: You mean the peace creeps? Well, I think most of them are just trying to stay out of the Army; they don't want to go to Nam. But I think the guys who are running the show really believe in what they are doing.... But I don't blame them. If I knew then what I do now, I'd be in Canada.[39]

That summer the paper printed a letter from a GI who wrote, "I am for staying and kicking Charlie's ass. I have lost too many friends to see it all wasted. I am thankful that I'm still in one hunk and still can look at both sides." The respectful editor's comment that followed demonstrates why *Vietnam GI* continued to be the place where GIs chose to air their thoughts:

> There's a lot of truth and honesty in what you say. Every time we lose someone to Charlie we want to do something about it. We're men, and we don't forget our own. But what should we do about the politicians back home who sent us into this stinking war? Are we man enough to settle our score with them?   SINCERELY, JEFF SHARLET[40]

The third issue included a letter from retired brigadier general Hugh B. Hester:

I strongly feel that anyone who has studied thoroughly the background and conduct of this war, as I have, and who has reached the conclusion, as I have, that the war is in violation of the basic interests of the American people, is not an enemy of our people when he refuses to accept service in Vietnam. On the contrary, he is exercising his loyalty to our people in its finest form.[41]

Even more remarkable than the fact that a retired brigadier general was endorsing mutiny was the fact that he chose *Vietnam GI* as the venue to state this opinion, for the same paper was running letters from grunts like the following:

As for Vietnam, all I can say is we're wrong for being here, no one knows what we're fighting for or who we're fighting against. The only true picture you get is that we are fighting every gook over here as all of them hate us and will go to no end to get the best of us. There is no loyalty or appreciation given to us for helping their shitty cause (whatever it is), all there is are gooks (young and old, men and women) planning and scheming to cut our throats so they can take our money and possessions. With all this going on they condemn a man for getting stoned occasionally. I would hate to think of being stuck in this shit hole for a whole year without the effects of hallucinogens to help me carry through it all, though don't get me wrong, as a hobby not a crutch.[42]

The delicate balancing act *Vietnam GI* was performing was graphically and horrifyingly presented in a large photo in the May 1968 issue, showing a GI with a maniacal grin holding the heads of two Vietnamese he had just decapitated. The boldface caption read:

The above picture shows exactly what the brass want you to do in the Nam. The reason for printing this picture is not to put down G.I.'s, but rather to illustrate the fact that the Army can really fuck over your mind if you let it.

It's up to you, you can put in your time just trying to make it back in one piece or you can become a psycho like the Lifer (E-6) in the picture who really digs this kind of shit. It's your choice.[43]

The above picture shows exactly what the brass want you to do in the Nam. The reason for printing this picture is not to put down G.I.'s but rather to illustrate the fact that the Army can really fuck over your mind if you let it.

It's up to you, you can put in your time just trying to make it back in one piece or you can become a psycho like the Lifer (E-6) in the picture who really digs this kind of shit. It's your choice.

Vietnam GI, May 1968: By focusing on the moral dilemmas of grunts on the ground, the paper quickly built up a large readership among GIs in Vietnam.

In a very short time, the expanding reach of *Vietnam GI* enabled it to publish more sophisticated assignments, like a spread in that same May 1968 issue which showed two articles by the same person: one written for the *Army Observer* and the other for *Vietnam GI*. In the second article, the author described how he had been made to lie when writing for the army paper.[44]

As opposition to the war among the troops became more widespread, the editors of *Vietnam GI* kept abreast of the practical concerns that came with this development:

A growing percentage of GIs are finding themselves in a position in which they may very well have to spend some time in a military brig or stockade. The purpose of this article will be to acquaint you with the conditions in a number of Navy and Marine Corps Brigs. Moreover, we hope to give you a few tips toward making your stay in confinement a bit easier to hack.[45]

The *Vietnam GI* reached a peak circulation of about ten thousand. But after just one year of publishing, Sharlet started to visibly tire. Friends didn't think he looked well. During an organizing trip in Florida, he checked into a VA hospital and died soon after. He was twenty-seven years old. The official cause of death was cancer, but vets who worked with him believe his death was caused by exposure to Agent Orange. *Vietnam GI* never recovered from his loss and published its last issue in June 1970.

Barton sums up *Vietnam GI*'s extraordinary run: "The truth of the paper was in the letters to the editor. These came in from all over South Vietnam and were a barometer of the paper's extraordinary reach, and the importance it held for those who read it."[46] One such letter reads:

Gentlemen:

It seems like every time you put a new issue out I have six or seven guys who want subscriptions after ripping my copy to shreds. Right now it's an even-money bet which is more popular in our unit, Playboy or Vietnam GI.... Enclosed are several more names for subscriptions.
—PCF, 198TH LIGHT INFANTRY[47]

* * *

On the Vietnamese New Year ("Tet" in Vietnamese) in 1968 (January 30 by the Western calendar), Viet Cong forces attacked nearly every military installation and city controlled by the U.S. Army and its South Vietnamese allies. The Tet offensive came as a total surprise to an American command that had reported almost uninterrupted progress to citizens back home. It was a shock from which the U.S. war effort never recovered.

The GI antiwar movement exploded. In 1967 there were three underground GI papers. By 1972, the Department of Defense reported, 245 had been published.[48] The breakneck pace of the press can be tracked by the mailings of the GI Press Service (GIPS), which was run by vets working out of the Student Mobilization Committee, a national peace group based in New York City. The first GIPS mailing contained 48 pages of stories mailed to 27 papers in June 1969. One month later, the mailing was going to 39 papers. By the end of the year, 208 pages of stories were being sent to 55 papers.[49]

The national papers, such as *Vietnam GI* and *The Bond,* had been largely superseded by papers located on particular bases. Some of these were no more than a few mimeographed sheets put out clandestinely by a few friends until they were caught, were transferred, or ran out of money. Others grew into major operations that broke stories before the mainstream press, mobilized large GI demonstrations, and had circulations in the thousands.

The names of the papers reflected the dark humor common among GIs: *Shakedown* at Fort Dix, *Attitude Check* at the Marine Corps' Camp Pendleton, *Fed-Up* at Fort Lewis, *All Hands Abandon Ship* at Newport Naval Station, *The Last HarAss* at Fort Gordon, *Left Face* at Fort McClellan, *The Star-Spangled Bummer* at Wright-Patterson Air Force Base, *Your Military Left* at Randolph Air Force Base, and on the submarine tender USS *Huntley,* the *Huntley Hemorrhoid,* which informed officers "We Serve to Preserve the Pain in Your Ass." The movement even penetrated Strategic Air Command Headquarters at Offut Air Force Base in Omaha, where the *Offul Times* was published. In the very Pentagon itself was *OM: The Best of the Worst,* one of the smallest papers but also one of the most spectacular.

OM was published briefly by Roger Priest, an apprentice seaman stationed in the Pentagon. Priest's objective was not to organize GIs but to pick a free speech fight with the Pentagon. He never hid the fact that he was the editor and publisher. On the contrary, he listed his name and address on every issue. And he followed military regulations to the letter in all other aspects of his behavior, ensuring that if the brass was going to get rid of him, they could not do it on a technicality. He then set about creating the most outrageous newsletter he could.

OM headlines included such items as "BOMB AMERICA. MAKE COCA-COLA SOMEPLACE ELSE" and "WE WILL STOP AT NOTHING TO STOP THE VIETNAM WAR, AND POWER ARRANGEMENTS THAT MADE IT POSSIBLE. WE TAKE THAT 'NOTHING' SERIOUSLY."

OM provided its readers with useful information such as, "If Spiro Agnew jumped (or was pushed) from the spire of the Empire State Building, and was caught by a favorable crosswind, he would hit 34th Street at a velocity of 281.6 feet per second" and "Thanks to Dow's napalm and modern technology, it is now possible to take the ovens to the people rather than the people to the ovens."[50]

The brass went ballistic, and Priest got the court-martial he wanted after the third issue was released. At trial it came out that the Pentagon had detailed twenty-five military intelligence agents to follow Priest at all times. The brass had furthermore moved the FBI and AT&T to tap his phone, the U.S. Post Office to intercept his mail, and finally the Washington, DC, Sanitation Department to collect his garbage and deliver it to the Pentagon. The garbage surveillance led to a very public flap between the capital's mayor and the Sanitation Department, with the mayor calling for a "full and complete investigation."[51]

The court-martial involved no evidence from Priest's garbage but centered on his published description of the chair of the House Armed Services Committee as a pig shitting and pissing on the country. (Meanwhile, Priest apologized to his readers for the "obscenities which are frequently used in OM, such as: army, brass, lifer, war, kill, gun, stockade or brig, barracks, 'duty,' and capitalism.") Despite facing the prospect of thirty-nine years of hard labor, Priest was not intimidated. He raised money for his defense by offering to sell trial souvenirs, including "Naval intelligence-approved garbage from Priest's own trash cans."[52]

Trial coverage in the mainstream press sent the brass into orbit. The *Washington Post* described Priest as "the young man from Texas with the Gomer Pyle accent and the undershot jaw":

> It takes more than four, single-spaced typewritten pages to enumerate all the bad things Roger has done, which include the charge that he "did wrongfully use contemptuous words against the Chairman of the Armed Services Committee to the House of Representatives, L. Mendel Rivers." How Roger managed to use contemptuous words against the Congressman wrongfully is not explained, but if he did, he's a very clever boy and they should make him an admiral.[53]

* * *

Priest's case highlighted the ambiguous legal terrain on which the underground GI press existed. According to the Universal Code of Military Justice (UCMJ), which ostensibly governed personnel in all branches of the military, GIs were free to express their views in print as long as they did it "off-post, on their own time, with their own money and equipment."

But the UCMJ also prohibited any "insubordination," or criticism of either superior officers or the chain of command, including the president, vice president, cabinet, and Congress.[54] Finally, a federal statute that applied to all citizens prohibited "all manner of activities (incitements, counseling, distribution or preparation of literature) intended to subvert the loyalty, morale, or discipline of the Armed Services" and carried a penalty of ten years in prison.[55] However, GIs were still U.S. citizens whose right to free speech was supposedly protected by the First Amendment.

The underground papers that appeared on base after base skated on this thin legal ice. In August 1968, the commanding general of the U.S. Continental Army Command asked the Department of the Army to furnish him with "guidance" on dealing with "subversive publications disseminated at military installations." The department's subsequent *Guidance on Dissent* reiterated that GI papers must be produced "off-post, on their own time, with their own money and equipment," but further stipulated that the papers also had to be submitted for the prior approval of the base commander.

In practice, the *Guidance* neither changed nor clarified anything. When commanders figured out who was behind the underground base paper, they found many ways to punish the perpetrators without directly mentioning the paper. Infractions could be invented. Transfers to undesirable posts could be arranged. And, of course, the guilty parties could be sent to Vietnam.

These threats were serious. A dishonorable discharge would hang over a GI's head for the rest of his life, making employment difficult. PFC Dennis Davis, one of the editors of *The Last HarAss*, was given such a discharge just fifteen days before he was scheduled to muster out honorably.[56] Patrick McCann of *A Four-Year Bummer* at Chanute Air Force Base got a dishonorable discharge and thirty days in the stockade.[57]

Others fared far worse. Many charges on which GIs were framed carried a penalty of substantial time at Fort Leavenworth doing hard labor. Andy Stapp served forty-five days at hard labor in 1967 and was threatened with much more. Pvt. Wade Carson was sentenced to six months for "intention" to distribute *Fed-Up* on Fort Lewis. Pvt. Bruce Peterson, the first editor of *Fatigue Press* at Fort Hood, was busted twice for the possession of quantities of marijuana so tiny that they "disappeared" under analysis. With only months to go before his discharge, he was sentenced to eight years' hard labor at Leavenworth.[58] Terry Irvin was even court-martialed for distributing copies of the Declaration of Independence at McChord Air Force Base on July 4, 1971.[59]

Incarceration in a base stockade or at Fort Leavenworth was a very serious matter. The torture of prisoners was commonplace. Randy Roland remembers that during his incarceration, "one night every prisoner in the hole got their legs broken. The guards came in and broke their legs.... Another time a sergeant sat on [a prisoner],

Terry Irvin (photographed in 1992) was busted for distributing
the Declaration of Independence on base on July 4, 1971. The
(Fort) Lewis–McChord Free Press put his case on the front page.

sat on him and bent his thumb back until his thumb broke. . . . They
put another guy's head in a cell door and slammed it, cracked his
skull."[60]

Roger Priest was unique in that he was not trying to use OM to *organize* anybody. He was using his location in Washington, the heart

of political power and a major media center, to wage a media battle with the military. Most underground GI publishers were on dusty bases in nowhere towns, where big media attention was far out of reach. They were trying to organize other GIs instead of the media, and if they were caught, the *Washington Post* was not going to rush to their defense. Not only did they refrain from putting their names on the mastheads, they frequently went to great lengths to conceal their identities.

Many of the smaller papers involved a handful of GIs and a couple of issues, like the *Desert Dissenter* at Williams Air Force Base in Arizona. Barry Miller remembers that he was inspired to launch the paper when he noticed the *Guidance on Dissent* posted on a bulletin board on base. "I was like, 'Hey, now that's a great idea.' "[61]

Miller rounded up three friends and suggested the idea of a paper. "We were *very* paranoid about being found out," he remembered. Miller and his friends made a trip to a peace center in Tempe where they met a Quaker named Joe Gerson, who agreed to print the paper for them. Gerson also got a post office box for the paper, as the airmen did not want to go to the post office in person. "We went to [the] mail room to see what box numbers there were, and we decided to mail one paper to every other box number until our money ran out. We pooled our money and had $60, which was a lot in those days."

The first issue was mailed in March 1970, and Miller and his buddies "went and hung around the mail room" to watch the response. "All the young guys loved it. The lifers *hated* it." After just one issue, letters started to pour in, "hate mail from the lifers, love mail from the younger guys." But after just two issues, the identities of the publishers were discovered and the publishers were transferred.

Curt Stocker and Tom Roberts identified themselves as "this reporter" and "that reporter" in *Aboveground,* their paper at Fort Carson, Colorado. Yet they were called in by military intelligence just two days after the first issue appeared. Though transferred to separate locations, they managed to keep the paper going for a while, due in part to a woman whose husband had been killed in Vietnam and who donated money from the GI life insurance she received.[62]

Other papers, however, became stable operations that published for extended periods. Almost invariably, these papers had the support of off-base coffeehouses supported by vets and civilians, which provided funds, a base of operations, and perhaps most important, continuity when active-duty personnel were busted or transferred. Whether a coffeehouse, a "peace center," or simply an office with a mimeograph machine, the place the paper was produced became the center of GI antiwar activity.

Gigline was an underground paper put out by GIs at Fort Bliss, Texas, and its office became a de facto GI counseling center.[63] "Many people would come into the office and say, 'I can't do it anymore. I can't put on the uniform anymore. What do I do?'" remembers *Gigline*'s David Cortright. "We had it down to a science: how many pills to take to make yourself really sick without actually killing yourself but get into the hospital to get your stomach pumped and then get out on section 8 suicide. This would happen once or twice a week."[64]

Rage, published at Camp Lejeune, North Carolina, the largest Marine Corps base in the world, was one of the most successful papers. The driving force behind it was a Vietnam vet named Paul Cox, and the story of his transition from gung ho Marine to underground publisher is worth examining in detail.[65]

> I was a young kid out of Oklahoma. I basically trusted our leaders. If LBJ said we need to be there to do that, then that was what we were going to do. I got my draft notice in '68. I talked to the Marine recruiter. I figured if I was going to war, I wanted to be with the best.
>
> I got there in February 1969. It was in those last six months that I got to see how wrong that war was. We were down in the rice paddies, the populated areas. We were the foreign legion. There was no raping and plundering, but there was plenty of pillaging.
>
> We were in areas that had been heavily contested since '65, clearly

VC-influenced. We would load entire villages up on trucks or helicopters and send them off to resettlement areas. Then we'd call in air strikes.

One day we went into a village and wiped them out.[66] The survivors filed a complaint saying that eighty-four people had died. I didn't kill anyone but I went into shock. I mean, there was no sniper fire, no battle, the captain just gave us permission to go in and kill everyone, said it was a free-fire zone.

That was the day I quit war.

There was an investigation. These fat lifers sat us down in the mess hall and gave us each a piece of paper and pencil and said, "Write down what you saw on this day." Then they took all our papers and nothing was ever heard about it.

I decided I wasn't going to kill anyone else unless it was a matter of life or death. I got into "sandbagging." One night we were sent out on an ambush three clicks.[67] We faked an encounter, fired some shots in the air, and ran back in, saying two guys walked into the kill zone. "We think we got 'em!"

We were pissed. This was during the beginning of the withdrawal. No one wanted to be the last guy to die in Vietnam.

We had a mutiny. They had us walking in line across these rice paddies. I think there were two VC setting booby traps right in front of us. We took twenty-six casualties out of a hundred. One guy got his whole lower body blown off. Our chicken-shit lieutenant took a tiny piece of shrapnel in his arm and took the Medevac out of there. We called into the company commander and said, "There are too many booby traps, we are going into squad columns and put a good guy in front." I mean, people were in shock, but some guys were good at keeping their heads in that kind of situation.

The colonel, who was flying overhead said no. The staff sergeant was apoplectic: "You can't refuse an order!"

I said, "Yes, I can. What are they going to do? Send me to 'Nam?"

The colonel flew down. He stood us at attention and threatened us with Leavenworth.

When I finally left the country, [I went] through Okinawa; that was the Marine transition point. They couldn't get people to get out of bed, to stand up. People would smoke in formation.

"PUT THAT CIGARETTE OUT!"

"FUCK YOU, SERGEANT."

Morale had fallen apart. And in the rear you could see the same thing. There was a hooch that had the Black Panther flag. Black GIs weren't putting up with a lot of shit.

I had to report to Camp Lejeune. I was really pissed. I did a lot of reading. Some antiwar books were being passed around. A bunch of us decided that the Marine Corps was evil, and that when we got back we would start an underground paper. We thought the Marine Corps would collapse if we printed the truth, because morale was so bad.

There were three of us. We started writing letters to everyone we could find, asking for help. Two hundred forty-three letters. We got two responses. One was from Bragg Briefs in Fayetteville and one was from Up against the Bulkhead in San Francisco.

We got a visit from people in Fayetteville, who recruited two guys to move into town. They got some money from somewhere and bought a house—they figured no one would rent to us—and opened a bookstore to support our work putting out this paper. There was a movement that was intent on assisting with the awakening of GIs. The U.S. Servicemen's Fund—we would send them a completed paper and they would send us $100.

The first one, we mimeographed five hundred. Then we found a printer and went to tabloid, printing a thousand.

We weren't very good writers. We either gleaned it from letters that we got or from antiwar newspapers. We were intimidated by writing, but we really wanted to do it. There are some good articles in there, but there is a lot of just invective. But we did the best we were capable of and we kept at it.

The fun part was getting rid of them. They didn't appear to know who we were. This is the cool part, one of the most fun things I have ever done in my life. We would load the bundles in the back of my car at two in the morning. [At the barracks] we would throw the papers out on the beds. We would do a whole barrack in two minutes.

Occasionally someone would say, "What are you doing?" We would give them the paper and say, "Read this." And they would say, "Far out." Eventually the MPs would be scrambling for us and we would split.

There were relatively few people that actually stepped forward. In the whole time I was there, there were probably twenty-four that really did. It was scary, and it was risky. Many guys got into trouble. Three months after I left, a local Klan guy bombed the building, really blew the hell out of it.

The paper did a lot of good for me. When I left Vietnam I was pretty fucked up, really down on myself, in a real crisis. I had a bunch of medals and shit, but when the chips were down that day I didn't have the courage to stand up and say, "This is wrong." It was very emotionally important to me to strike back, to redirect my anger away from myself. It gave me a lot of stuff to read, and a way to reclaim my humanity. I didn't know anything about the Vietnam war even though I had been there for eighteen months: didn't know how it started, didn't know how we got there, didn't know anything.

The early issues of Paul Cox's *Rage* paint a portrait of the GI movement at its peak. The first issue features an article describing the life of prisoners in the brig, or camp jail.[68] By this time the military was jailing thousands of its own troops.

The second issue reports on an insurrection among prisoners held in the stockade of Fort Gordon, in which a barrack was burned.[69] Another article is "a plea for support of the Marines and Sailors stationed on the USS *Coral Sea* and explains their imminent mutiny. . . . The crew of the *Coral Sea*, an attack aircraft carrier, have decided to help stop the war by stopping their ship." There is also a report on an antiwar march at the gates of Fort Campbell which included 400 active-duty GIs, 320 of whom had just returned from Vietnam.

Two issues later came a report of a jail revolt at Camp Lejeune itself, during which a leg was broken off a table and used as a flagpole for a homemade flag with the word "revolution" scrawled across it. The prisoners held the flag out of the jail's window during the revolt.[70]

Throughout the pages one finds a very active sense of movement. There is a detailed, well-written column about the rights of GIs in the Marine Corps and how to use the rules to stand up to the brass. Another column deals with drug addiction. There are articles supporting union strikes both locally and around the country, news of the Attica uprising, reviews of *Johnny Got His Gun* and the *Autobiography of Malcom X*. Articles addressing racism in the marines appear more than once in every issue. Other articles address women marines. Some of these are well written, some are jargonistic, and others veer into fairly wacked-out stuff, like a history of money that informs us that money was invented by capitalists as a means of mind control.[71]

What jumps out more than anything is how *radical* this movement was. The civilian antiwar movement was endlessly debating whether to adopt a "single-issue" focus on the war or a broader, "multi-issue" agenda, which was seen as the more radical option. This debate never occurred in the GI movement, where everyone agreed that stopping the war meant stopping the military, which would require very radical, militant action and major social upheaval.

Some papers not only sustained large circulations over extended periods but broke real news stories and became the focal point of widespread dissent and protest. *Fatigue Press* was one of these, published at the sprawling Fort Hood in Texas, where about half the troops were on their way back from Vietnam, and the other half were preparing to go there.

Fatigue Press was published out of a GI coffeehouse with the unlikely name of the Oleo Strut. "When they opened the Oleo Strut coffeehouse, the idea of the publication was that it was the first effort to pull GIs together," says Dave Cline, a soldier who was wounded three times in Vietnam before returning to Fort Hood. "The two people who organized the Oleo Strut had been SNCC organizers before that.[72] They were into the idea of empowering people. The oleo strut was the shock absorber on a helicopter. [The coffeehouse] was to be a shock absorber from the military."[73]

> We started writing the paper, and the idea was for people just to write their ideas. When you would go into the coffeehouse, [they] would say, "Why don't you write an article?" Most people in the army are not writers. Maybe they write a letter home, but that was about the extent of it. It was mimeographed, and the production was piss poor, but the idea was that we were putting something out.

The coffeehouse made for a stable base of operations, which enabled the *Fatigue Press* to keep going despite constant turnover in staff, as GIs were either shipped off to Vietnam or processed out of the service. It also provided some degree of shelter from army harassment. "They would put out these reports that the Oleo Strut was off-limits, which it wasn't," recounts Cline. "There are rules for making a place off-limits, which have to do with prostitution and crime. But they would repeatedly tell people we were off-limits."

The coffeehouse suffered continual harassment from civilian conservatives. "Our windows only lasted six months, then became plywood," Cline recalls. "Someone threw a dead skunk in. They would fill our cars with stink bombs, and then leave KKK stickers on them. Once we were going down to Houston for a rally. A car came by, and a guy leaned out with an M16 and started shooting at our front tires. He missed the tires but hit the oil filter."

Through the paper, an "Armed Farces Day" demonstration was organized on Armed Forces Day, 1970. One thousand active-duty GIs attended. A second Armed Farces Day the following year was even larger, though the participation of civilians made a count of GIs difficult.

Fatigue Press's big scoop came during the buildup to the 1968 Democratic Convention in Chicago. The army began secretly training soldiers at Fort Hood for deployment against demonstrators in

Chicago, an operation code-named Garden Plot. Breaking the heads of peace activists was not what most GIs thought they had signed up for when they went into the service. Opposition to riot-control duty ran especially strong among black soldiers. Just months before, in the wake of the murder of Martin Luther King Jr., army troops had occupied black neighborhoods in cities across the country in response to the biggest wave of rioting and insurrection the nation had ever experienced. With King gone, "black power" politics swept through the African American population, including those in the military. Soon army bases around the country, and even some in Vietnam, would have their own, internal race riots to deal with.

> The Fatigue Press *began running articles against Garden Plot. We held a meeting right in the middle of the base, on the bleachers of the baseball diamond, [and] had over one hundred guys. We had black nationalists who would not talk to white guys on principle. We had hippies. It was a broad spectrum. We came up with a simple plan. We [sent one guy] to Chicago to tell the demonstrators that there was an opposition movement among the GIs, and we made stickers with a black hand and peace sign. If they put us on the streets of Chicago, we were going to put the stickers on our helmets to show the whole world. It was that simple a plan: to show that the military ain't with the military.*
>
> *Military Intelligence found out about this, and put out that if anyone was caught possessing a sticker, they would be court-martialed, which was completely illegal. Then they went through and took everyone suspected of being subversive and took them out of Garden Plot. In the end, the troops never got deployed, the Chicago police rioted, and the rest is history.*

*   *   *

Soldiers of all races were rebelling against the military at the end of the sixties, but the rebellion was sharply segregated along racial lines. The activists of the GI underground press were overwhelmingly white. In part, this was due to the soldiers' disparate social backgrounds. A study commissioned by the army command found that "the better educated do not engage in direct confrontations with individual superiors from whom they would presumably receive punishment, but they rather confine their dissidence to coffeehouse and protest meeting attendance, contributions to underground newspapers, and other covert...activities." Outright resistance, such as "combat refusals" (when soldiers refused to obey orders) and "fraggings" (when soldiers would kill their officers, often with fragmentation grenades, and thus the term "fraggings"), however, were more likely from "ill-educated, undisciplined individuals."[74] Stockade riots, race rebellions on bases, and insurrections in the field in Vietnam were generally led by black soldiers. Underground newspapers were generally published by whites.

Timing also played a role. By the time the GI movement was gaining momentum, the "civil rights" phase of the black struggle had run its course, and the "black power" phase was in full swing. The Student Non-Violent Coordinating Committee (SNCC) had sent its white members away, and the Black Panther Party had captured the imagination of the left—black, white, and brown. The segregation of the movement at home was mirrored in the segregation of troops in Vietnam into "brothers" (blacks), "la raza" (Latinos), and "heads" (whites). Black soldiers were more likely to view the Black Panther Party's newspaper as theirs than an underground GI paper published mostly by whites. The Panthers, however, were slow to pick up their cause.

In September 1968, a black GI wrote a letter to the *Black Panther* with a plea for the Panthers to understand the difficult situation of blacks in the military. The paper ran the letter in the back pages, with no editorial comment or reply.[75] There was no further mention of black soldiers for months. The following January saw a brief article on a speaking tour by the Fort Hood Three, who were released from over two years in jail (but were no longer in the army),[76] as well as major coverage of the Stop the Draft Week in Oakland (focused on those not yet in the service); but there was still nothing on blacks serving in the military.[77]

In February the paper printed another letter, this time from a group of black servicemen on the USS *Ranger,* who wanted "all of our 'Black People' to know that we too are fighting for the Brothers who may be unfortunate and may make the same foolish move."[78] Again, the editors made no comment. Instead, regular coverage was given to stories about the heroic Vietnamese fighting the U.S. soldiers and their leaders.[79]

Through the spring of 1969, coverage picked up a bit, mostly through brief articles provided to the paper by Andy Stapp and the American Servicemen's Union (ASU).[80] A soldier wrote to the paper describing an incident in which racist white soldiers clashed with black soldiers and beat a black GI nearly to death. The writer closed by asking the editors, "Please, we need your help." Inexplicably, there is no comment or reply from the editors.[81]

In August another letter appeared about racist violence against black GIs that went unpunished.

> This morning, we, the Black brothers, have to go and see the battalion commander to talk things over, but we have tried to do this already. No more talk either: we just kill them off or they kill us off. That's just how bad it is here. . . . I have 19 days left in the army, but right now my brothers need me to stand by them. I know for a fact that I want to get out of the white man's army to come home and join the Black Liberation Army. But before I come back to the States, if it takes 19 days or 19 years, I will stand side by side with my Black brothers until I have used every breath in my body to fight those white dogs.[82]

Once again, the editors offered no comment. The letter comprises less than one column, on a page filled with a long-winded analysis of the National Liberation Front (NLF) of Vietnam. Incredibly, the editors seemed more interested in the minutiae of the Vietnamese movement than in black American soldiers declaring their readiness to commit mutiny and join the Panthers.

Coverage of GI resistance continued to increase incrementally over the next weeks, with the ASU files supplemented by Liberation News Service (LNS) stories and, for the first time, briefs sent by

Black Panthers themselves. More letters appeared from different branches of the military. Finally, by the end of September, the editors seemed to have taken notice of the GI movement. The *Black Panther* ran three full pages of news on GI resistance, and letters from black GIs appeared in every issue. The last issue of the month included the first call to join the party addressed to black GIs, but it is in a letter *to* the editor, not *from* anyone in the party. "We the people and the Black Panther Party need the continued support from brothers who have served in the fascist military machine. We need the skills, the technical know-how you possess."[83]

October saw the heyday of the relationship between the *Black Panther* and black GIs. At long last the paper had become a forum where radicalized black soldiers could learn about the movement of which they were a part. Numerous pages were devoted to the movement. One section led off with the *Panther*'s first article addressed to black GIs.[84] A letter titled *"Dung Lai (Halt) GI: To My GI Brothers"* indicated that the writer assumed that the *Black Panther* was the paper his GI brothers were actually reading.[85] An article reported on a black GI framed and busted at Fort Dix. A report from Goose Air Force Base (in northern Canada) told of efforts by black airmen to organize and included their multipoint program demanding education, appropriate entertainment, and racial justice.[86] An "Open Letter to President Nixon" complained, in formal prose, of a transfer of a black seaman for racist reasons.[87] Finally, a long letter sent from Japan denounced racism in the U.S. military there.[88] None of these stories came from LNS or the ASU. They were all sent to the paper by black soldiers or activists.

> *I have been in the grasp of the pig for 10 years and I must admit that for at least 5 of those years I was asleep. I had allowed myself to fall into the groove that many of us have allowed ourselves to be placed or brainwashed into and that is that the pig in time would treat us right. . . . But brother, don't be fooled like I was . . . use this time to arm yourselves mentally, read, discuss, and think.*
>
> FROM THE 354TH COMBAT SUPPORT GROUP[89]

The *Panther* even included a letter from a white GI concerning the stockade insurrection at Da Nang:

During the time we were in control we took good care of the segregation cell blocks where they put you for punishment; we burned the whole place down.

The leaders of the rebellion were black guys. After we had taken over the brig they began to hold court on white guys who had shown racism and I got worried about the situation. Most of the black guys were friends of mine but you couldn't talk to them then.

It looked as if it might turn out bad. But it didn't work out that way. Instead, after it was over there was a new and deeper sense of unity among the guys, black and white. There was also a new feeling of strength. We'd taken over the brig. Sure, they had overpowered us this time.

But who knows what might happen next time?[90]

Yet after just one month, coverage of the GI movement disappeared completely from the *Panther*'s pages, as the party and its paper were overwhelmed by the assault they faced from the FBI. Nearly the entire leadership had been murdered, was on trial, or had fled the country. Messages from exiled leaders, and articles following the numerous trials under way, pushed all other content from the paper.

Then, at the start of 1970, the paper ran "Black Soldiers as Revolutionaries to Overthrow the Ruling Class: Statement from Bobby Seale, in Jail, to Black GI's." The tone of the party chairman's appeal was almost bizarrely out of touch with the radicalism sweeping blacks in the military, but at least he had noticed them: "We'll be glad when you come home. We oppose the war.... It's important Black brothers that we understand the need to come home."[91]

But the paper also printed another appeal to black troops, "To My Black Brothers in Vietnam," by another party leader, Eldridge Cleaver, whose tone was even stranger. Cleaver demanded that black GIs "either quit the army now, or start destroying it from within.... You need to start killing the racist pigs who are over there with you giving orders. Kill General Abrahms [sic] and his staff, all his officers." There is no hint that Cleaver was aware that this struggle was already under way, that black soldiers *were* killing their officers. Instead, Cleaver called his readers names. "I know that you niggers have your minds all messed up about Black organizations, or you wouldn't be the flunkies for the White organization—the U.S.A.—for whom you have picked up the gun."[92]

After these appeals, the paper's coverage of the GI movement became increasingly sporadic. Instead, the paper was dominated by trial reports, descriptions of guns, increasingly pompous proclamations from Panthers in exile, increasingly bizarre tributes to "the wise and brave leader of 40 million Korean People, Comrade Kim Il Sung,"[93] and purges and counterpurges of membership and leaders. The nadir came in June when the paper ran an article titled "From Mercenary to Servant of the People," which called black GIs "lackeys and bootlickers." "Black America says that if you continue to act in the manner of hired killers, we will not welcome you back into the Black communities of Babylon."[94] What black GIs thought of all this can only be inferred, for they had stopped writing letters to the paper.

Incredibly, during these very months, *New York Times* correspondent Wallace Terry II was traversing Vietnam conducting a substantial survey of the opinions of black GIs. He found that a full 30.6 percent of black GIs in Vietnam planned to join the Black Panther Party upon their return to the States, and another 17.1 percent said they might, for an astounding total of *half* of all black soldiers considering joining an organization committed to the armed overthrow of the U.S. government. An even higher percentage, 49.2, answered "yes" when asked if they would use weapons to secure civil rights back home, and another 13 percent answered "maybe."[95] This totals thousands of black soldiers who were looking to the Panthers for leadership. None was forthcoming.

On a practical level, the GI papers were the place where soldiers found out about protests and other antiwar activities. More than that, the papers helped isolated GIs connect with a sense of movement and community. "It was a tremendous personal affirmation, being so isolated and getting this little rag every once in while to see that there were other soldiers who felt the same way," says David Cortright.[96]

Even more than that, the underground papers were often a bridge GIs used to cross over from private misgivings to public opposition, despite their profound distrust of the student antiwar movement. Former air force pilot Jim Willingham remembers, "I was exposed to a lot of dissent in college. I would walk through demonstrators in my ROTC uniform." Willingham felt no connection to the movement, until friends at Randolph Air Force Base gave him copies of *Your Military Left*. "It really impacted on me personally. I had no other contact at that time with anyone who was antiwar."[97]

Through much of American history, social movements have launched newspapers to publish news that mainstream newspapers refused to print. In the case of the GI movement, however, it was genuinely difficult, particularly in the movement's early days, for the civilian press to even know what was going on in the barracks and on the battlefield. The GI papers became a major conduit for what little news of GI opposition to the war made it into the mainstream press.

"The command would never want to spread this information, so reporters would not receive it," says Cortright. "Many bases are in isolated places. And the actors are all young, inexperienced people, often 19–20 years old. We didn't know what the hell we were doing. We didn't know how to go about press relations very well. We were 'fighting the green machine.' And there is an intrinsic cognitive dissonance for reporters to even *conceive* of soldiers speaking out against war. It is *very* subversive."[98]

Just how subversive? One veteran writing in *Aboveground* equated distributing the newspapers with sabotage. "You don't have to pass out *Aboveground*...to hurt the army. You can rip off supplies, break trucks...punch holes in walls, go AWOL.... Every one of you could come up with hundreds of ideas. If we all tried our best to slow down the Army at least once each day—in whatever way we choose—it would go a long way toward causing the Army's death."[99]

Many papers professed more allegiance to the "enemy" than to the U.S. military. *Gigline* reported the death of Vietnamese leader Ho Chi Minh on the front page: "We who deeply regret our nation's longstanding interference in the affairs of the Vietnamese people wish to express our great sadness at the death of Chairman Ho Chi Minh, whose dedication to the welfare of his people and their liberation from foreign domination should be an inspiration to the leaders of all nations."[100]

"In Vietnam," proclaimed the *(Fort) Lewis–McChord Free Press*, "the Lifers, the Brass, are the true Enemy." Another paper proclaimed: "Don't desert. Go to Vietnam and kill your commanding officer."

In Vietnam *GI Says*, a mimeographed bulletin circulated in the 101st Airborne Division, offered $10,000 to any soldier who would kill Colonel W. Honeycutt, who had ordered the infamous May 1969 attack on "Hamburger Hill," in which 56 GIs were killed and 420 wounded.[101]

After the Tet offensive in early 1968, the handful of underground papers that had emerged with the return of the first vets from Vietnam had multiplied several times over. They multiplied again in 1969, after President Richard Nixon announced his policy of "Vietnamization" and eventual withdrawal, as GIs contemplated the thankless possibility that they, or someone they knew, might be the last American to die in Vietnam, in a war the United States was obviously going to lose, yet which was being prolonged to serve the political interests of the Nixon administration. *Rage* announced a "Last Man to Die in Vietnam Contest" with "Prizes!" First prize included a Medal of Honor for the winner's parents and a plot in Arlington Cemetery. Second prize was a Silver Star and lifetime membership in the VFW. And so on.[102]

By the early 1970s activism ranging from dissent to mutiny had reached almost every U.S. installation at home, abroad, and at sea.

Even young officers joined the movement, organizing the Concerned Officers Movement (COM), which published *COMmon Sense*, with a circulation of three thousand. The Pentagon itself had a COM chapter.[103]

GI resistance reached such levels that decades later accounts by movement participants seem scarcely believable. By this time, however, the military brass was in a panic and was conducting its own investigations into internal dissent. The first report was a two-volume study (1970 and 1971) of soldier dissidence produced for army commanders by the Research Analysis Corporation.[104] The first public discussion of the crisis came at the same time, when Colonel Robert D. Heinl Jr. published "The Collapse of the Armed Forces" in the *Armed Forces Journal*, two years *before* the final withdrawal of U.S. troops.[105] Two additional seminal works came later: *The Rise and Fall of an American Army* [106] and *Self-Destruction*, a book attributed to "Cincinnatus," the pseudonym for a senior officer at the Pentagon who, even in 1981, preferred not to have his name associated with the bad news his book purveyed.[107] These military sources painted the following picture:

- Twenty-five percent of US soldiers participated in "dissidence" (expressing opposition to the war), and 25 percent participated in "disobedience" (refusing orders, going AWOL, sabotage, attacking officers). Thirty-seven percent of all soldiers participated in one of the two, and 32 percent did so more than once. If drug use is considered an act of disobedience or dissidence, the total comes to 55 percent.[108]
- The term "fragging" refers to attempts by troops to kill their own officers, a term that did not even exist until the Vietnam War. The army alone reported 551 fraggings from 1969 to 1972, with 86 dead and 700 injured. Other scholars put this number at between 800 and 1,000.[109] These numbers include only fraggings with grenades, the weapon of choice, since they left no fingerprints. If shootings with firearms were included, the total would be much higher.

- "Combat refusal" was another term coined in Vietnam, referring to a refusal of orders to advance during combat. In every
other war in U.S. history, this was deemed treason and punishable by death. In Vietnam, in the elite First Cavalry Division
alone, considered the army's top unit, there were thirty-five
combat refusals in 1970, some involving entire units.[110]

- "Widespread breakdowns in troop discipline forced the military police into a front-line role serving as assault troops
against other soldiers. These actions were typified by two instances. Composite military police [were] engaged in a rather
spectacular standoff on September 25, 1971. Fourteen soldiers
...had barricaded themselves in a bunker and were holding
out with automatic weapons and machine guns.... A month
later, another military police strike force air-assaulted onto the
Praline Mountain signal site.... Two fragmentation grenades
had been used in an attempt to kill the company commander
two nights in a row. Initial escorts had proved insufficient protection, and military police had to garrison the mountaintop
for a week until order was restored."[111]

- The biggest mutiny in the history of the U.S. Air Force occurred
at Travis Air Force Base in May 1971. The base was in chaos for
four days. Three hundred eighty MPs and police were called
in, the officers' club was burned, dozens were injured, 135 GIs
were arrested, and the base remained in a state of siege for
days.[112]

- By 1972 sabotage was crippling the U.S. Navy's participation in
the war. In 1972 the House Armed Services Committee reported "literally hundreds of incidences of damaged Naval
property wherein sabotage is suspected."[113] A massive fire on
the USS Forrestal caused $7 million's worth in damage and a
two-month delay in deployment, making it the costliest sabotage in naval history. Three weeks later, sabotage on the USS
Ranger caused $1 million's worth in damage and delayed de-
ployment for three and a half months.[114]

- The USS *Kitty Hawk*, sent to replace the *Forrestal* and *Ranger*, had a riot on board the day operations began. Hundreds of armed sailors clashed with marine guards, with dozens injured. A few weeks later on the carrier *Constellation*, more than one hundred, mostly black sailors organized by the Black Fraction staged a sit-down strike.[115]

The role of the GI press in these events can hardly be overstated. When President Nixon ordered U.S. troops to invade Cambodia in May 1970, sixteen soldiers from Fire Base Washington refused to go. No one would have known about the incident had the soldiers not fired off a letter to *Up Against the Bulkhead*: "We have no business here. We have enough trouble in Vietnam. Sixteen of us refused to go. We just sat down."[116] The following year two hundred soldiers assembled at the headquarters of the 101st Airborne to protest the use of Cobra gunships because they resulted in so many civilian casualties. The protesters mailed a report of the event to *The Ally*, and GIs throughout the services heard about it.[117]

As GI resistance skyrocketed, the number of penalties administered to the culprits declined. By the end of the war, actions that at the outset would have resulted in court-martials went unpunished. This was due in no small part to the publicity the GI press was bringing to the formerly hidden world of GI resistance. When Barry Miller and his buddies at the *Desert Dissenter* were busted, they were transferred—but not to Vietnam. By this time the brass knew it was losing control and preferred to send troublemakers to isolated, low-profile outposts rather than to Vietnam, where they would compound "morale problems." (Miller figures that getting caught publishing an underground paper kept him out of Vietnam.) However, even these transfers were failing to have the desired effect. The *(Fort) Lewis–McChord Free Press* was one of numerous papers started by a GI who had been transferred from his previous post in an effort to break up an underground paper there, only to start a new paper at his new post.[118]

The brass was losing its appetite for court-martials as well. By 1969 the army had seven thousand soldiers locked up in its stockades, which were turning into hotbeds of antiwar organizing and drug use. Riots rocked numerous stockades, both stateside and in Vietnam.[119] Randy Roland, a GI imprisoned for participating in a sit-down strike on base, was sentenced to Leavenworth, where he befriended another prisoner who was jailed for killing his commanding officer. "That totally influenced me," Roland says. "I went into Leavenworth as a pacifist and came out as a radical."[120]

In 1971 the government reported that 15,000 young men refused induction, 100,000 failed to appear for physicals, and local draft offices had sustained 190 attacks. For every 100 GIs, 17 had gone AWOL and 7 had deserted: one-quarter of the U.S. military had walked off the job, the highest rate ever.[121]

Colonel Heinl summed up the situation thus:

> By every conceivable indicator, our army that now remains in Vietnam is in a state approaching collapse, with individual units avoiding or having refused combat, murdering their officers and non commissioned officers, drug-ridden, and dispirited where not near mutinous.... [These] conditions have only been exceeded in this century by . . . the collapse of the Tsarist armies in 1916 and 1917.[122]

As Paul Cox put it, "The Vietnamese didn't drive us into the sea, but they would have eventually, 'cause people just weren't doing it."[123]

By the early 1970s, civilian antiwar activists were reeling. The Nixon administration's "Vietnamization" strategy had sapped the movement's strength on campuses. Efforts by student radicals to develop a social base in factories had gone nowhere.[124] Organizers felt their movement was collapsing.

The movement did not collapse, however. It changed form. The same Vietnamization that took the wind out of the student movement sent the GI movement into overdrive. What's more, the

increasing reliance on the air force and navy implied by Vietnamization (U.S. bombing missions from both air and sea increased dramatically as U.S. ground troops withdrew) caused the crisis in the
U.S. military to spread from the army and marines to the air force
and navy. This movement not only finally brought down the U.S. adventure in Vietnam but nearly shattered the U.S. Armed Forces as
an institution.

Here was the militant, working-class, multi-issue, and interra-
cial movement student radicals had hoped for, but activists hardly
noticed. In part, this was because the GI movement was largely invisible to civilians. Much of the information contained in this chapter was simply not available at the time. But a lot of it *was* available
—through the GI press. Apparently very few people, other than
the GIs themselves and those spying on them, were reading the
GI press.

By the yardstick conventionally employed to measure revolutions,
the sixties have been judged a failure. The gates of the White House
were never stormed. No revolutionary government was formed. The
most prominent organizations the movement had created shattered under the combined weight of state repression and sectarian
politics.[125]

But perhaps the yardstick needs to be reconceptualized. If instead of looking at flags and governments we look at real-life human relationships, things appear quite different. Male-female,
parent-child, black-white, teacher-student, boss-worker, straight-
gay, rich-poor, and, yes, even officer-soldier: almost every human relationship emerged from the sixties profoundly changed, and in
every case the change was toward greater equality.

Many of these changes have proven remarkably resilient over
the years. It is inconceivable that relations between men and
women, or straights and gays, for example, could ever return to
what they were before the sixties. Race issues still bedevil American society of course, but they do so differently today than before.

At the very least, the segregated South has been banished from the national stage. Ground that was won in the economic field, however, was lost and then some in the 1980s, when the gap between rich and poor widened dramatically.

But in no terrain were the victories of the sixties reversed so dramatically as in the field of imperial power. From a state of total collapse in 1973, the U.S. military has been rebuilt and projected around the globe with an intensity that could scarcely have been imagined as the last troops straggled home from Vietnam. How was this possible? At the end of the Vietnam War, the country was confronted with a radicalized core of Vietnam vets who had become the most public face of antimilitarism in the nation. These few spoke for thousands more who shared their views but were too exhausted or emotionally damaged to speak out. A 1975 survey showed that 75 percent of Vietnam vets opposed the war.[126]

And then, they disappeared.

They disappeared into VA hospitals with constant pain from war wounds; into a nightmare of Agent Orange complications; into support groups for posttraumatic stress disorder; into cardboard boxes under highway overpasses because they were too stressed out to hold jobs; and overall, into political retreat and silence as the country moved to the Right and people just didn't want to hear anymore about the horrors of their country's debacle in Southeast Asia.

Their absence from the historical stage made room for a stunning rewriting of history. The very real image of angry vets marching together to oppose the war in which they fought was replaced by a make-believe image of the solitary, "forgotten" vet being spat on by peace activists. Paul Loeb, who studied student ambivalence toward political involvement in the 1990s, found that

> [in 1994] students at school after school volunteered stories of protesters spitting on soldiers as their central image of the Vietnam-era peace movement. At every kind of college, in every corner of the country, the slightest mention of antiwar activism of that time would impel them

...to describe how peace marchers spat on soldiers.... "You might be right about the need to get involved," [said one student,] "but I just can't approve of people going out and spitting on soldiers."[127]

The problem is that this never happened. Peace activists did not spit on vets. It is a myth. There is not one news account (despite extensive press presence at peace marches) or police report (despite extensive police surveillance of the movement) or military intelligence report or photo or even an account of a veteran claiming such a thing happened until more than a decade after the troops were home—*after* the image had been purveyed through the mass media and manipulated by national political leaders beating the drums of war.[128]

In fact, peace activists held demonstrations in Oakland, from where GIs were shipped to Vietnam. At the San Francisco airport, to which soldiers returned, they were met by activists passing out copies of *The Ally*. "We would sometimes have conversations with these guys," remembers *The Ally's* Clark Smith. "Sometimes they weren't too friendly...but I don't recall anyone ever refusing the paper."[129] What *did* happen, and was reported in numerous published accounts at the time and even shown on television at the 1972 Republican Convention, was that antiwar veterans were spat on—by right-wingers who viewed them as unpatriotic and as cowards for losing the war.

Nevertheless, by the turn of the century, the image of brave and angry vets throwing their medals back at the politicians who had sent them to war had been replaced in the popular imagination by a phony image of peace activists spitting on vets, a politically calculated hoax.

The real Americans who actually fought the war stand as isolated from history today as they were from their contemporaries back home when they were in Vietnam. There is no more powerful argument for the importance of a movement press than this: the movement press allows the actual makers of history to tell their own story.

Addendum: More Myth

On October 14, 2003, the Gannett News Service reported that army battalion commander Lt. Col. Dominic Caraccilo was responsible for sending five hundred letters to hometown newspapers promoting his soldiers' rebuilding efforts in Iraq. Though the letters were identical, they were signed with different signatures. "At least one soldier contacted by Gannett News Service said he never signed the letter that appeared in his hometown paper in Charleston, W.Va. Several parents said they knew their sons had not written the letters that appeared in local papers."

Caraccilo said he wanted to "share [his troops'] pride with people back home."

The letter-writing campaign coincided with a publicity blitz conducted by President Bush and other administration officials to emphasize "successes" in Iraq, as polls showed that American opinion on the war was souring. Commenting on the phony letters, White House spokesman Scott McClellan said, "The intention was good but the delivery system was probably not a good way to do it because of misperceptions that could be taken. You don't want anybody out there saying I never saw that letter."

The Environmental Movement

In 1890 the U.S. Census showed a contiguous line of settlement of no fewer than two people per square mile stretched from coast to coast.[1] As the great frontier closed, Americans began to see wilderness as something to preserve instead of conquer. Just two years later, Scottish naturalist John Muir founded the Sierra Club, "to explore, enjoy, and render accessible the mountain regions of the Pacific Coast; to publish authentic information concerning them; to enlist the support and cooperation of the people and government in preserving the forest and other natural features of the Sierra Nevada Mountains."[2]

Perhaps the visionary Scotsman had no idea of the breadth this movement would acquire one century later, but perhaps he did: it would take nearly a century for the movement he helped launch to catch up with his observation that "to pick out anything by itself, we find it hitched to everything else in the universe."[3]

The subsequent history of the movement appears as a gradual unfolding of Muir's claim.[4] The fight to preserve scenic wilderness has grown into a struggle to preserve biodiversity and watershed integrity, exceedingly complex phenomena at the cutting edge of several scientific disciplines. Yet even banning logging and mining in pristine mountain lands may not accomplish much if the area is blanketed in a global wash of toxic chemicals from industrial processes far away, pollinated with genetically engineered seeds carried by the wind from factory farms, and exposed to the unknown ravages of global climate change. To John Muir's maxim, we might add: *to pick out anything in the environmental movement by itself, we find it hitched to everything else in society.*

No one has done an exact count, but there are hundreds of environmental journals in the country today, ranging from the Sierra Club's *Sierra* magazine with a circulation of 728,000 to the photocopied newsletters of local environmental groups in hundreds of locales around the nation, each one addressing a different piece of the increasingly complex and daunting environmental puzzle. This chapter can cover but a few.

Although Muir was a self-taught naturalist who lived in poverty by choice, those gathered around him in the early days of the Sierra Club were a high and mighty group, including the president of Stanford University, the publisher of a popular national magazine, and the future mayor of Oakland. Powerful but hardy. They might not have kept up with Muir, who wandered the Sierras for years with very little in the way of provisions and gear, but they were outdoors people cut from a cloth they don't make anymore, pioneering wilderness skiing, mountain climbing, and wilderness hiking in an era before Gore-Tex, freeze-dried dinners, or even maintained trails.

The *Sierra Club Bulletin,* which began publication in January 1893, was full of reports of these adventures: favored routes, what to wear and eat, and climbing techniques. Much of modern "backpacking" was invented by these sturdy souls and fleshed out in the pages of the *Bulletin.* Club "outings," as they came to be called, were seen not as an escape from politics but as an entrance to it. Muir's idea of organizing was to bring people to the Sierras to share the rapture he found in the wilderness. Muir did not travel to Washington to lobby his concerns. Washington came to him, and he in turn took Washington to the mountains, including President Teddy Roosevelt and California governor James Pardee, who accompanied Muir to Yosemite in 1903 as part of the Sierra Club's successful campaign to expand Yosemite National Park to include Yosemite Valley.[5]

The Sierra Club leadership's combination of wealth, power, and education was typical of other early conservation groups as well.[6] These people saw themselves not spearheading a social movement but working together with federal agencies in the Department of the Interior to advance the cause of wilderness preservation and the "rational" development of natural resources. As the years passed and Muir's influence faded, the tenor of the organization became increasingly sedate. A March 1948 *Bulletin* editorial by Sierra Club president William Colby concerning the kinds of activities that should be permissible in Yosemite National Park is a good indicator of the organization's tone and temperament at midcentury: "Moving pictures . . . and good music would all be in the spirit of the place, while 'jazz' and 'ballyhoo' are not. Dancing comes closer to the borderline. Personally, I do not object to it in moderation."[7]

The explosion of economic and infrastructural development in the United States following World War II shattered the conservation movement's complacency and its cozy relation with the Department of the Interior. The pivot point of the divorce was a 1951 federal proposal to build a dam that would flood the Echo Park area of Dinosaur National Monument, following on a previous proposal to build a dam in Glacier National Park.

The man who led the fight against the Echo Park dam was David Brower, a Sierra Club mountain climber who first became editor of the club's *Bulletin* and then the club's first executive director. Brower first transformed the *Bulletin*, then used the revitalized journal to transform the Sierra Club. Concerns about jazz in national parks were scrapped for lobbying campaigns and citizen engagement. Urgency took the place of complacency. With the *Bulletin* in the lead, Brower brought twentieth-century activism to the conservation movement.

Under Brower's prodding, the Sierra Club not only engaged in a full-force lobbying effort but attempted a much broader public mobilization as well. The latter included direct mail, the production of two movies, raft trips in which hundreds of members floated through the region of the proposed dam,[8] and a special issue of the *Bulletin* (which by then was sent to eight thousand members). Largely due to Sierra Club press work, the dam proposal became front-page news in magazines and newspapers around the country.[9]

Defeating the Echo Park dam eventually involved a quid pro quo in which the Sierra Club acquiesced in the construction of the Glen Canyon dam on the Colorado River, a remote red-rock labyrinth not protected by national park status, yet rivaling the Grand Canyon in beauty and spectacle. The flooding of Glen Canyon (creating what is now Lake Powell) on January 21, 1963, caused many in the movement to question even more deeply their practice of collaboration and compromise with federal land bureaucracies.

Conservationists began to press for the ambitious and far-reaching idea of a system of wilderness areas in which development would not take place. This approach was comprehensively laid out in the *Leopold Report* in 1963, a collaborative work of several wildlife biologists who advocated ecologically oriented management of the national park system. The *Report* was influential—in part because Brower published it in its entirety in the *Bulletin*.[10]

Brower had built a very effective collection of tools that worked synergistically, and publishing was a key element. He had bumped the *Bulletin* up to a larger format to make better use of nature photos. As part of the fight against the Echo Park dam, he had rushed into publication a book of essays and photos, *This Is Dinosaur,* by noted western writer Wallace Stegner.[11] This was followed by a series of Exhibit Format Sierra Club books combining color photos and essays, including *The Place No One Knew,* which documented the haunting scenery of Glen Canyon just before it was flooded.[12] At nearly the same time, during the successful campaign to designate California's Point Reyes a National Seashore, the club published *Island in Time: The Point Reyes Peninsula* and placed one on the desk of every member of Congress.[13]

In the years before desktop publishing and the massive increase

SIERRA CLUB BULLETIN

October 1963

. . . our civilization is rapidly becoming one in which
only two values are recognized: power and amusement.
It would be a pity if the last refuges where man can enter
into another kind of relation with the natural world
should be improved out of existence . . .

—JOSEPH WOOD KRUTCH
in *Grand Canyon*

Twilight for the Grand Canyon?

Twilight for old-school conservationism: David Brower uses the
Sierra Club Bulletin *to usher in the age of environmental activism.*

in outdoor recreation, these books were many people's introduction to what the American wilderness actually looked like, and their effect on the dam battles in particular and on Americans' understanding of their continent in general is difficult to overstate.

No sooner had Glen Canyon died than a new plan was announced to build two dams in the Grand Canyon. Brower turned up the heat in a multifaceted campaign that would define the parameters of mainstream environmentalism. For four years the subject of the dams was hammered in nearly every issue of the *Bulletin*. Brower organized specialists to testify in Congress while spearheading an unprecedented media campaign everywhere else. Club members around the country argued with the editorial boards of their local papers. Letters poured into Washington by the hundreds of thousands. Brower entered copies of *The Place No One Knew* into the congressional record, along with a new book, *Time and the River Flowing: The Grand Canyon*. Brower explained to Congress, "Ten years ago I was testifying in favor of a higher Glen Canyon dam, and I wish I had been struck dead at the time."[14]

The coup de grâce came on June 9, 1966. Responding to a tip that a move was afoot to railroad the dams through, Brower beat the dam proponents to the punch, running full-page ads in the *New York Times, Washington Post, San Francisco Chronicle,* and *Los Angeles Times.* "NOW ONLY YOU CAN SAVE THE GRAND CANYON FROM BEING FLOODED...FOR PROFIT." Another round of ads followed a month later.

The Brower juggernaut brought results. The dam proposals were defeated. Sierra Club membership nearly doubled, from 39,000 to 67,000, and then doubled again to 135,000 by 1967. But there was fallout as well. Within twenty-four hours of the first round of ads, the IRS had revoked the Sierra Club's tax-exempt status. Brower himself was in hot water at the Sierra Club. Losing the tax exemption made the board nervous, especially since the Exhibit Format books had come to dominate the club's budget. Though clearly a success politically, they were also expensive. In 1966 alone the publishing program lost more than $100,000.[15]

As early as 1959, the club board had tried to rein Brower in by passing a "gag rule" that forbade club representatives to "expressly ...criticize the motive, integrity, or competence of an official or bureau."[16] In 1969 the internal struggle became intolerable when Brower led a campaign against the board's decision to endorse Pacific Gas and Electric's proposal to build a nuclear power plant at

Diablo Canyon. Brower's personal style did not help. Under the glare of publicity and the heat of battle, the shy mountain climber had evolved into a sometimes egotistic, sometimes paranoid, and always impatient autocratic leader. Before the turn of the decade, Brower was out.

By the time of Brower's departure from the Sierra Club, a new thread had emerged in the environmental movement which had nothing to do with mountain climbers, hobnobbing with the high and mighty, or spectacular landscape photographs. The youth counterculture was spawning a "back-to-the-land" movement that entailed some two thousand rural communes and five thousand collectives by the mid-1970s.[17]

If David Brower was too far out for the Sierra Club, the back-to-the-landers wanted to create an entirely new society. Out of the counterculture kaleidoscope of lifestyle experimentation, criticism of actually existing society, and psychedelic-drug use, emerged one of the most startlingly innovative journals in the history of publishing in America: the *Whole Earth Catalog*.

The *Catalog* was as quirky in its genesis as it was in its pages. The project was conceived in 1966 by Stewart Brand after hearing Buckminster Fuller lecture on the earth as a holistic, integrated system. After the lecture, Brand took LSD and had a vision that if humans could only see their planet from space—a tiny, beautiful globe floating in a sea of space—they might begin to think and live as if they were part of the holistic, integrated system Fuller had described. Brand launched a one-person crusade calling upon NASA to release such a photograph of the entire surface of the earth. He made a button that asked "Why Haven't We Seen a Photograph of the Whole Earth Yet?" and distributed it to senators, congresspeople, NASA officials, and even Soviet space experts. Soon NASA did release such photographs, and a photograph of Earth as seen from space became the instantly recognizable cover of the *Whole Earth Catalog*, the icon of counterculture environmentalism, the logo for the first Earth Day on April 22, 1970, and eventually the ubiquitous Earth flag.[18]

Beginning in 1968 with nothing but an idea and a photograph of the earth, in 1972 the Last Whole Earth Catalog *ran 447 pages and sold more than 1.5 million copies worldwide.*

The *Catalog*'s success was as unprecedented as everything else about it. Beginning in 1968 with nothing but an idea and a photograph of the earth, the *Catalog* published twice a year from 1968 to 1971, followed by the *Last Whole Earth Catalog* in 1972, the *Whole Earth Epilogue* in 1974, and the *Next Whole Earth Catalog* in 1980. The first

Catalog had 31 pages and a circulation of 15,000. Four years later there were 447 pages and sales of more than 1.5 million worldwide. Occasional *Supplements* sold fewer copies and were more narrowly targeted to real back-to-the-landers.[19]

The *Catalog* was so utterly unique that it is almost impossible to summarize its dizzying kaleidoscope of contents. Brand himself described the unifying thread in the "Purpose" statement that ran on the inside cover:

> *We are as gods and might as well get good at it. So far remotely done power and glory—as via government, big business, formal education, church—has succeeded to the point where gross defects obscure actual gains. In response to this dilemma and to these gains a realm of intimate, personal power is developing—power of the individual to conduct his own education, find his own inspiration, shape his own environment, and share his adventure with whoever is interested. Tools that aid this process are sought and promoted by the WHOLE EARTH CATALOG.*

Like other issues, the *Last Whole Earth Catalog* was divided into sections. "Understanding Whole Systems" led off with the works of Buckminster Fuller, followed by coffee-table photo books of space, and then a hodgepodge of scientific, ecological, and spiritual publications promoting the concept of integrated systems. The rest of the sections include "Land Use," "Shelter," "Industry," "Craft," "Community," "Nomadics," "Communications," and "Learning." In these pages one could learn about edible plants, buy a bulldozer, learn to build a tepee, order a Futuro (the world's "first well-detailed, commercially available, foam and fiberglass dwelling"), subscribe to *American Pyrotechnics Fireworks News*, obtain study guides for becoming an airplane pilot, learn how to build a pipe organ or buy a Moog synthesizer, purchase a .22-caliber rifle, study Eastern philosophy, and learn to build a covered wagon.

Jumbled up with everything else are poems, stories, letters, manifestos, and helpful tips and diagrams (such as a cutaway rendering of the mouth of a cow for telling its age). Every item offered is reviewed by the *Catalog* staff, and though many reviews indicate real knowledge of the relevant item or subject, the second page of the *Catalog* offers the following caveat: "We are a bunch of amateurs ...[though] the judgments in the reviews are wholly sincere, I wouldn't rely on them too far. Try to see through them."

The *Catalog* closes with a section called "Money," which details the budget of the whole operation, and "How to Do a Whole Earth Catalog," which tells you just how they do everything in case you want to make one yourself.

"Conservationists had been all about changing policy," recalls one long-time activist. "The counterculture came to the realization that maybe solving environmental problems is not just about changing policy, maybe we have to change our lives, how we live."[20] What those changes would be was anyone's guess. Given the spirit of the times, people set out to learn the answer by *doing,* and the *Catalog* was just eclectic and inspiring enough to be their clearinghouse.

In 1972 Brand formed the non-profit Point Foundation to distribute grants to the hundreds of Whole Earth–inspired endeavors that cropped up throughout the 1970s. In its first two years, the Point Foundation handed out $1.5 million to grass-roots experiments and launched a publishing project centered on *CoEvolution Quarterly.*[21] The *Quarterly* continued the *Catalog*'s emphasis on access to information, book and tool reviews, guest essays, and interviews. One early issue was guest edited by the Black Panther Party.[22] Over the years, ideas such as the Gaia hypothesis, watershed awareness, medical self-care, environmental restoration, and, perhaps most important, bioregionalism have received some of their earliest public airing in its pages.

The journal was still going strong at the close of the century, renamed the *Whole Earth Review.* The *Review* maintains an eclectic mix, ranging from articles predicting that digital technology will trigger wondrous special transformations to a piece titled "Reshaping Erotic Bellydancing."[23] A special issue on environmental restoration in the spring of 1990, featuring numerous articles on the tools, knowledge, and knuckles-in-the-dirt know-how necessary to begin restoring a local stream or wetland, continued in the very best *Whole Earth* tradition, providing usable information and a hopeful world vision hard to find elsewhere in the environmental press.

* * *

The energy that swirled around the *Whole Earth Catalog* spawned new publications such as *RAIN,* which appeared in the Northwest in 1975. *RAIN* was a sort of *Whole Earth* without the eccentricity and eclecticism.

"The practice of giving access to information in publications did not exist before *Whole Earth,*" recalls *RAIN* cofounder Tom Bender. "If someone wrote an article on nuclear power, and you wanted to find out about the plans, or the approval process, there would be no information in the article, or if you contacted the press and inquired, it was frowned upon. *Whole Earth* said our primary thing is to connect people and information. Want to build a compost toilet? Set up a community bank? Here it is, go do it. This was the first time this had happened."[24] *RAIN* even went through a fight with the U.S. Postal Service, who did not want to grant it a magazine postal permit because it distributed useful information instead of news.[25]

"The subscribers were doers," Bender continues. "I reviewed the cost performance of a nuclear power plant. I wrote that this was ignoring the decommissioning costs, etc. etc. Two issues later people had written in detailing those costs. Everything had an effect, a response, each spark seemed to light a fire." The *RAIN* publishers coordinated with an organic farming group called Oregon Tilth, with whom they collaborated in constructing a parabolic solar greenhouse and a dairy farm methane plant, among other projects.

RAIN folded in the mid-1980s, but by then many of the ideas it developed had their own specialized publications, including alternative energy, horticulture, organic food and materials, recycling, living spaces, and physical community structure. Oregon Tilth now has its own bimonthly, *In Good Tilth*.

Appearing at the same time as RAIN, the back-to-the-land journal Mother Earth News had more than one million subscribers by the end of the 1970s, and its Eco-Village, a six-hundred-acre research center, drew twenty thousand visitors each summer. With the advent of the Reagan era and the fading of 1960s idealism, subscriptions and advertising plummeted, journal-sponsored trips and tours were dropped, and the Eco-Village closed. Owen Lipstein, founder of the commercially successful Health magazine, came onboard as publisher. By 1988, with new slick packaging and color photos, Mother Earth News had the "fastest growing advertising revenues of any magazine in the country."[26] Like the Whole Earth Review, Mother Earth News continues to this day, but with banners like "20 Must-Have Country Tools" across its glossy cover.[27]

As the 1960s turned into the 1970s, the environmental movement achieved spectacular growth. A series of very high-profile environmental disasters, including a massive oil spill off the coast of Santa Barbara and the worsening smog in American cities, pushed the environment to the center of the political stage. The tide of public opinion turned Democrats and even Republicans into "environmentalists": it was a Republican president, Richard Nixon, who signed off on the Endangered Species Act, the National Environmental Policy Act, and the creation of the Environmental Protection Agency and gave the first "Message on the Environment" to Congress.

The journals of the major conservation groups, including the Audubon Society, the Wilderness Society, The Nature Conservancy, and of course the Sierra Club, all kept publishing but seemed out of step with the youthful energy of the times. The Sierra Club did not even go on record opposing nuclear power, one of the hottest issues of the times, until 1974.[28]

In the institutionalized environmental movement, the activist energy moved with David Brower out of the Sierra Club and into his new organization, Friends of the Earth (FOE), and its journal, Not Man Apart. Friends of the Earth lacked the money, membership, institutional history, and access to power of the Sierra Club. *Not Man Apart* turned all these deficiencies to its advantage.

"We had no budget," remembers editor Tom Turner. "We didn't pay for writing or photography, but there were wonderful people all over who would send us stuff because they cared about it. We had regular correspondents. Then as Friends of the Earth grew and established field offices in essentially random places where people would turn up who were willing to work for $25 a month, the field reps would become correspondents as well."[29]

Not Man Apart looked more like a newspaper than an environmental journal, and Brower wanted it to function like one. "Brower's dream was always to have it weekly," says Turner. "You got a big break on postage if you came out weekly. We were publishing monthly. In '74 Brower said, 'Let's split the difference and go every other week.' I said, 'OK, but let's have a little help around here.'" The staff for the biweekly went up to ten, some of whom worked part-time.

"We were free to take positions on things," Turner continues. "By the time Brower left the Sierra Club, he had to show all his copy to the director. I didn't have to run our stuff by anybody. I had running battles with the lobbyists in Washington and with the fund-raising department. They always wanted the paper to be more an organ of the organization and to talk about Friends of the Earth achievements, and we did that. But we covered things Friends of the Earth didn't have much to do with as well. There was no grand plan. We never told anyone that 'it was a good story but it doesn't fit into any of our departments.' We didn't have departments."

Not Man Apart covered the Super Sonic Transport (SST), the Alaska pipeline, and nuclear power plants, all of which were FOE priorities. But it also ran some of the earliest pieces about global warming, before FOE or any other organization had a campaign about it, and the fight against the Black Mesa coal mine in northern Arizona, an issue that local activists in the region raised to prominence.

By 1985 the increasingly egocentric Brower had burned through another organization, and Friends of the Earth sent him packing. FOE moved from San Francisco to Washington, DC, and focused on lobbying. Brower stayed in San Francisco and launched yet another organization, the Earth Island Institute, and the *Earth Island Journal* picked up where *Not Man Apart* had left off.

By this time there had been a sea change in environmental politics in the United States, with the inauguration of President Reagan and the ascension of his combative secretary of the interior James Watt. "Environmentalism" was no longer a bipartisan issue. Watt set the tone at his Senate confirmation hearing by implying that long-term planning on federal lands was unnecessary, since the arrival of the Messiah was imminent.[30] "There are people who want to bring their motorcycles and snowmobiles right into the middle of Yellowstone National Park," he later told a group of Park Service employees, "and our job is to make sure they can."[31]

In the end, Watt's biggest success was fueling an unprecedented growth in membership for the organizations opposed to him. The Sierra Club's membership had grown from 178,000 in 1978 to 181,000 in 1980. In just three years of Watt's tenure, the club's membership nearly doubled, to 346,000. The Wilderness Society more than doubled, from 48,000 before Watt to 100,000 at the time of his resignation, then tripled to 333,000 in 1989 and doubled yet again to 600,000 in 1995. The newcomer National Resources Defense Council had just 6,000 members in 1972 but increased to 45,000 by 1983 and to 105,000 by the end of the Reagan era.[32] Greenpeace dwarfed them all: by the end of the 1980s, Greenpeace USA had a membership base of 2.5 million, which was growing by 77,000 a month.[33]

The "membership" of these organizations consisted mostly of people who had responded with cash to the vast quantities of direct mail the national offices sent out. Short of asking for more money, and for letters to government officials concerning critical issues, no one was really sure what these members should *do*, but the organizations certainly wanted to keep in touch with them while the matter was sorted out. Organizational magazines were the mechanism that was relied on. Clip out the coupon, send in your check, and a magazine arrives in your mailbox for the rest of the year, telling you what wonderful work your money is doing, until you get hit up again for the next check at the end of the year. The huge influx of "members" thus sent the house organs of institutionalized environmentalism quickly rising from nobodies to significant players in American journalism.

The anomaly in the trend was *Orion* magazine, launched in 1982 with a different emphasis entirely. *Orion's* aim was to become the "literary, artistic and philosophical voice of the environmental movement."[34] At a time when most environmentalists felt a nearly unbearable urgency, *Orion* took a very long-term view. While others looked for results, *Orion* looked for good writing.

Publishing an entire issue on "ceremonial acts and festivals," including puppetry and storytelling, may have seemed tangential to some activists locked in battles to protect wilderness areas from imminent clear-cuts, who probably questioned the assertion of an organizer quoted in the issue that "the most radical thing you can do today is to be, with joy, on your streets." But *Orion* developed a devoted following with a circulation of twenty-five thousand and a very high-powered stable of writers, including Barbara Kingsolver, Wendell Berry, and others.

"We are in an environmental crisis," explains *Orion's* Laurie John Lane-Zucker, "and the solutions to that crisis, and the ways in which human culture is going to find its path to sustainability, will take much more than scientific or technological fixes. It will entail a far-reaching envisioning of human relationships with the planet. In order to do that, one must approach this search for a new way of living through as many ways of knowing that people have. For us, this means the finest writing that we have, as well as the finest art."[35]

The idiosyncrasies of *Orion*, however, paled in comparison with those of the *Earth First! Journal. Earth First!* appeared in 1980 and was unlike anything the environmental movement had seen. It was organized—to the degree that it was in fact *organized*—by a group of disaffected wilderness activists frustrated by the increasingly slick and professional tenor of the big organizations, which had come to be known as the "gang of ten," and the failure of these organizations to deliver in the political fights over designation of wilderness areas in the 1970s. They decided it was time for someone to liven up the party.

Whereas most environmental groups lobbied, Earth First! blockaded logging roads, spiked trees, and did guerrilla theater. Mainstream environmental magazines followed up articles about campaigns with sidebars calling for letters to legislators; Earth First! leaders published a guide to sabotage, *Eco-Defense: A Field Guide to Monkeywrenching* (1985), which includes instructions on how to spike trees, down power lines, plug discharge pipes, disable heavy machinery and aircraft, and "trash condos." Its 350 pages of small print and diagrams reveal a very real, indeed obsessive familiarity with the nuts and bolts of "ecotage"—real enough that the book was banned in Australia. By the time the reader gets to the chapter on security, with its discussion of the subtle differences between using a $12,000 Starlight Scope and the even more expensive Thermal Imager for night vision on moonlight ecotage raids, it is easy to wonder whether one is reading a work on environmental activism or a paranoid paramilitary fantasy.[36]

Other environmental groups filled the mail with membership solicitations; Earth First! didn't *want* any members. The "organization" pretty much consisted of a core of activists who traveled around the West putting on the environmental equivalent of a revival meeting, with country-and-western music, impassioned speeches, and howls at the moon. Other than that, the way to "join" was to *do* something and then say it had been done by Earth First!

The *Earth First! Journal* was just as unusual. Dave Foreman, the organization's ideologue, described "three vacant journalistic niches in the conservation movement" he hoped the journal would fill: "to report on and discuss the militant, no-compromise environmental movement (both direct action and the presentation of visionary wilderness proposals); to provide a forum for analysis, criticism and debate over strategy, tactics and goals of the conservation movement; and to articulate, discuss and explore the philosophical bases [of] preservation."[37]

The journal may have come up short on the latter two objectives, but its pages were full of images of people doing exciting stuff, like hanging from ropes 170 feet in the air and dangling "Save the Old Growth" banners from redwoods. The paper also included a generous dose of humor, which was in desperately short supply in every other environmental periodical. A front-page photo of a man in a ski mask and gloves holding a wrench was captioned "Civic-minded Earth First!ers across the country enthusiastically participated in an informal public comment period."[38]

Earth First! Journal's subscribers numbered between five thousand and ten thousand, which author Susan Zakin notes was

> *an impressive number considering the publication's strange combination of dry scientific writing and gonzo politics: An article with the headline "DENVER BEARS PROTEST YELLOWSTONE" written by someone named "Gainesburger" began this way: "Dogmeat the Beserker had spoken and Colorado Earth First! appeared at the National Park Service Regional Headquarters in Denver to answer the call. At the Park Service sign in a landscaped decorator "environment," complete with token pines, we unfurled Brush Wolf's banner: US PARK SERVICE: GRIZZLY KILLERS. In the same issue, ethnobotanist, author, and MacArthur fellow Gary Paul Nabhan would exhibit some of his least user-friendly prose. "Whereas the tropical agroforester has few growth-forms, but many tree species from which to choose, desert agroecologists are actively investigating the genetic resources of water-efficient cacti, drought-evading annuals, drought-escaping perennial tubers, and salt-tolerant shrubs.*[39]

While the rest of the environmental movement was trying to move into mainstream publishing with glossy covers and professional staffs, Earth First! was publishing a zine. "We got a lot of attention because of the rise of the zines and all," says Earth First! cofounder Mike Roselle. "We hit it perfectly. If we tried to launch it now, no one would notice."[40]

Tensions accumulated, however. "The [Earth First!] campaigns were almost exclusively about biological diversity, bread-and-butter conservation issues," says Roselle, "though we were attracting people from the alternative progressive side of the spectrum. Foreman had envisioned a group that included cowboys, bikers, and hippies. We did a much better job of getting the hippies, and we got hardly any bikers or cowboys, and at a certain point the joke kind of wore off."

The self-described "redneck" Foreman had the highest profile of the bunch and reacted to the increasingly countercultural milieu of Earth First! by becoming more "redneck" than he actually was. The tension culminated in a 1987 *Journal* article titled "Is AIDS the Answer to an Environmentalist's Prayer?" "The aim of my article was to point out that the AIDS epidemic, rather than being a scourge, is a welcome development," the author explained.[41]

Foreman resigned not long after.

The publishing world of the 1990s was booming with glossy magazines, and several entrepreneurially minded publishers saw an available niche in environmentalism. Efforts by the publishers of *Rolling Stone* and *Penthouse* fell flat, however. The corporate-oriented *Trilogy* lasted but a year. *Buzzworm*, *Garbage*, and *E Magazine* gave it a better run, but in the end only *E Magazine* survived, and then only because the editor, Doug Moss, was willing to subsidize it with a second mortgage on his house and a printing business that was willing to accumulate IOUs.[42] His timing was right as well. The 1989 launch coincided with the *Exxon Valdez* spilling oil into Prince William Sound in the Pacific and medical waste washing up onto the shore of New Jersey in the Atlantic. "We rode the coattails of those events and got a lot of subscriptions right off the bat," Moss says. "Subscriptions have stayed flat ever since."[43]

That circulation sits at forty thousand, divided equally between subscriptions and newsstand sales.[44] Though advertising revenue brings in $40,000–$45,000 per issue, *E* is heavily dependent on foundation funding.

Newsstand distribution has been tough. "When we launched, the newsstands didn't know what to do with us," says Moss. "*Audubon* was over with the bird magazines. *Sierra* was in the outdoor section. Barnes and Noble moved us around according to what was on our cover that month. Our religious issue was in the religious section, while political covers might be with *Mother Jones*, animal stories with pets. They don't have the idea of an environmental section."[45]

E's circulation is substantially augmented by syndicating to the mainstream press. The *Los Angeles Times* buys 10–15 articles from each issue, and the *New York Times* buys 4 or 5; thus more people read E articles in other newspapers than in E. E also publishes two nationally syndicated columns, whose reach peaked at 20 papers but dropped to 10 after the September 11 World Trade Center attack, as newspapers focused on war and terrorism.

E also overprints in large numbers for targeted outreach beyond the circulation base. "We just did an issue on religion and the environment," he explains. "We purchased lists of churches, mosques, and synagogues, not just churchgoers but the leadership as well. We sent them copies with a wrapper around it, explaining why we were doing it. We do this with almost every issue. With the religious issue we printed twenty-five thousand over, but we have done as many as forty-thousand over. Foundations give specific funding for this, but not general operating expenses."[46]

Flying mostly below the national radar are a range of regional publications that have gradually grown from the most modest of beginnings to respectable circulations and whose influence outweighs what one would expect from their absolute numbers. These journals include *Cascadia West*, the *Northern Forest Forum*, the *Adirondack Explorer*, and most prominently the Rocky Mountain's *High Country News*. Their editorial stances run the gamut from militant no-compromise to practical coalition-building, but they share a field of vision that follows ecological rather than political boundaries. They are the publishing embodiment of the "bioregional" idea.

"This kind of publishing effort has a potentially very effective place," says Tom Butler, editor of the nationally circulated *Wild Earth*. "So many Americans have no idea where they are. Every strip mall, every interstate looks the same. These kinds of publications help develop a *sense of place*."[47]

Earth Island Journal editor Chris Clark agrees. "Environment is not about anything if it is not about place: living appropriately in the place that you live. The species loss that most concerns me is the species that I might actually have a chance of seeing if they do not go extinct."[48]

The most successful of the regionals is *High Country News* (HCN), founded in 1971 by Tom Bell, a Wyoming rancher of a different sort: a deeply religious man who revered the land on which he ranched. Bell was the environmental movement's version of an old-time preacher, and, as current *HCN* publisher Ed Marsten notes, he

> used High Country News as his pulpit. In Old Testament tones, he preached his gospel of evil men—ranchers, miners, loggers, politicians, bureaucrats—destroying the natural world.... Because he felt the destruction of land and wildlife so deeply, and because he was so much a part of the society he was attacking, Bell eventually succumbed to emotional exhaustion. He moved to Oregon in 1974, leaving the paper in the hands of what were to become several overlapping generations of younger people.... Interestingly, with the exception of a Denverite, Bell's successors were all from the coasts or the Midwest, from cities or suburbs.... With the departure of Bell, the paper stopped thundering and has not thundered since.
>
> But Bell's successors had an important strength: They did not realize the extent to which they were living in the debris of what had been —a century ago—an intact, natural world. And so they lacked Bell's enormous sense of loss, and also his heartfelt anger and bitterness against those who had turned a golden land into an exhausted, wasted land.... They had come from much more ravaged places, and they could set about fighting for the West's still-clean air, the surviving forests, and the small communities with more optimism and less sense of doom than Bell.[49]

In 1983 Marston and *HCN* editor Betsy Marston moved to the Rockies from the East. They have built the journal into a force to be reckoned with. The paper boasts a circulation of twenty-one thousand, but the list is heavily weighted with policymakers, educators, and public land managers. A thousand are teachers who use the paper in their classes. Hundreds are reporters who watch it for story ideas.[50] More than five hundred live in Washington, DC.

The Marstons have added a half-hour radio program, *Radio High Country News,* which appears on almost a dozen public radio outlets in Colorado, Utah, and New Mexico, and a "Writers on the Range Program," which has presented the views of 150 commentators in newspapers large and small across the region.

The Marstons' *HCN* has positioned itself as a bridge builder between environmentalists and ranchers. "People are ready for a less ideological perspective, a less angry perspective," Ed Marston explains. "On the one hand, we are an environmental newspaper and have to be true to our roots, but on the other, we want to have a dialogue.... When we came here, there was absolute consensus, everyone agreed on what the West was, what it lived off of, and what its values were, except for a few fringe naysayers in the environmentalists. That economy, consensus and myth have all crashed."[51]

Marston sees condominiums as a far greater threat to the West than the ranching, logging, and mining that have been more typical targets of environmental criticism. "My sense of the West," adds Marston, "is that it's balanced between becoming suburbia, another ring of L.A., and something else. For me that something else is a productive landscape."[52]

This line of thinking has won the attention of people like Mike Gauldin, press spokesman for former interior secretary Bruce Babbitt. "You can open [HCN] up and read something from a bearded hippie freak or a cowboy-hatted rancher, who seem to have more in common than one might have thought." But it has also drawn criticism from those who feel that ranching remains the central threat to the streams and critical wildlife habitat of the region. "They have an unduly romantic image of anyone who wears a cowboy hat and a big belt buckle," says Scott Groene, a longtime wilderness advocate in Utah. "They are soft on cows."[53]

The back-to-the-land movement of the sixties and seventies needed advice and tools for organic farming, but by the 1980s the complexity of issues confronted by environmental activists required considerable scientific knowledge and technical expertise. Specialized journals that explain technical issues in everyday language emerged to meet this need, playing a similar role for the environmental movement to that which *AIDS Treatment News* and the *Project Inform Perspective* played for AIDS activists. The Northwest Coalition for Alternatives to Pesticides began publishing the *Journal of Pesticide Reform*, and the Institute for Energy and Environmental Research began publishing *Science for Democratic Action*, which deals with nuclear power and weapons.

RACHEL's Environment and Health Weekly is spearheaded by Peter Montague. Montague was a visiting scholar at Princeton University in New Jersey when it was discovered that across the border in New York, the community of Love Canal was sitting on top of twenty thousand tons of toxic chemicals. Montague realized that toxic waste would become a huge issue and started publishing a newsletter called the *New Jersey Hazardous Waste News*. In 1986 he changed the name and went national.[54] Montague explains:

> *Right from the beginning [RACHEL's] was thought of as a service to help people get new technical information. Scientific studies would be reviewed in everyday language: new studies, new revelations, whatever people needed to know.*
>
> *When landfills went out of fashion after the Love Canal catastrophe, government turned to incinerators. We started providing information about incinerators. It became clear that "risk assessment" had been developed by government and industry as a club to beat people over the head, so we spent five or six years on that. These guys would come out*

there with degrees and computer printouts, and say, "This dump will not hurt more than one in a million people. Can you prove me wrong?" That was the legal limit set by the federal government. They'd be wearing lab coats. People had to learn how risk assessments were flawed, filled with bogus assumptions. It took a lot of doing, a big fight against the embedding of all environmental health decisions in a wrapper of science that made it appear that citizens have no rights in the decision-making process.[55]

After years of this work, it was obvious that the movement needed to propose an alternative. Montague hired Mary O'Brien as staff scientist and raised money for her to write *Making Better Environmental Decisions,* a book published by MIT Press together with Montague's Environmental Research Foundation. In place of "risk assessment," O'Brian proposed "alternatives assessment." "The key," says Montague, "was to figure out what it is you are really trying to accomplish, look at all the options, and pick the least damaging alternative. It seems so obvious, but we had to stand on our heads to get the simplest ideas across."

Other scientists were thinking along the same lines. Eventually these threads came together in the "precautionary principle," which has gained widespread support among many scientists in the United States and elsewhere: "When an activity raises threats of harm to human health or the environment, precautionary measures should be taken even if some cause and effect relationships are not fully established scientifically. In this context the proponent of an activity, rather than the public, should bear the burden of proof."[56]

At the dawn of the new millennium the environmental press has grown to a scale that dwarfs the press of any other social movement in U.S. history. It has won big-time mainstream recognition. *Audubon Magazine* has won five National Magazine Awards and been a finalist sixteen times.[57] The *New York Times* called it "the most beautiful magazine in the world."[58] *USA Today* is one of several mainstream papers that have covered the rise of HCN, reporting that "for those involved in the never-ending debate over Western land-use issues, *High Country News* is must reading."[59]

Yet even with all the recognition, the multiplication of journals, and the huge increases in circulation, there is a palpable sense among movement publishers and activists that it is not enough. One reflection of this is that nearly everyone is "upgrading." The Earth Island Institute, The Nature Conservancy, the Audubon Society, the Natural Resources Defense Council, and the Orion Society all recently completed redesigns and relaunches of their publications.

In fact, despite a vast amount of good journalism, there have been few truly influential environmental journals. Histories of the abolitionist, woman suffrage, and gay and lesbian movements are full of detailed discussions of the journals the movements produced. Histories of the environmental movement fail to even mention them.[60] The canon of the environmental movement is composed of books, not magazines: Aldo Leopold's *Sand County Almanac*, Rachel Carson's *Silent Spring*, Barry Commoner's *Closing Circle*, and others.[61]

One big factor the environmental press has had to deal with that is atypical for a movement press is the coverage environmental issues receive in the mainstream press. Of course, in one sense it is not a "problem" at all. The abolitionist and woman suffragist press would have loved to have the problem of competing with the mainstream press for the attention of readers on the subject of ending slavery or giving women the vote. The gay and lesbian press had to go to the Supreme Court to win the right to simply mention the subject of homosexuality in a journal that was sent through the mail.

The environmental press has had to compete with the corporate media from the start. This coverage suffers from all the problems inherent in the corporate press. In addition to obvious bias and direct corporate influence, environmental issues are generally covered only when they boil over into crises, and environmental advocates are presented as "special interest groups"—a particularly infuriating moniker, given that environmental organizations are trying to save the health and sustainability of the planet for future generations and thus may be the closest thing to "*general* interest groups" that human society has produced.

However, the environmental press has had a major influence on the corporate press, and stories consistently migrate from the former to the latter. The editor of nearly every journal mentioned here can point to a list of stories he or she has published that were later picked up by a corporate outlet. The reporter who covers the Rocky Mountains for the *Washington Post* went so far as to admit: "I steal from them [*High Country News*] all the time. They're a great tip sheet."[62] As mentioned, E *Magazine* and HCN have formalized their contributions to the mainstream press through their syndicated stories and columns.

Other problems are specific to the particular form the environmental movement has taken: most movement journals are produced at least in part as rewards for cash donations. This has given some journals very impressive circulation numbers, but serious problems as well. One drawback is the lack of an independent editorial stance that comes with being a house organ, or more precisely, the *perception* of lack of independence. In fact, very few of the journals sponsored by the established organizations are held on a very tight leash by their sponsors. For example, *On Earth,* the new name for the journal sponsored by the National Resources Defense Council, has designated "NRDC pages" that reflect NRDC positions and campaigns, but the rest of the journal is run independently.

Yet many of the editors interviewed for this chapter listed their independence from tight organizational control as one of the unique characteristics of *their* publication. If the editors of the big environmental journals are so independent, why do they seem to be under tight organizational control, even in the eyes of their peer editors?

The role these journals play in the fund-raising schemes of their sponsoring organizations does indeed color their image, just as corporate ownership shapes the mainstream press despite the lack of blatant censorship. As the editor of a major, institutionally sponsored journal admitted off the record, "House organs don't like controversy, or rather, they don't like controversy that touches the house. If they touch on controversy that touches the organization, then you start hearing phrases like 'dirty laundry,' or you only cover one side of it after the issue has already been decided."

Almost every environmental battle ends in some sort of compromise. Every wilderness area has a boundary. Every emissions cap has a number. Where does one draw the line? When is a compromise acceptable? These complexities have made the environmental movement one of the most internally contentious social movements ever, but one would never know it from reading its press.

Another national editor speaking off the record added, "They all have a formula and you need to follow it: a slick look, lots of nice pictures, 'eco-porn.' It is easy-listening, coffee-table stuff. You can read it in the bathroom and not be challenged too much. *Earth Island* is one of the best; they never followed the eco-porn formula."

Never one to mince words, Earth First! and Greenpeace activist Mike Roselle summed it up succinctly: "They are boring to read. They are mostly donor services to keep their members active and informed. Greenpeace decided it wasn't worth the effort." Roselle was referring to Greenpeace USA's decision to terminate publication of *Greenpeace*, which had been regarded as one of the higher-quality organizational journals. "Back in 1991 we had 1.1 million members; imagine the cost of mailing that magazine to all those people. The purpose was to keep the donors informed. It was a good magazine, but in the end we couldn't justify the expense."[63]

These problems are inherent in a social movement rooted in activism yet led by large, professionally staffed institutions, and they will not go away. No matter how much noise is made in the street, environmental battles are nearly always settled in legislative bodies, the administrative hearings of government agencies, or the courts. Playing in these arenas requires professional expertise. Professional expertise requires money, and people who give money expect something back. Furthermore, movement victories are rarely permanent. Slavery is not going to come back to the United States, and women's right to vote will not be rescinded. But win a decision saving a local wetland from subdivision and sprawl, or a national wildlife refuge from oil drilling, and the developer will just come back in ten or twenty years when the deciding body has different members. The environmental movement will thus continue to be dominated by large, permanent institutions that are building up for a very long haul.

There have certainly been moments when particular journals stood out. The *Sierra Club Bulletin* during the Brower years is one of them. "*Not Man Apart* in the 1970s came as close to being the official voice of the environmental movement as anything," notes *Earth Island Journal*'s Chris Clark.[64] The *Whole Earth Catalog* invented an entirely new kind of journal, in the process pioneering a new publishing niche that was subsequently developed by *RAIN* and then made commercially viable by *Mother Earth News*. *High Country News* has shown what is possible while thinking about ecological regions rather than political ones.

All the organizationally affiliated journals have relied on the financial support of their sponsors to stay afloat except for one. The *Earth First! Journal* funded the organization instead of the other way around. *EFJ* "attracted a large reader base that paid for it," says Roselle. "We had no membership, no foundation money. We actually made money; we were the only environmental magazine that did this. And we had almost no ads, [except] for hippie musicians." (This is in stark contrast to *Sierra*, which features full-page glossy ads from Toyota, Nike, and even Eastman Chemical.)

Orion is unique in a different way. "Usually an organization starts with the organization, and then needs a voice piece and creates a magazine," says *Orion*'s Laurie John Lane-Zucker. "We went the other way. We started the magazine in 1982. As our tenth year approached we decided, in part at the urging of a growing community of writers and artists, to create this organizational entity, the Orion Society." As the magazine brought together more readers active in local environmental groups, the Orion Grassroots Network was launched. With more than five hundred affiliates, it became the "first communications and support network that recognizes the full diversity of place-based work that has been exploding around the country."[65]

Despite their diversity, these journals have several things in common. None was created by a large organization (except for the *Sierra Club Bulletin,* where the most creative period ended in the editor's dismissal). None had a large budget. In fact, some were started —and ended—with virtually no money at all. All were written with a more personal, at times humorous voice (though none has gone as far as the *Earth First! Journal,* which described its editor as an "ecobrute and macho Daniel Boone [who] can't sit idly by with such fine opportunities at which to aim his typically bombastic, misanthropic pontifications" and titled its merchandising page "Trinkets and Snake Oil"). With the exception of the *Whole Earth Catalog,* none had a large circulation, yet all wielded influence far in excess of what their circulation would have implied.

The tendency of environmental journals to be boring has been discussed, but there is a contradictory problem as well. Given the scale of the environmental catastrophe, how does one make magazines that are readable and entertaining instead of numbing and infuriating? "We have not wanted to publish a magazine that after a while you just can't open up," says *One Earth*'s Kathrin Day Lassila. "People say they cannot even read it; they have to close it halfway through because they are just so mad."[66]

The problem of seeming too boring on the one hand and too infuriating on the other may be contradictory, yet it is real nonetheless. Many of these journals *are* boring and overwhelming at once. While researching this chapter, I was actually put to sleep reading through them, but then had real nightmares about the crisis the journals depicted.

The root of the problem is the sheer magnitude of the crisis. The world's myriad environmental problems are adding up to systemic catastrophes that are much larger in scope than homophobia, women's rights, imperial wars, or even slavery. What's more, they have arrived with their own time line. Slavery ended in the United States after the Civil War, but if it had not ended then, it *could* have ended fifty years later. If women had not won the vote in the twentieth century, they *could* still win it in the twenty-first. Yet the time window in which to act to prevent the polar ice caps from melting due to global warming is coming to a close. The window of time for the preservation of biodiversity is even shorter; for thousands of species, it is already past.

People who read environmental magazines are generally familiar with the broad outlines of all this. Learning more of the gory details may not create new meaning for them, and writing a letter to a congressperson may seem to be a depressingly inadequate response. In part, this may reflect a lack of creativity on the part of the environmental movement and its press, but it also reflects the reality of a planet slipping toward catastrophe and a human society that seems to have no answers.

No one magazine can offer its readers answers, but the most successful ones at least offer meaningful things to do—not in the sense of writing a letter to a congressperson, but in the sense of offering an idea of how to meaningfully engage with a disaster of such epic proportions. Brower's *Bulletin* invited the reader to join in the idealistic early days of the movement. The *Whole Earth Catalog* and *RAIN* invited readers to change their own lives, living spaces, and habits. *High Country News* invites readers to engage with the crisis on the slightly larger, but still manageable, scale of the region in which they live, the water they drink, and the land on which they walk. *Orion* offers an opportunity to imagine an alternative to the whole mess of industrial society; *Earth First! Journal* invites you to slash its tires and make off with the spark plugs.

Despite the unique qualities of the environmental movement,

the recipe for a successful journal seems to be no different from that of other movements: big money, big advertising, big organizations, and big circulation are beside the point. What is required is simply a vision of what people can do to make their lives more meaningful.

A Note from the
Independent Press Association

Where are the social movements of the twenty-first century? I posed this question to Bob Ostertag (or maybe he posed it to me) during an intense and provocative discussion we held late one Friday afternoon in a historic San Francisco bar—the kind of place where the city's journalists, politicians, and rabble-rousers have been gathering for the last hundred years or so to debate the issues of the day. As the din surrounded us, we hit upon a critical point: Social movements as we have known them, and the social movement press as we have come to expect it to function and engage with the public, are changing in ways one may not immediately recognize.

It's a remarkable fact that one of the most prominent social movements to emerge in this new century is the media reform movement itself. In 2003, twenty years after Ben Bagdikian published his groundbreaking but much-ignored book *The Media Monopoly*, millions of citizens bombarded the halls of government to protest the Federal Communication Commission's decision to radically lower the barriers to corporate media consolidation. That seemingly spontaneous protest succeeded, and two years later, Free Press, an organization founded by prominent media critic Robert McChesney and responsible for much of the grass-roots organizing that led to that victory, brought more than twenty-five hundred media reform activists together for a national convention to celebrate the movement's success and to chart its future.

As Bob Ostertag notes in his introduction, corporate media consolidation has emerged as one of the most socially corrosive forces we face today. It has robbed local communities of their voice in national public affairs, and it has turned debate over complex national issues into a shouting match over deliberately polarized views. The result is a dichotomy only George Orwell could have predicted: The majority—those who nominally have a voice in local and national civic affairs—have come increasingly to view the public stage as a reality TV set, where they have a ticket to watch but not to take part; and the minority—those for whom American civic society is daily held up as a promise in mainstream newspapers, magazines, books, movies, TV shows, and Web sites—find themselves standing offstage, portrayed as actors in a drama they could never have imagined on their own.

Whereas there have been moments in the past, however brief, when social movements could leverage mainstream media to echo and amplify their successes in grass-roots organizing, today's social movements face the uncomfortable fact that mainstream, corporate media are overwhelmingly indifferent to complex social debate. Bagdikian anticipated this outcome: "The result of the overwhelming power of relatively narrow corporate ideologies has been the creation of widely established political and economic illusions in the United States with little visible contradiction in the media to which a majority of the population is exclusively exposed" (*Media Monopoly*, 6th ed., p. 44).

Hence the need for media reform of a kind not envisioned in the 1980s, when Bagdikian first stated his case, and certainly not in recent years, when the profusion of Internet content has seemed to make media reform an idea whose time has come—and gone. Today's media reform movement is characterized by a growing recognition that a strong, diversified, professional, and independent press is a critically needed factor in the contemporary media environment, essentially replacing mainstream, corporate media in the role of echoing the insights of social movements to the larger society and creating the conditions under which social activism is possible.

This book is a tribute to the vision of the Independent Press Association's (IPA) founders, and especially its founding executive director, John Anner, who in 1996 launched the organization specifically to support the emergence of independent publishing as a powerful new force on the media and social movement scenes. In 2002, at the suggestion of the New World Foundation's president Colin Greer, Anner enlisted Bob Ostertag to write a brief narrative on the history of the social movement press in order to document its central influence in bringing about the great social advancements of the nineteenth and early twentieth centuries, which we now take for granted. With encouragement, advice, and generous support from Dayna Cunningham and Andre Oliver of the Rockefeller Foundation, Anner and Ostertag expanded the initial manuscript into the full-length book you hold in your hands. The IPA's Jeremy Smith shepherded the manuscript through a critical period of gestation; and Joanne Wyckoff and Brian Halley of Beacon Press recognized the significance of this work and brought it to completion. To all these people—especially to Bob Ostertag and our colleagues at the Rockefeller Foundation—we owe a debt of gratitude.

RICHARD LANDRY
Executive Director
Independent Press Association

Author's Note

This book began as a report commissioned by the Independent Press Association (IPA), and it was the IPA again that offered the support to expand the report into the present book. In particular, I would like to thank former IPA executive director John Anner for initiating the project, and current IPA executive director Richard Landry for seeing it through to its conclusion. Without the gracious support of John and Richard, this book would never exist.

Many of the journals I have researched for this book cannot be found in official archives or library collections. They are more likely to be found in cardboard boxes in someone's attic. That someone will be a veteran of years of selfless dedication to one of the movements about which I have written, and somehow, in the midst of the chaos and overwork of social movement activism, he or she will have thought to squirrel away copies of movement papers on the faint chance that someone like myself might come looking for them decades later. Thomas Barton is one such person; he photocopied and then shipped to me a complete collection of the *Vietnam GI* at his own expense. Paul Cox did the same with *Rage*. Clark Smith provided whatever copies of *The Ally* he could, as did Steve Rees with *Up against the Bulkhead*. Tatiana de la Tierra provided all the copies of *esto no tiene nombre* and *Conmoción* she had managed to save from

Hurricane Andrew. Sydney Brinkley offered me full access to his private collection of black gay and lesbian journals.

I have benefited immensely from the comments of both academics and activists who have reviewed various drafts of different chapters. These include Eric Foner, Frances Fox Piven, Harriet Barlow, Hank Wilson, Joan Nestle, and the University of California Davis Queer Studies Research Cluster.

Trauma Flintstone has done detailed proofreading and copyediting whenever I asked. Jane McAlevey, my political soul mate, introduced me to the IPA and then, as she has done for years, discussed anything and everything about the world of politics with me at all hours of the night.

Brian Halley, my editor at Beacon Press, has been a joy to work with.

My most sincere thanks to you all.

There is one more thank-you that requires special mention. I have interviewed many people about their personal histories in social movement activism. Most people who have gone through such experiences love to talk about them, as they are often reminiscing about the best days of their lives. This is not the case with Vietnam vets. Vietnam was a dark time for them. Many spent decades trying to put those terrible experiences behind them and would rather talk about almost anything than dredge up those memories one more time. To those who were willing nevertheless to be interviewed for this book, I owe my deepest gratitude.

Notes

Introduction

1. Possibly the only book-length work on the topic is Lauren Kessler's brief survey from 1984: *The Dissident Press: Alternative Journalism in American History* (Newbury Park: Sage Publications, 1984). In terms of the twentieth-century movements examined in this book, see Rodger Streitmatter, *Unspeakable: The Rise of the Gay and Lesbian Press in America* (Boston: Faber and Faber, 1995). For the underground GI press, see James Lewes, *Protest and Survive: Underground GI Newspapers during the Vietnam War* (Westport, CT: Praeger, 2003). I know of no study of the press of the environmental movement.

2. Streitmatter, *Unspeakable*.

3. U.S. Census Bureau, "50th Anniversary of 'Wonderful World of Color' TV" (Washington, DC: U.S. Census Bureau, 2004).

4. Ben H. Bagdikian, *The New Media Monopoly* (Boston: Beacon Press, 2004).

5. Quoted in *Free Culture: How Big Media Uses Technology and the Law to Lock Down Culture and Control Creativity*, by Lawrence Lessig (New York: Penguin, 2004), 162.

6. *Crossfire*, CNN, October 15, 2004.

The Nineteenth Century:
Abolitionists and Woman Suffragists

1. William Lloyd Garrison, "To the Public," in *The Abolitionists: A Collection of Their Writing*, ed. Louis Ruchames (New York: G. P. Putnam's Sons, 1963), 30.

2. Oswald Garrison Villard, *Some Newspapers and Newspaper-Men* (New York: A. A. Knopf, 1923), 302–3.

3. Henry Mayer, *All on Fire: William Lloyd Garrison and the Abolition of Slavery* (New York: St. Martin's Press, 1998), xx–xxi.

4. Jeremy Reimer, www.Pegasus3d.Com/Total_Share.html (Pegasus.com, 2005).

5. *Console Market Share* (IT Facts.biz, September 2, 2003); available from www.itfacts.biz/index.php?id=P23.

6. National Association of Theatre Owners, *Number of U.S. Movie Screens* (2004); available from www.natoonline.org/statisticsscreens.htm.

7. U.S. Census Bureau, "50th Anniversary of 'Wonderful World of Color' TV."

8. Central Intelligence Agency (CIA), "The World Factbook" (2005).

9. Michael Schudson, *Discovering the News: A Social History of American Newspapers* (New York: Basic Books, 1978), 13. Newspaper Association of America, "Facts about Newspapers: A Statistical Summary of the Newspaper Industry, 2004" (Newspaper Association of America, 2004).

10. Ellen Carol DuBois, *Feminism and Suffrage: The Emergence of an Independent Women's Movement in America, 1848–1869* (Ithaca: Cornell University Press, 1978), 34.

11. E. Claire Jerry, "The Role of Newspapers in the Nineteenth-Century Woman's Movement," in *A Voice of Their Own: The Woman Suffrage Press, 1840–1990*, ed. Martha M. Solomon (Tuscaloosa: University of Alabama Press, 1991), 28.

12. Phil Barber, *A Brief History of Newspapers*; available from www.historic-pages.com/nprhist.htm. See also S. H. Steinberg and John Trevitt, *Five Hundred Years of Printing* (London: British Library, 1996), 139–40.

13. Louis Filler, *The Crusade against Slavery, 1830–1860* (New York: Harper, 1960), 17.

14. The somewhat curious title of Lundy's publication comes from John Philpot Curran, an Irish lawyer and statesman who advocated for the emancipation of British Catholics from civil disabilities. "I speak in the spirit of the British law, which makes liberty commensurate with,

and inseparable from, the British soul—which proclaims, even to the stranger and the sojourner, the moment he sets foot upon British earth, that the ground on which he treads is holy, and consecrated by *the Genius of Universal Emancipation*." See Ralph Korngold, *Two Friends of Man: The Story of William Lloyd Garrison and Wendell Phillips and Their Relationship with Abraham Lincoln* (Boston: Little, Brown, 1950), 24.

15. Ibid., 24–25.
16. Jacqueline Bacon, "The History of Freedom's Journal: A Study in Empowerment and Community," *The Journal of African American History* 88 (2003): 1.
17. Robert S. Levine, "Circulating the Nation: David Walker, the Missouri Compromise, and the Rise of the Black Press," in *The Black Press: New Literary and Historical Essays,* ed. Todd Vogel (New Brunswick, NJ: Rutgers University Press, 2001), 23–24.
18. Peter P. Hinks, *To Awaken My Afflicted Brethren: David Walker and the Problem of Antebellum Slave Resistance* (University Park: Pennsylvania State University Press, 1997), 91–93.
19. Elizabeth McHenry, "Rereading Literary Legacy: New Considerations of the 19th-Century African-American Reader and Writer," *Callaloo* 22, no. 3 (1999).
20. Levine, "Circulating the Nation," 22.
21. Roy E. Finkenbine et al., *Witness for Freedom: African American Voices on Race, Slavery, and Emancipation* (Chapel Hill: University of North Carolina Press, 1993), 2.
22. Hinks, *To Awaken My Afflicted Brethren,* 103.
23. Finkenbine et al., *Witness for Freedom,* 7.
24. Bacon, "History of Freedom's Journal," 8.
25. Lauren Kessler, *The Dissident Press: Alternative Journalism in American History* (Newbury Park: Sage Publications, 1984), 29.
26. As quoted in *To Awaken My Afflicted Brethren,* by Hinks, 92.
27. Hinks's definitive study seems to debunk certain theories, such as the idea that Walker died mysteriously at the hands of Southern slaveholders. Yet even Hinks cannot fix Walker's birth, education, movements, or exact death. See ibid.
28. Here is just one example of Walker's detailed attention to Jefferson:

> "Will not a lover of natural history, then, one who views the gradations in all the races of animals with the eye of philosophy, excuse an

effort to keep those in the department of MAN as distinct as nature has formed them?" I hope you will try to find out the meaning of this verse— its widest sense and all its bearings: whether you do or not, remember the whites do. This very verse, brethren, having emanated from Mr. Jefferson, a much greater philosopher the world never afforded, has in truth injured us more, and has been as great a barrier to our emancipation as any thing that has ever been advanced against us. I hope you will not let it pass unnoticed. He goes on further, and says: "This unfortunate difference of colour, and perhaps of faculty, is a powerful obstacle to the emancipation of these people. Many of their advocates, while they wish to vindicate the liberty of human nature are anxious also to preserve its dignity and beauty. Some of these, embarrassed by the question, 'What further is to be done with them?' join themselves in opposition with those who are actuated by sordid avarice only."

For my own part, I am glad Mr. Jefferson has advanced his positions for your sake; for you will either have to contradict or confirm him by your own actions, and not by what our friends have said or done for us; for those things are other men's labours, and do not satisfy the Americans, who are waiting for us to prove to them ourselves, that we are MEN, before they will be willing to admit the fact; for I pledge you my sacred word of honour, that Mr. Jefferson's remarks respecting us, have sunk deep into the hearts of millions of the whites, and never will be removed this side of eternity. For how can they, when we are confirming him every day, by our groveling submissions and treachery?

> David Walker, *Walker's Appeal, in Four Articles; Together with a Preamble, to the Coloured Citizens of the World, but in Particular, and Very Expressly, to Those of the States of America* (Chapel Hill: University of North Carolina, Academic Affairs Library, 2001)

29. All excerpts are from *Walker's Appeal*.
30. Hinks, *To Awaken My Afflicted Brethren*, 155–56.
31. Ibid., 143.
32. Ibid., 118–19.
33. Ibid., 134–35.
34. Ibid., 150.
35. Ibid., 168.

36. *Boston Daily Evening Transcript*, September 28, 1830, as cited ibid.

37. Louis Ruchames, ed., *The Abolitionists: A Collection of Their Writing* (New York: G. P. Putnam's Sons, 1963), 16. Also Hinks, *To Awaken My Afflicted Brethren*, 112–13.

38. Ruchames, *Abolitionists*, 16.

39. William Lloyd Garrison, "Words of Encouragement to the Oppressed," in *Abolitionists*, ed. Ruchames, 38.

40. Filler, *Crusade against Slavery*, 60.

41. Stephen Currie, *The Liberator: Voice of the Abolitionist Movement* (San Diego: Lucent Books, 2000), 30–33.

42. Finkenbine et al., *Witness for Freedom*, 4.

43. Garrison, "To the Public."

44. Filler, *Crusade against Slavery*, 52.

45. Sherman W. Savage, *The Controversy over the Distribution of Abolition Literature, 1830–1860* (New York: Negro Universities Press, 1938), 15.

46. Filler, *Crusade against Slavery*, 67.

47. Sherman, *Controversy*, 9.

48. Ibid., 14.

49. Filler, *Crusade against Slavery*, 97.

50. Eric Foner, *The Story of American Freedom* (New York: Norton, 1999).

51. Gregory P. Lampe, *Frederick Douglass: Freedom's Voice, 1818–1845* (East Lansing: Michigan State University Press, 1998), 44.

52. William W. Brown, *Narrative of William W. Brown, an American Slave: Written by Himself* (Chapel Hill: University of North Carolina Press, 1996).

53. Solomon Northup, *Twelve Years a Slave: Narrative of Solomon Northup, a Citizen of New-York, Kidnapped in Washington City in 1841, and Rescued in 1853* (Chapel Hill: University of North Carolina Press, 1997).

54. Armistead S. Pride and Clint C. Wilson, *A History of the Black Press* (Washington, DC: Howard University Press, 1997), 50.

55. Ibid.; Robert Fanuzzi, "Frederick Douglass's 'Colored Newspaper': Identity Politics in Black and White," in *The Black Press: New Literary and Historical Essays*, ed. Todd Vogel (New Brunswick, NJ: Rutgers University Press, 2001), 65.

56. Frederick Douglass, "The Meaning of July Fourth for the Negro," in *The Life and Writings of Frederick Douglass, Volume II: Pre–Civil War Decade, 1850–1860*, ed. Philip S. Foner (New York: International Publishers, 1950).

57. Melvin R. Sylvester, *Negro Periodicals in the United States Series I, 1840–1960*, www.liu.edu/cwis/cwp/library/historic.htm#20.

58. Filler, *Crusade against Slavery*, 197.
59. Jane Smiley, introduction to *Uncle Tom's Cabin* (New York: Modern Library, 2001).
60. Ibid., xviii.
61. Ibid., xx.
62. William S. McFeely, *Frederick Douglass* (New York: W. W. Norton, 1991), 269–70.
63. Currie, *Liberator*, 71.
64. Ibid., 31–33.
65. Finkenbine et al., *Witness for Freedom*, 4.
66. Kessler, *Dissident Press*, 24.
67. Pride and Wilson, *History of the Black Press*, 51.
68. Fanuzzi, "Frederick Douglass's 'Colored Newspaper,' " 64.
69. Maria Stewart, "Religion and the Pure Principles of Morality, the Sure Foundation on Which We Must Build," *The Liberator* (1831).
70. Maria Stewart, "Lecture Delivered at Franklin Hall, Boston, September 21, 1832" (Boston, 1832).
71. Maria Stewart, "An Address Delivered at the African Masonic Hall" (Boston, 1833).
72. Robert James Branham and Philip S. Foner, *Lift Every Voice: African American Oratory, 1787–1900* (Tuscaloosa: University of Alabama Press, 1998), 7.
73. Maria S. Stewart, "Farewell Address" (New York City, 1834).
74. Angelina E. Grimké, "Slavery and the Boston Riot," *The Liberator* (1835).
75. Angelina Grimké Weld, "Angelina Grimké Weld's Speech at Pennsylvania Hall," in *History of Pennsylvania Hall Which Was Destroyed by a Mob on the 17th of May, 1838* (New York: Negro Universities Press, 1969).
76. Martha M. Solomon, "The Role of the Suffrage Press in the Women's Rights Movement," in *A Voice of Their Own: The Woman Suffrage Press, 1840–1910*, ed. Martha M. Solomon (Tuscaloosa: University of Alabama Press, 1991), 12.
77. DuBois, *Feminism and Suffrage*, 49.
78. Waldo E. Martin Jr., *The Mind of Frederick Douglass* (Chapel Hill: University of North Carolina Press, 1984), 145.
79. Flexner, *Century of Struggle*, 15.
80. Solomon, "Role of the Suffrage Press," 21. Prior to this, there had been journals that did treat the issue of woman suffrage, though it was not their primary focus. For example, *The Lily* (1849–1856) started as a tem-

perance journal but evolved to focus on female suffrage. See Edward A. Hinck, "*The Lily*, 1849–1856: From Temperance to Woman's Rights," in *A Voice of Their Own: The Woman Suffrage Press, 1840–1910*, ed. Martha M. Solomon (Tuscaloosa: University of Alabama Press, 1991).

81. For the complete resolutions of one such convention, see Aileen S. Kraditor, *Up from the Pedestal: Selected Writings in the History of American Feminism* (Chicago: Quadrangle Books, 1968), 220–22.

82. As quoted in "The *Una*, 1853–1855: The Premiere of the Woman's Rights Press," by Mari Boor Tonn, in *A Voice of Their Own: The Woman Suffrage Press, 1840–1910*, ed. Martha M. Solomon (Tuscaloosa: University of Alabama Press, 1991), 49.

83. According to the *Oxford Universal Dictionary*, the word *feminism*, in reference to the advocacy of women's rights, was first used in England in 1895.

84. Claire E. Jerry, "The Role of Newspapers in the Nineteenth Century Woman's Movement," in *A Voice of Their Own: The Woman Suffrage Press, 1840–1910*, ed. Martha M. Solomon (Tuscaloosa: University of Alabama Press, 1991), 19.

85. As quoted in *Feminism and Suffrage*, by DuBois, 23.

86. As quoted in "Role of Newspapers," by Jerry, 22.

87. As quoted in *Feminism and Suffrage*, by DuBois, 95.

88. Ibid., 103.

89. Ibid., 104.

90. Ibid., 178.

91. Lynn Masel-Walters, "Their Rights and Nothing More: A History of *The Revolution*, 1868–1870," *Journalism Quarterly* 53 (Summer 1976): 251.

92. As quoted in "The *Revolution*, 1868–1870: Expanding the Woman Suffrage Agenda," by Bonnie J. Dow, in *A Voice of Their Own: The Woman Suffrage Press, 1840–1910*, ed. Martha M. Solomon (Tuscaloosa: University of Alabama Press, 1991), 85.

93. DuBois, *Feminism and Suffrage*, 122.

94. Ibid., 189.

95. See Susan Schultz Huxman, "*The Woman's Journal*, 1870–1890: The Torchbearer for Suffrage," in *A Voice of Their Own: The Woman Suffrage Press, 1840–1910*, ed. Martha M. Solomon (Tuscaloosa: University of Alabama Press, 1991), 87–109.

96. As quoted in "*Woman's Journal*," by Huxman, 96.

97. Ibid., 99.

98. E. Claire Jerry, "Clara Belwick Colby and the Women's Tribune, 1883–1909," in *A Voice of Their Own: The Woman Suffrage Press, 1840–1990*, ed. Martha M. Solomon (Tuscaloosa: University of Alabama Press, 1991).

99. Huxman, "Woman's Journal," 97.

100. Jerry, "Role of Newspapers," 23–24.

101. Altina L. Waller, *Reverend Beecher and Mrs. Tilton: Sex and Class in Victorian America* (Amherst: University of Massachusetts Press, 1982), 1.

102. Ibid., 2.

103. As quoted in "The *Women's Column*, 1888–1904: Extending the Suffrage Community," by Marsha L. Vanderford, in *A Voice of Their Own: The Woman Suffrage Press, 1840–1910*, ed. Martha M. Solomon (Tuscaloosa: University of Alabama Press, 1991), 130.

104. Ibid., 131.

105. Ibid., 137–48.

106. Kessler, *Dissident Press*, 78.

107. Jerry, "Role of Newspapers," 26.

108. For nuanced discussions, see DuBois, *Feminism and Suffrage*, 106, and Linda Steiner, "Evolving Rhetorical Strategies / Evolving Identities," in *A Voice of Their Own: The Woman Suffrage Press, 1840–1910*, ed. Martha M. Solomon (Tuscaloosa: University of Alabama Press, 1991), 189.

109. Dubois, *Feminism and Suffrage*, 30.

110. Solomon, "Role of the Suffrage," 15.

The Gay and Lesbian Press

1. The meaning of these terms reveals how different prewar homoerotic male life was from the latter half of the century. *Fairies* were the only publicly identifiable face of homoeroticism. *Fairies* wore male clothes but women's makeup and adopted extremely feminine mannerisms. *Fairies* were a normal feature of working-class neighborhood street life, at least in New York City. *Queers* were middle-class, masculine-acting men who sought out sex with other men. In a complete inversion of today's gay scene, middle-class *queers* had to sneak off to the working-class neighborhoods to have a gay night out. *Trade* referred to basically all other men, as it was assumed that under the right circumstances, almost any man would happily consent to sex with a *fairy*. Descriptions of sailors leaving ships to waiting groups of *fairy* prostitutes suggest that this assumption was largely valid. See George Chauncey, *Gay New York:*

Gender, Urban Culture, and the Making of the Gay Male World, 1890–1940 (New York: Basic Books, 1994).

2. On the emergence of the "homosexual," see Michel Foucault, *The History of Sexuality: An Introduction*, vol. 1 (New York: Vintage, 1990). On the emergence of "queers" in the 1990s, see Frank Browning, *The Culture of Desire: Paradox and Perversity in Gay Lives Today* (New York: Vintage, 1994).

3. Michel Foucault, *The Use of Pleasure: The History of Sexuality*, vol. 2 (New York: Vintage, 1990).

4. Gilbert Herdt, *Same Sex, Different Cultures* (Boulder, CO: Westview Press, 1997).

5. See Neil Miller, *Out of the Past: Gay and Lesbian History from 1869 to the Present* (New York: Vintage, 1995). Also see Chauncey, *Gay New York*, and History Project, *Improper Bostonians: Lesbian and Gay History from the Puritans to Playland* (Boston: Beacon Press, 1998).

6. Gregory Sprague, "60 Years Ago—America's First Gay Rights Group," *Gay Life* (1984).

7. Ibid.

8. Jim Kepner, "Review of Streitmatter," *International Gay and Lesbian Review* (1998).

9. Rodger Streitmatter, *Unspeakable: The Rise of the Gay and Lesbian Press in America* (Boston: Faber and Faber, 1995), 341.

10. Ibid., 1.

11. Ibid., 4.

12. The historian in question was Rodger Streitmatter, who apparently remained unaware of the woman's real name when he published *Unspeakable*, the most comprehensive study of the gay and lesbian press to date.

13. Kenneth Pobo, "Journalism and Publishing," in *GLBTQ: An Encyclopedia of Gay, Lesbain, Bisexual, Transgender, and Queer Culture* (Chicago: glbtq: An Encyclopedia of Gay, Lesbian, Bisexual, Transgender, and Queer Culture, 2002).

14. D'Emilio, *Sexual Politics*.

15. Ibid., 70.

16. Ibid., 73.

17. Ibid., 77–79.

18. *The Ladder* 1, no. 1 (1956): 2.

19. Jonathan Katz, *Gay American History: Lesbians and Gay Men in the USA*, 2nd ed. (New York: Meridian, 1992), 425.

20. *ONE* 1, no. 1 (1953).

21. Ibid., 12.

22. *ONE* 6, no. 1 (1958): 4.

23. Streitmatter, *Unspeakable*, 45.

24. *The Ladder* 1, no. 2 (November 1956).

25. Del Martin, "Dob Speaks for Lesbian," *The Ladder* 4, no. 1 (1959).

26. D'Emilio, *Sexual Politics*, 113.

27. Streitmatter, *Unspeakable*, 27.

28. *ONE* , no. 1 (January 1953): 17. See also D'Emilio, *Sexual Politics*, 117.

29. Katz, *Gay American History*, 425.

30. D'Emilio, *Sexual Politics*, 164.

31. *The Ladder: A Lesbian Review* 8, no. 6 (1964).

32. Barbara Gittings, "Looking Back on a Life of Activism, a Pioneer Is Still on the Go," *The Advocate*, July 9, 1981.

33. Katz, *Gay American History*, 427.

34. Streitmatter, *Unspeakable*, 51, 56.

35. Chasin, *Selling Out*, 64–65.

36. "SIR Statement of Policy," *Vector* (1964).

37. D'Emilio, *Sexual Politics*, 191.

38. Streitmatter, *Unspeakable*, 61.

39. Ibid., 73.

40. Ibid., 84.

41. Ibid., 88.

42. Ibid., 117.

43. Ibid., 124.

44. Ibid., 118.

45. See Winston Weyland, ed., *20 Years of Gay Sunshine: An Anthology of Gay History, Sex, Politics, and Culture* (San Francisco: Gay Sunshine Press, 1991).

46. Streitmatter, *Unspeakable*, 121, 141.

47. Ibid., 124.

48. *The Ladder* 16, nos. 7 and 8 (April/May 1972).

49. Del Martin, "Is That All There Is?" *Motive* (1972).

50. The Furies, *The Furies* 1 (1972): 1.

51. Ibid.

52. Author's interview with Jeanne Córdova, March 11, 2005.

53. Streitmatter, *Unspeakable*, 158.

54. As cited in "Lesbian Feminism," by Elise Chenier, in *GLBTQ: An Encyclopedia of Gay, Lesbian, Bisexual, Transgender, and Queer Culture* (Chicago:

glbtq: An Encyclopedia of Gay, Lesbian, Bisexual, Transgender, and Queer Culture, 2004).

55. Streitmatter, *Unspeakable*, 172.

56. Author's interview with Jeanne Córdova.

57. See the *Lesbian History Project: A Lesbian History Research Site*, http://isd.usc.edu/~retter/main.html.

58. Author's interview with Jeanne Córdova.

59. Streitmatter, *Unspeakable*, 185.

60. *Fag Rag* 1 (June 1971): 14.

61. *Fag Rag* 7+8 (Winter–Spring 1974): 8.

62. *Fag Rag*, no. 9 (Summer 1974): 3.

63. *Fag Rag*, no. 1 (June 1971): 5.

64. See "To Be 27, Gay, and Corrupted," *Fag Rag* (Fall 1971): 6, and "Hustler: A Boy for All Seasons—an Interview with a Hustler and His Customer," *Fag Rag*, no. 4:3.

65. Streitmatter, *Unspeakable*, 189.

66. Ibid., 183, 186.

67. Ibid., 192.

68. Ibid., 184.

69. Chasin, *Selling Out*, 81.

70. Scott Anderson, "The Gay Press Proliferates—and So Do Its Problems," *The Advocate*, December 13, 1979, 19–20, as cited in *Selling Out*, by Chasin, 81–82.

71. S. Brinkley, "The Bottom Line," *Blacklight* 1, no. 1 (1979): 2.

72. Ibid., 1.

73. *Blacklight* 2, no. 1.

74. An overview of the work of Vaginal Davis can be found at www.vaginaldavis.com.

75. Correspondence with the author, February 28, 2005.

76. Ibid.

77. Streitmatter, for example, ignores all but *BLK*, which he somewhat inexplicably lumps together with the shallow gay glossies of the 1990s.

78. Streitmatter, *Unspeakable*, 214.

79. Randy Shilts, *The Mayor of Castro Street* (New York: St. Martin's Press, 1982).

80. Streitmatter, *Unspeakable*, 241.

81. As quoted ibid., 214.

82. Ibid., 216.

83. Ibid., 236.

84. James Kinsella, *Covering the Plague: AIDS and the American Media* (New Brunswick, NJ: Rutgers University Press, 1990).

85. *New York Native*, May 18–31, 1981, 7.

86. Ibid., July 13–26, 1981, 1.

87. *The Advocate*, July 23, 1981, 12.

88. Streitmatter, *Unspeakable*, 249.

89. Author's interview with Randy Alfred, October 30, 2002.

90. In the United States, health authorities eventually closed the baths in most cities, and authors like Randy Shilts *(And the Band Played On)* were influential in vilifying the institution. Baths in Europe, Canada, and Australia, however, were never closed. The fact that the HIV infection rates among gay men in those places has consistently stayed far lower than in the United States indicates that the emphasis on the baths may have been simplistic.

91. Streitmatter, *Unspeakable,* and Randy Shilts, *And the Band Played On: Politics, People, and the AIDS Epidemic* (New York: St. Martin's Press, 1987).

92. Author's interview with Randy Alfred.

93. One prominent author has raked the *Sentinel* over the coals for a front-page headline announcing "Most Tubs, Clubs Safe." The story investigated the adequacy of fire exits at the baths, which seems trivial and misleading in hindsight, given the proportions the AIDS epidemic eventually took (Streitmatter, *Unspeakable,* 254). But in fact the story was the result of pressure from Bay Area Gay Liberation (BAGL). "We had businesses like the Midnight Sun [a gay bar] with two hundred people and no fire exits. We had that incident in New Orleans where many people died [in a fire in a gay bar]. BAGL was very conscious of safety; we picketed the Midnight Sun. The gay press gave us energy because we saw our activism reflected on the front page. It's hard when you do stuff and you don't see it reflected in the media" (author's interview with Hank Wilson, October 25, 2002).

94. Shilts, *And the Band Played On,* 244–45.

95. *New York Native*, March 17–24, 1983, 1.

96. Streitmatter, *Unspeakable,* 256.

97. Shilts, *And the Band Played On,* 74.

98. *New York Native*, July 13–26, 1981, 1.

99. Testimony of John S. James before the Presidential Commission on the HIV Epidemic, New York City, February 20, 1988.

100. Author's correspondence with Gordon T. Menzies, October 10, 2002.

101. *Los Angeles Times*, November 4, 1991.

102. Author's interview with Randy Alfred.

103. Ibid.

104. Streitmatter, *Unspeakable*, 312–13.

105. Grant Lukenbill, *Untold Millions: Positioning Your Business for the Gay and Lesbian Consumer Revolution* (New York: HarperCollins, 1995).

106. Mike Wilke, "Commercial Closet: Ads Drop, Gay Themes Rise," *Gay Financial Network*, October 14, 2002.

107. J. Nicholson, "Big National Advertisers Are Eyeing Gay Press," *Editor and Publisher* 132, no. 11 (1999): 30.

108. Streitmatter, *Unspeakable*, 319.

109. Author's interview with William Waybourn, March 4, 2005.

110. "Genre Magazine, Window Media and Unite Media Join Forces," *Write News* (2004).

111. *Totally Gay*, VH1, 2003 (www2.commercialcloset.org/cgi-bin/iowa/themes .html?brand=751).

112. Witeck-Combs Communications, "Gay Buying Power Projected at $610 Billion in 2005" (Washington, DC: Witeck-Combs Communications, 2005).

113. *Out Magazine* (March 2005).

114. *The Advocate*, March 15, 2005.

115. *Out Magazine* (March 2005): 37. Emphasis added.

116. *Totally Gay*.

117. See, for example, Chasin, *Selling Out*.

118. See www.gayshamesf.org.

119. See Vito Russo, *The Celluloid Closet* (New York: Harper and Row, 1981).

120. GLAAD Mission Statement, www.glaad.org/about/index.php.

121. Author's interview with Jeanne Córdova.

122. Chasin, *Selling Out*, xvi.

123. Ibid., 55.

124. See Mitch Walker, "Contradictory Views on Radical Faerie Thought," *White Crane*, no. 34 (1997).

125. *RFD*, no. 79 (Autumn 1994): 24.

126. Tatiana de la Tierra, "Activist Latina Lesbian Publishing: *Esto No Tiene Nombre* and *Conmoción*," in *I am Aztlán: The Personal Essay in Chicano Studies*, ed. Chon A. Noriega and Wendy Belcher (Los Angeles: UCLA Chicano Studies Research Center Press, 2004), 172.

127. Ibid., 200.
128. See www.i.1asphost.com/xrdistro/.
129. *Homocore*, no. 1 (September 1988).
130. Ibid., no. 2 (December 1988).
131. Ibid., no. 3 (February 1989).
132. Ibid., no. 6 (May 1990).
133. Ibid., no. 7 (February 1991).

The Underground GI Press and the Vietnam War

1. Richard B. Moser, *The New Winter Soldiers: GI and Veteran Dissent during the Vietnam Era* (New Brunswick, NJ: Rutgers University Press, 1996), 113–14.
2. *Going Upriver: The Long War of John Kerry*, directed by George Butler (New York: Palisades Pictures, 2004).
3. Members of the Vietnam Veterans Against the War (VVAW) had traveled around the country visiting underground GI papers and handing out cash for special issues to be published about the action in Washington and how to get there. Author's interview with Dave Hettick, October 15, 2003.
4. A 1975 survey found that 75 percent of Vietnam vets were opposed to the war. Jerry Lembcke, *The Spitting Image: Myth, Memory, and the Legacy of Vietnam* (New York: New York University Press, 1998), 106. These numbers dwarf even the most generous assessment of antiwar sentiment among students at any point in the war. See Terry H. Anderson, *The Movement and the Sixties: Protest in America from Greensboro to Wounded Knee* (Oxford and New York: Oxford University Press, 1995).
5. The exact number of Vietnamese casualties has been the subject of considerable dispute. Without doubt many sources have skewed the data for political reasons. In addition to deliberate manipulation, when millions of people die in a poor agricultural country in the midst of a war, record keeping is an approximation at best. On April 4, 1995, the Vietnamese government released what appeared to be its final figures: more than four million civilian deaths, and more than one million combatant deaths. The government admitted that "[t]hese figures were deliberately falsified during the war by the North Vietnamese Communists to avoid demoralizing the population." Agence France-Presse, April 4, 1995.
6. Raymond Mungo, *Famous Long Ago: My Life and Hard Times with Liberation News Service* (Boston: Beacon Press, 1970), 3.

7. David Armstrong, *Trumpet to Arms: Alternative Media in America* (Boston: South End Press, 1984), 2. As Armstrong notes, Sony's introduction of the video recorder Portapak, a few years later in 1968, had a comparable impact on video and television and led almost immediately to the emergence of an SDS-affiliated documentary film collective called Newsreel (idem, 71).

8. Armstrong, *Trumpet to Arms*, 60.

9. Abe Peck, *Uncovering the Sixties: The Life and Times of the Underground Press* (New York: Citadel Press, 1991), 44.

10. Ibid., 147.

11. Ibid., 86.

12. Ibid., 187.

13. Armstrong, *Trumpet to Arms*, 60.

14. Mungo, *Famous Long Ago*. Mungo uses the word "magic" to describe LNS functioning throughout the book.

15. Peck, *Uncovering the Sixties*, 78.

16. Ibid., 244.

17. Ibid., 176.

18. Ibid., 132.

19. Ibid., 142.

20. "The war drove us crazy." SDS and Weather Underground activist Mark Rudd in *The Weather Underground*, film directed by Sam Green and Bill Spiegel (Waterville, ME: Shadow Distribution, 2003).

21. Moser, *New Winter Soldiers*, 43.

22. Donald Duncan, "The Whole Thing Was a Lie," *Ramparts* 4, no. 10 (February 1966): 12–24. His scathing memoir of his time in Vietnam was published two years later. See *The New Legions* (New York: Random House, 1967).

23. Terry H. Anderson, "The GI Movement and the Response from the Brass," in *Give Peace a Chance: Exploring the Vietnam Antiwar Movement*, ed. Melvin Small and William D. Hoover (Syracuse, NY: Syracuse University Press, 1992), 93–115.

24. *Joint Statement by Fort Hood Three*, www3.niu.edu/~tdoraf1/history468/feb2603.htm.

25. Moser, *New Winter Soldiers*, 71, and Anderson, "GI Movement," 95–96.

26. Anderson, "GI Movement," 97.

27. *The Bond* was originally briefly published by two civilian activists in Berkeley. The two quickly split in political disagreement, and one of the

two hooked up with Stapp, taking the fledgling paper with him. Author's interview with Clark Smith, October 7, 2003. See also Andy Stapp, *Up against the Brass: The Amazing Story of the Fight to Unionize the United States Army* (New York: Simon and Schuster, 1970).

28. Moser, *New Winter Soldiers,* 72.

29. Dick Perrin and Tim McCarthy, *G.I. Resister: The Story of How One American Soldier and His Family Fought the War in Vietnam* (Victoria, Canada: Trafford, 2001). See also www.lib.umb.edu/archives/perrin.html.

30. Moser, *New Winter Soldiers,* 104.

31. "Jeff Sharlet Dies," *Vietnam GI* (August 1969): 3.

32. Author's interview with Thomas Barton, October 4, 2003.

33. *The Ally,* published in San Francisco by civilians and vets, targeted GIs in both Vietnam and the United States.

34. Author's interview with Dave Cline, September 30, 2003.

35. *Vietnam GI* (February 1968): 4.

36. Ibid.

37. Ibid. (May 1968): 4.

38. Ibid., 1.

39. Ibid. (June 1968).

40. Ibid. (August 1968): 2.

41. Ibid. (April 1968): 2.

42. Ibid. (May 1968): 3.

43. Ibid., 3.

44. Ibid., 8.

45. Ibid., 6.

46. Author's interview with Thomas Barton.

47. *Vietnam GI* (June 1968): 8.

48. Anderson, "GI Movement," 96.

49. GI Press Service 1, no. 1, June 26, 1969, through 1, no. 14, December 25, 1969.

50. *OM: The Best of the Worst,* April 1, May 1, and June 1, 1969.

51. *New York Times,* July 23, 1969.

52. James Lewes, *Protest and Survive: Underground GI Newspapers during the Vietnam War* (Westport, CT: Praeger, 2003), 83.

53. *Washington Post,* June 25, 1969.

54. Lewes, *Protest and Survive,* 89, 142.

55. Mathew Rinaldi, "The Olive-Drab Rebels: Military Organizing during the Vietnam Era," *Radical America* 8, no. 3 (1974).

NOTES TO PAGES 136–147

56. FTA, no. 8 (May 1969).

57. Author's interview with Patrick McCann, September 29, 2003.

58. Author's interview with Dave Cline.

59. William Short and Willa Seidenberg, *A Matter of Conscience: GI Resistance during the Vietnam War* (Andover, MA: Addison Gallery of American Art, 1992), 44.

60. Author's interview with Randy Roland, October 15, 2003.

61. Author's interview with Barry Miller, September 25, 2003.

62. Short and Seidenberg, *A Matter of Conscience*, 44–48.

63. The term *gigline* refers to the visual line made by the buttons on a GI's shirt and the fly of his or her trousers, which must be in a straight line when facing inspection.

64. Author's interview with David Cortright, September 17, 2003.

65. Author's interview with Paul Cox, October 7, 2003.

66. The village was named Gonoi, near Hoyan.

67. Kilometers.

68. *Rage* 1, no. 1 (October 1971).

69. Ibid., no. 2 (November 1971).

70. Ibid. 1, no. 4 (November 1972).

71. Ibid., no. 2 (November 1971).

72. SNCC, the Student Non-Violent Coordinating Committee, had been the main student organization in the civil rights movement in the South.

73. Author's interview with Dave Cline.

74. Study from 1970–71 by the Research Analysis Corporation, cited in the chapter "GI Resistance During the Vietnam War," by David Cortright, in Melvin Small and William D. Hoover, eds., *Give Peace a Chance: Exploring the Vietnam Antiwar Movement* (Syracuse, NY: Syracuse University Press, 1992), 116–29.

75. "Letter from a Black Soldier," *Black Panther*, September 28, 1968, 23.

76. *Black Panther*, January 4, 1969, 3.

77. Ibid., January 15, 1968.

78. Ibid., February 2, 1969.

79. See, for example, the "New Year's Message from Ho Chi Min," *Black Panther*, March 3, 1969.

80. "Four Anti-War GI's Thrown into Ft. Jackson Stockade," *Black Panther*, April 6, 1969, 15. The April 27 issue featured a brief report of a black man drafted and sent to Vietnam unwillingly after his request for com-

manding officer status was rejected. Finally, the May 4 issue ran a piece on the Fort Jackson 8.

81. *Black Panther*, July 26, 1969, 6.
82. Ibid., August 16, 1969, 9.
83. Ibid., September, 27, 1969, 8–10.
84. Ibid., October 4, 1969, 14.
85. Ibid.
86. Ibid., 15.
87. Ibid., October 18, 1969, 10.
88. Ibid., 18.
89. Ibid., October 11, 1969, 16.
90. Ibid., 14.
91. Ibid., January 3, 1970, 6.
92. Ibid. The same appeal was reprinted in the March 22, 1970, issue.
93. Ibid., June 27, 1970, 8. Writing from North Korea, Eldridge Cleaver proclaimed,

> We are truly amazed by the achievement of the Korean people.... Nowhere have we encountered such beautiful people, so vigorously mobilized, so efficiently organized, moving with the harmony of one man, one will, and one dedication.... We came to Korea in search of something. We have been searching all over the world for it. The whole of our lives has been given to this search. And all of the oppressed people of the world are searching for this thing. We have found it here in Korea.... Comrade Kim Il Sung has provided [it]. I see the earth as one big piece of land with one big body of water. I see one territory. And I see Comrade Kim Il Sung speaking to all the people in this territory, and I see them listening to him and understanding him. (*Black Panther*, January 3, 1970, 16)

94. *Black Panther*, June 20, 1970, 15.
95. Wallace Terry II, "Black GI's—Bringing the War Home," *San Francisco Chronicle*, July 4, 1970, 18.
96. Author's interview with David Cortright.
97. Author's interview with Jim Willingham, October 2, 2003.
98. Author's interview with David Cortright.
99. *Aboveground* (March 1970).
100. *Gigline* 1, no. 3 (1969).

101. Col. Robert D. Heinl Jr., "The Collapse of the Armed Forces," *Armed Forces Journal*, June 7, 1971.

102. *Rage* 1, no. 5 (February 1972).

103. Anderson, "GI Movement," 106.

104. "Determination of the Potential for Dissidence in the U.S. Army" and "Future Impact of Dissident Elements within the U.S. Army," cited in "GI Resistance," by Cortright, 117.

105. Heinl, "Collapse of the Armed Forces."

106. Shelby L. Stanton, *The Rise and Fall of an American Army: U.S. Ground Forces in Vietnam, 1965–1973* (New York: Presidio Press, 1985).

107. Cinncinatus, *Self-Destruction: The Disintegration and Decay of the United States Army during the Vietnam Era* (New York: Norton, 1981).

108. As cited in "GI Resistance," by Cortright, 117.

109. See Moser, *New Winter Soldiers*, 48.

110. Stanton, *Rise and Fall of an American Army*, 124.

111. Ibid., 357.

112. Cortright, "GI Resistance," 125.

113. Ibid., 126.

114. Ibid., 127.

115. Ibid.

116. Moser, *New Winter Soldiers*, 45.

117. *The Ally*, no. 38 (November 1971), as cited in *New Winter Soldiers*, by Moser, 57–58.

118. Author's interview with Randy Roland.

119. Anderson, "GI Movement," 112.

120. Author's interview with Randy Roland.

121. Anderson, "GI Movement," 110.

122. Heinl, "Collapse of the Armed Forces."

123. Author's interview with Paul Cox.

124. SDS, the largest student organization of the sixties, ran a special program for years called the Economic Research and Action Project (ERAP), which sent student organizers into factories and ghettos. Many of the small Marxist-Leninist parties had similar programs.

125. The most extreme version of this view conflates the *organizations* of the new left, and SDS and the Black Panthers in particular, as the movement *itself*. The crumbling of these organizations is thus misconstrued as the crumbling of the movement. See Todd Gitlin, *The Sixties: Years of Hope,*

Days of Rage (New York: Bantam, 1987). Also see Sale Kirkpatrick, *SDS* (New York: Vintage, 1974).

Students for a Democratic Society split acrimoniously in 1969 into two factions. One was directed by the neo-Leninist Progressive Labor Party. The other formed the nihilistic Weatherman. More recent scholarship has challenged this view, arguing that the locus of the movement was in local organizing, not national organizations, and that this organizing often continued unabated as national organizations rose and fell. See in particular Anderson, *The Movement and the Sixties*. This has been a good corrective but has not gone far enough, for it does not challenge the view that the sixties overall were a "failure."

126. Lembcke, *Spitting Image*, 106.
127. Ibid., 124, citing Paul Loeb, *Generation at the Crossroads* (New Brunswick, NJ: Rutgers University Press, 1994).
128. Lembcke, *Spitting Image*. Lembcke's extraordinary study not only exhaustively refutes the allegations of peace activists spitting on vets but also examines the image of the spat-upon veteran at the level of mythology, underscored by the similarities in the reported incidents: the location was always the San Francisco airport, the spitter was always a woman who always called them a "baby killer," and more.
129. Author's interview with Clark Smith.

The Environmental Movement

1. Hal K. Rothman, *Saving the Planet: The American Response to the Environment in the Twentieth Century* (Chicago: Ivan R Dee, 2000), 14.
2. "Sierra Club Centennial," *Sierra* (May/June 1992): 53.
3. Susan Zakin, *Coyotes and Town Dogs* (New York: Penguin, 1993), 7.
4. Dating the environmental movement to the launch of the Sierra Club will meet objection in some quarters. Henry David Thoreau and others presaged the writings of Muir, for example. And some present-day activists, most notably Dave Foreman, insist that the "conservation" and "environmental" movements are separate and distinct. Given that this book is concerned primarily with the press, we shall leave these arguments to the side.
5. "Sierra Club Centennial," *Sierra* (May/June 1992): 53.
6. Other early groups include the Izaak Walton League, and later the Na-

tional Wildlife Federation, the Audubon Society, and the Wilderness Society.

7. "The Sierra Club *Bulletin*: One Hundred Years of Activism and Adventure," *Sierra* (September/October 1993): 60.

8. Ibid., 67.

9. Hal K. Rothman, *The Greening of a Nation? Environmentalism in the United States since 1945* (New York: Harcourt Brace, 1998), 42.

10. Ibid., 53.

11. Wallace Stegner, *This Is Dinosaur: Echo Park Country and Its Magic Rivers* (New York: Knopf, 1955).

12. Eliot Porter, with David Brower, *The Place No One Knew: Glen Canyon on the Colorado* (San Francisco: Sierra Club Books, 1963).

13. Harold Gillam and Philip Hyde, *Island in Time: The Point Reyes Peninsula* (San Francisco: Sierra Club, 1962). See also Eliot Porter, with David Brower, *In Wildness Is the Preservation of the World* (San Francisco: Sierra Club, 1962); Ansel Adams and Virginia Adams, *Illustrated Guide to Yosemite and the Valley* (San Francisco: Sierra Club, 1963); Robinson Jeffers, *Not Man Apart: Photographs of the Big Sur Coast* (San Francisco: Sierra Club, n.d.); and Dave Bohn, *Glacier Bay: The Land and the Silence* (San Francisco: Sierra Club, 1966).

14. See Zakin, *Coyotes and Town Dogs*, 162–69.

15. "Sierra Club Centennial," 68–69.

16. Ibid., 67.

17. Data are from a *New York Times* survey cited in "The Seers of Menlo Park: Heroizing the Reflexive Consumer in the Whole Earth Catalog," by Sam Binkley, undated manuscript.

18. Binkley, "Seers of Menlo Park."

19. Ibid.

20. Author's interview with Harriet Barlow, December 12, 2002.

21. Binkley, "Seers of Menlo Park."

22. See www.wholeearthmag.com.

23. *Whole Earth Review*, no. 85 (Spring 1995).

24. Author's interview with Tom Bender, December 5, 2002.

25. Ibid.

26. Sara Pacher, "The Story of Mother Earth News," *Mother Earth News* (March–April 1990).

27. *Mother Earth News* (May 2001).

28. "Sierra Club Centennial," 71.

29. Author's interview with Tom Turner, January 2, 2003.

30. Rothman, *Greening of a Nation?* 186.

31. Ibid., 170.

32. Ibid., 180–81.

33. Bob Ostertag, "Greenpeace Takes Over the World," *Mother Jones* (March/April 1991).

34. Author's interview with Laurie John Lane-Zucker, December 23, 2002.

35. Ibid.

36. Dave Foreman, *Eco-Defense: A Field Guide to Monkeywrenching* (Chico, CA: Abzug Press, 1985).

37. Dave Foreman, "Around the Campfire," *Earth First! Journal* 8, no. 1, November 1, 1987, 2.

38. *Earth First! Journal*, June 21, 1988, 1.

39. Zakin, *Coyotes and Town Dogs*, 281.

40. Author's interview with Mike Roselle, December 23, 2002.

41. Daniel Conner, "Is AIDS the Answer to an Environmentalist's Prayer?" *Earth First! Journal*, December 22, 1987, 14.

42. Author's interview with Doug Moss, December 19, 2002.

43. Ibid.

44. Ibid.

45. Ibid.

46. Ibid.

47. Author's interview with Tom Butler, December 12, 2002.

48. Author's interview with Chris Clark, December 20, 2002.

49. Ed Marston, "An Improbable Newspaper Reaches an Improbable Age: A Tough Weed Takes Root in the Devastated West," *High Country News* 21, no. 18, September 25, 1989.

50. *Boston Globe*, undated, untitled clipping from 1999.

51. Tom Kenworthy, "Small-town Newspaper Has Grand Ambitions," *USA Today*, May 10, 2000.

52. *Boston Globe*, undated, untitled clipping from 1999.

53. Kenworthy, "Small-town Newspaper."

54. The name *RACHEL's* comes from a digital data bank Montague initially used.

55. Author's interview with Peter Montague, January 6, 2003.

56. See Nancy Myers and Carolyn Raffensperger, eds., *Precautionary Tools for Reshaping Environmental Policy* (Cambridge, MA: MIT Press, 2005). See also *Our Stolen Future: Are We Threatening Our Fertility, Intelligence and Survival?*

(New York: Plume, 1997). The back section of the book describes the evolution of the "Wingspread Statement," the first articulation of the precautionary principle in the United States.

57. Author's interview with David Seideman, December 20, 2002.

58. "Audubon Society History," www.audubonsociety.org.

59. Kenworthy, "Small-town Newspaper."

60. See Rothman, *Saving the Planet*; Samuel P. Hays, *A History of Environmental Politics Since 1945* (Pittsburgh: University of Pittsburgh Press, 2000); and Rothman, *Greening of a Nation?*

61. Aldo Leopold, *A Sand County Almanac* (Oxford: Oxford University Press, 1966); Rachel Carson, *Silent Spring* (Greenwich, CT: Fawcett, 1962); Barry Commoner, *The Closing Circle: Nature, Man, and Technology* (Westminster, MD: Random House, 1971).

62. *Boston Globe*, undated, untitled clipping from 1999.

63. Author's interview with Mike Roselle.

64. Author's interview with Chris Clark.

65. Lane-Zucker estimates there are 25,000–30,000 environmentally oriented local organizations in the country. The phrase "place-based work" refers to the idea that environmental activists should focus on specific local problems that do not easily fit within national campaigns or programs.

66. Author's interview with Kathrin Day Lasilla, December 31, 2002.

Index

AASS (American Anti-Slavery Society), 43, 44–45

abolitionist movement: adversarial response, 43–44; African American and white presses, 50–52; Douglass's role in, 4, 44–47; historical trajectory of, 11, 12; introduction, 23–27; mainstreaming of, 5, 43, 48–49, 70; press influence on, 4; and print innovations, 26–27; shifts in press focus over time, 13; and woman suffrage movement, 52–62, 69–71. See also *Freedom's Journal*; *The Genius of Universal Emancipation*; *The Liberator*; *National Era*; *Walker's Appeal*

Aboveground, 138–39, 151–52

ACS (American Colonization Society), 31–32

ACT, 125

advertising revenue: and corporate media influence, 16; as criterion

for periodical success, 2; environmental publications, 172, 178; gay and lesbian press, 86, 94, 105–10

The Advocate (African American newspaper), 33

The Advocate (gay and lesbian publication): activist beginnings of, 77; and AIDS crisis, 100; commercialization of, 6–7, 94, 108; growth of, 106; return to activism in 1980s, 98

African-American Female Intelligence Agency, 52

African Americans: in abolitionist movement, 26, 29–39, 41, 44–47, 50–52, 53; black power movement, 120, 146–50; as Civil War soldiers, 49; gay and lesbian publications, 95–98; in GI antiwar movement, 124, 145–50; and women's movement, 52, 60, 61–62, 64

conservation groups. *See* environmental movement

consumerism as social context for corporate media, 17, 19. *See also* advertising revenue

conventions and women's rights movement, 57–58, 60

Córdova, Jeanne, 90, 92, 98, 109

Cornish, Samuel E., 29, 31, 32–33, 40

corporate culture: influence on environmental movement, 184–85; motivations vs. social movement press, 2–4, 16–18, 19. *See also* commercialization

Cortright, David, 151

counterculture, 1960s. *See* sixties counterculture movements

Covina, Gina, 7

Cox, Paul, 139–42, 156

Crude, 96, 97

Daily Planet (Miami), 122

Daughters of Bilitis (DOB), 80, 90

Davis, PFC Dennis, 136

Davis, Vaginal, 96–97

DeGeneres, Ellen, 110–11

De la Tierra, Tatiana, 112, 114–15

Democratic National Convention (1968) protests, 121, 144–45

democratization of reading and print technology, 26–27

Desert Dissenter, 138, 155

desktop publishing, 9, 115

Diablo Canyon nuclear power plant, 166–67

Dinosaur National Monument, 163

Diseased Pariah News, 103–4

dishonorable discharges for antiwar GIs, 136

distribution: and African American community networks, 38; authorized agent method, 29–30, 33, 41; as criterion for periodical success, 2; early gay and lesbian presses, 76–77, 90; environmental publications, 173; GI underground press, 126–27, 138–39, 141–42; and Latina publication struggles, 114–15; personal delivery method, 28–31; sixties counterculture publications, 120; subscription-based publications in abolitionist movement, 26–27, 29–30, 48, 58; of *Walker's Appeal*, 37–38. *See also* circulation

DOB (Daughters of Bilitis), 80, 90

Douglass, Frederick, 4, 20, 44–47, 49, 57

Dowager, 96–97

Drum, 85–86

Duncan, MSgt. Donald, 123

Dyke, 90

Earth First! Journal, 3, 13–14, 175–78, 187

Earth Island Institute, 174

Earth Island Journal, 174, 180, 186

East Village Other, 120

Echo Park dam project, 163–64

Eclipse, 106

Eco-Defense: A Field Guide to Monkey-wrenching, 176

"ecotage," 176

Eco-Village, 172